THE AMATEUR'S LATHE

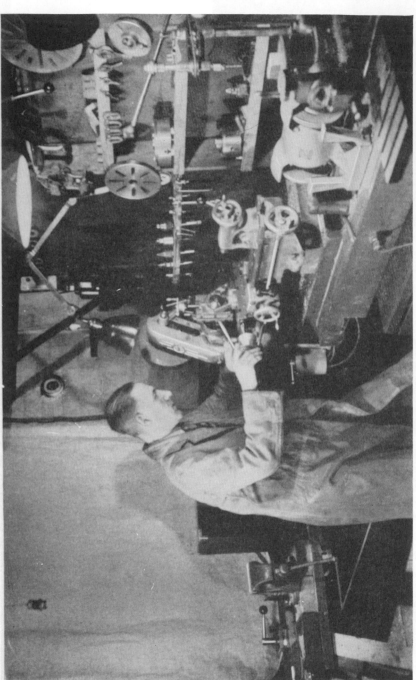

The Author in his home workshop. Milling a piece of work set up on the vertical slide in the lathe. Note the application of cutting lubricant to the work by means of a brush. The picture shows a lathe, bench grinder and small drilling machine mounted on a single bench, while in the extreme right-hand corner may be seen part of a small motorised bench shaper. With the addition of a large pillar drill, not shown in the photograph, these machines constitute the whole of the machine equipment.

THE
AMATEUR'S LATHE

By

LAWRENCE H. SPAREY

With a Foreword by
D. A. RUSSELL, M.I.Mech.E.

Special Interest Model Books

Special Interest Model Books Ltd
P.O. Box 327
Poole
Dorset
BH15 2RG

First Edition 1948

This edition published by Special Interest Model Books Ltd 2002
Reprinted 2003, 2005, 2007

ISBN 978 085242 288 5

Printed in Malta by Progress Press Co. Ltd

FOREWORD

As the small lathe in the hands of the skilled amateur is capable of so much more than just ordinary turning and screwcutting operations, it follows that a book on the Amateur's Lathe is virtually a book on an entire machine shop! It deals not only with the lathe, but the milling machine, shaper, and grinder. These unique possibilities which the small lathe possesses call for a much wider treatment of the lathe—and lathe practice—than has hitherto been accorded this item of machinery.

In previous publications the amateur's problems have been handled as if they were a " scaled down " version of those of the professional, with the result that many kinds of machine work of which the small lathe is capable have been omitted. It is here that Mr. Sparey's book establishes the practice of lathe work on an entirely new basis.

Mr. L. H. Sparey is that somewhat rare combination—a Professional Engineer with what he himself calls " the amateur's outlook ". By this he means that, in spite of many years' practical experience of machine practice, a number of which have been spent on the largest of " full-size " machines, he has still kept his " amateur " outlook and appreciation of the difficulties of the average owner, with his small workshop and small lathe; but with a very wide range of objects to be machined on it!

It is a good many years ago since I first met Mr. Sparey and I was impressed then, as I am impressed now, not only with the high degree of enthusiasm with which he approaches any project, but the thorough and practical way in which he deals with his work.

It is a fact that practically every photograph in this book has been taken by Mr. Sparey himself—no mean indication of his capabilities as a photographer, as well as an engineer. In every one of his photographs the machine " set-up " as shown therein is his own, and has been carried out in his own workshop—typically an "amateur's " workshop.

The further one progresses through this book the more one realises that it is suitable, not only for the amateur mechanic, but for the professional also. For the apprentice, the young engineer and the garage engineer, with limited machine equipment, no better book could be possible, if only because it reveals, in a never-ending variety of examples, the resourcefulness and ingenuity for which the amateur engineer is famous.

This book, therefore, in my opinion, is unique in Engineering Literature. It will be invaluable, not only in the amateur's workshop, but in Technical Institutes, Schools and Garages throughout the country; and from my personal knowledge of Mr. Sparey, the many fine models he has built, and of his workshop facilities, I can thoroughly recommend it.

D. A. RUSSELL, M.I.Mech.E.

CONTENTS

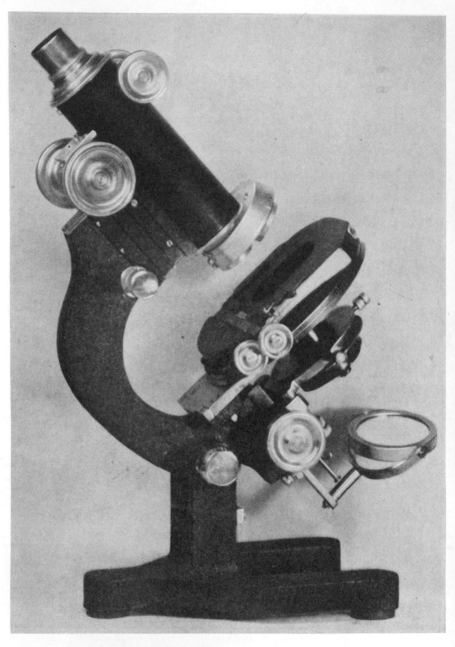

Research Microscope made by the Author entirely on his 3½-in. lathe. This sample of home engineering is particularly interesting as it contains examples of turning, milling, gear and rack cutting, and slotting, thus proving the versatility of the amateur's machine.

CHAPTER 1

THE LATHE

IN common with that of most other foundations of civilisation, the origin of the lathe is lost in the darkness of time. Quite rightly may we speak of the lathe as one of the bases of human progress, for it has proved to be the most wonderful and powerful tool ever put into the hands of man. A brief study of the everyday things around us will quickly show how deeply the mark of the lathe has been impressed on our culture and our surroundings—from the pistons and shafts of your motor car to the legs of your table and the very buttons on your jacket.

Probably one of the oldest mechanical contrivances is the potter's wheel—which is really only a kind of lathe—and although we cannot trace the history of the lathe with equal certainty, it may be safely assumed that wherever we find the potter's wheel there also existed its natural and logical development—the lathe. The products of the potter's wheel are, by their very nature, almost as durable as stone itself, whereas most of the work of the primitive turner, being of wood and, to a lesser extent, metal, have long since perished. Nevertheless, most ancient civilisation shows evidence of the lathe's influence; until, in mediaeval times, it had become a comparatively universal and well-known tool. Many of our most ancient cathedrals and abbeys offer examples of turning in wood and stone; many quite massive stone columns having been turned on some form of lathe.

Although it is impossible to be sure, certain evidence points to China or India as the probable place of origin, but it is quite possible that the invention may have occurred independently in several places; yet, whatever continent may claim the honour, the fact remains that the lathe still holds pride of place in our modern economy. It is quite true to say that without it life, and even mankind itself, would be quite different things from those which we know to-day, and that almost the whole of our somewhat materialistic modern civilisation is due to its influence. To the casual observer this may seem a far-reaching statement, but if we reflect that almost all the inventions, all the engines, all the turbines and dynamos, and all the wonderful machines which make the thousands of varied articles in daily use are only possible because of the lathe, we may then begin to see it in its true perspective.

It is little wonder, therefore, that to those of us with any mechanical bent whatsoever the lathe should exert such a strong appeal. The addition of a small lathe to the home workshop does, indeed, open up vistas and possibilities hitherto only dreamed of. It has always been a source of wonder that, for the cost of a few pounds, one may obtain not only an obedient servant, but an unfailing friend, through whom one may find the greatest creative expression, a lifelong companion, and a solace for most cares.

Although it is a far cry from the lathe of the Egyptian hieroglyphics to the modern efficient tool, the principle remains the same: namely, that of rotating a piece of work against a cutting tool. How this was accomplished in the primitive lathe those so inclined may discover for themselves; meanwhile it is our purpose to indicate the various parts of the modern machine, and the uses for which they are designed.

Let us, then, come directly to the illustration in Fig. 1, where may be seen a representation of a typical amateur's lathe, with its various parts numbered. It is not claimed that the machine illustrated shows all the best features of lathe design; rather does it indicate the type of machine which the amateur's pocket will most likely allow. Nor need this lack of perfection worry the amateur unduly, for it may be safely said that many hundreds of examples of perfect engineering have been produced on just such machines as this.

(1) **The Bed.** This is invariably a heavy casting, and is the backbone of the lathe. Upon it are machined the locations for the various lathe components.

(2) **The Ways.** These are highly finished surfaces, machined parallel and flat to line up with the headstock seating. Further remarks upon these will be found in Chapter 2.

(3) **The Headstock Casting.** In many lathes the headstock is sometimes made integral with the bed casting, but this is not generally a good arrangement. In the type illustrated the headstock casting is a separate unit, with a machined undersurface which bolts to the lathe bed. This allows the headstock to be lined up with the lathe ways, so that an adjustment of accuracy may be obtained.

(4) **The Gap.** This is a cutaway portion of the bed near the headstock, and its purpose is to allow work to be swung which is larger than would normally clear the lathe ways. Some lathes continue the ways right up to the headstock, but

this may be a limitation in an amateur's machine.

(5) **The Cross-slide.** This is a component which moves at right-angles to the lathe ways, and is actuated by a short feedscrew connected to the handle (20). It operates on " V "-shaped slides, the tightness of which may be adjusted by means of screws in the side of the slide. The cross-slide should contain a number of " T " slots, one of which may be seen in the illustration at the extreme end of the slide.

(6) **The Carriage and Apron.** This component slides along the lathe ways, and its tightness may also be adjusted by setscrews. The carriage is the part of the lathe upon which the cross-slide runs. The portion which extends down the front of the lathe is the apron, and carries the automatic and manual sliding mechanism. Sometimes the carriage is provided with a bolt, by means of which the carriage may be locked to the bed in any position. This is useful to prevent the carriage from being forced backwards by the pressure of the cutting tool when facing work.

(7) **The Mandrel.** A shaft which revolves in the headstock, and which carries the driving pulleys (8), and the backgear cogwheels (9). The nose of the mandrel carries a thread to which may be attached the faceplate (14) and various forms of chucks. It is also bored with an internal taper to accommodate various accessories.

(8) **Driving Pulleys.** In the illustration, these are shown for flat belt drive. They may, however, be of " V " shape, to accommodate the " V "-type belt. The pulleys are not connected directly to the mandrel (7), but are free to revolve independently.

(9) **The Bull Wheel.** This gearwheel forms part of the backgear mechanism. It is connected rigidly

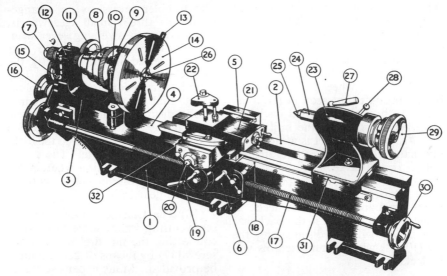

Fig. I

Typical Amateur's Lathe and its Components—(1) Bed; (2) Ways; (3) Headstock Casting; (4) Gap; (5) Cross-slide; (6) Carriage and Apron; (7) Mandrel; (8) Driving Pulleys; (9) Bull Wheel; (10) Backgear Pin; (11) Backgear; (12) Head Bearings; (13) Backgear Operating Lever; (14) Faceplate; (15) Tumbler Reverse Lever; (16) Change Wheels; (17) Leadscrew; (18) Rack; (19) Carriage Engagement Lever; (20) Cross-slide Handle; (21) Top Slide; (22) Toolpost; (23) Tailstock Casting; (24) Tailstock Barrel; (25) and (26) Lathe Centres; (27) Tailstock Barrel Clamping Lever; (28) Tailstock Clamping Lever; (29) Tailstock Handwheel; (30) Lead-screw Handwheel; (31) Tailstock Cross Adjustment; (32) Top Slide Swivelling Device.

with the mandrel (7), and always revolves with it.

(10) **The Backgear Pin.** A small pin which slides in the bull wheel, and which may be locked in the *in* or *out* position. It fits into a suitable register in the pulley (8), so that when the pin is engaged the pulleys also become locked to the mandrel (7), thus giving a direct drive.

(11) **Backgear.** The illustration shows only part of the backgear arrangement. The large gearwheel, which may be seen, is connected to a shaft, on the other end of which is a smaller gearwheel, all rigidly connected together. This small gearwheel corresponds in size to the small gear which may be seen on the mandrel, forming part of the pulley arrangement (8). The backgear shaft

may be moved on an eccentric motion, by means of the lever (13), so that the two gears on the backgear shaft may be swung in or out of engagement with the gears on the mandrel (7).

Operation of the Backgear

By means of the backgear a reduction in the speed at which the mandrel (7) revolves may be obtained. We have seen that the pulleys (8), together with small attached gearwheel, are free to revolve on the mandrel shaft (7), but may be locked to the mandrel by engaging the backgear pin (10). If the pin is, therefore, disengaged, the mandrel shaft will not turn, although the pulleys and attached gear may be revolving freely under the drive from the motor. If, however, the backgear wheels

(11) are swung into engagement with those on the mandrel, we have brought into operation a double reduction gear train. The drive to the mandrel (7) now takes place from the small pulley-wheel-gear, *via* the large backgear wheel (11), along the backgear shaft (not seen in the illustration), through the small backgear gearwheel, and so to the bull wheel (9). As the bull wheel is attached to the mandrel this will, therefore, revolve. It will be seen, however, that the speed has been stepped down twice, according to the ratio in size of the large and small gearwheels. It should be noted that if the backgear is engaged without disengaging the pin (10) the whole head assembly will be locked.

(12) **Head Bearings.** In the next chapter these will be considered at more length, as they are of considerable importance to the accuracy and life of the machine.

(13) **Backgear Operating Lever.** The type shown here is the most usual. Other designs of backgear are sometimes used, such as that wherein the backgear shaft lies directly below the mandrel. Some advantages are claimed for the variations, although all of them operate on the same system.

(14) **Faceplate.** This is always supplied as standard equipment, whereas chucks, collets and other forms of holding devices are usually listed as extras. The faceplate should be as large as will swing in the gap. The uses of the faceplate are discussed in detail in a later chapter.

(15) **Tumbler Reverse Lever.** When the leadscrew (17) is connected to the mandrel (7) by means of the change wheel gears (16) it is often desirable to reverse the direction in which the leadscrew is turning while the mandrel continues to revolve as before.

The tumbler reverse is an arrangement of three small gearwheels, mounted on a swinging lever arm, which allows an intermediate gear to be inserted in the train by the simple operation of a lever. This lever has some form of locking plunger, so that the gears may be secured in the desired position. Below the lever, in the illustration, may be seen two shallow slots into which the locking plunger may locate. The centre slot provides a position wherein the mandrel is disconnected entirely from the gear train.

(16) **The Change Wheels.** On all screwcutting lathes some method of connecting the mandrel to the leadscrew (17) by means of gearing must be provided. Many expensive lathes have self-contained gearboxes, providing a selection of screwcutting gear ratios. In the amateur's lathe, however, the gear trains are invariably set up by hand as required, for which purpose a bracket (known as the **banjo**) is provided. Into this, movable studs, carrying the selected gears, may be bolted. The matter is dealt with fully in the chapter devoted to screwcutting.

Lathes in which the backgears and leadscrew are absent are known as **plain lathes,** because their use is confined purely to plain turning operations.

(17) **The Leadscrew.** This is a long shaft, running in bearings, along the whole length of the lathe, and having a thread of comparatively coarse pitch, and of square or acme form, cut into it. By means of the change wheel gears, it may be coupled to the lathe mandrel, so that the leadscrew revolutions may be in a predetermined ratio to the revolutions of the mandrel. In some types of lathes the leadscrew is carried through the centre of the lathe bed, and not along the front as shown.

(18) **The Rack.** As may be seen, this is a long, toothed rack, which is screwed to the lathe bed. By means of a shaft and handle, situated in the lathe apron, a small pinion engages with the rack. Thus, by turning the handle, the lathe carriage may be made to move along the lathe ways. For the sake of clarity, a single pinion coupling has been shown, but for reasons to be discussed later, some form of intermediate pinion is desirable.

(19) **Carriage Engagement Lever.** Sometimes called the **Screwcutting Lever.** If a suitable nut is provided on the lathe carriage (6) so as to engage with the leadscrew (17), it is obvious that if the leadscrew is turned the lathe carriage will be moved along the lathe ways. It is by this method that screwcutting is, in fact, accomplished. While essential for this purpose, it is not always convenient thus to have the saddle and leadscrew connected together. It is usual therefore, to have a lever arrangement which actuates a **split** or **half-nut,** which may be engaged or disengaged from the leadscrew at will. Some lathes, however, do have the leadscrew and carriage permanently in engagement, but some form of

clutch is usually provided which disengages the leadscrew from the gear train. More about this later.

(20) **Cross-slide Handle.** This has been mentioned before, but attention is again drawn to it so that we may note the graduated index dial which is affixed. This dial is marked off into divisions, which indicates that the cross-slide has been moved a certain number of thousandths of an inch, according to how much the feed handle has been turned. A similar index dial will be noted on the handle of the top-slide feed screw.

(21) **The Top-Slide.** To the cross-slide is bolted the top-slide, in such a manner that it may be swivelled to within the limits of the slots, shown at (32). Various swivelling systems are to be found, and that shown is not, probably, the best, as the amount of movement is restricted. Some

Fig. 2

Myford TRI-LEVA speed selector suitable for fitting to M.L.7 type lathes. Any of three speeds may be obtained by depressing the appropriate lever.

14

Fig. 3A

The Box-Ford 4½ in. centre lathe with roller bearing headstock, and spindle bored to take ⅜ in. bar. This machine has eight direct speeds, and a quick-operating lever reverse for screw-cutting. (*Courtesy Denfords Engineering Co. Ltd.*)

deviation from a central position. A tailstock which will not keep its alignment with the head at any position on the lathe bed, is a grave nuisance and handicap. Once moved, the tailstock may be clamped to the ways by means of the nut shown in the recess. This necessitates the use of a spanner, and a better arrangement is that whereby the tailstock may be secured by a locking lever (28) which actuates an eccentric clamping arrangement. Both types are indicated in the drawing, although they are not combined in actual practice.

On the base at (31) will be seen an arrangement for moving the tailstock across the bed of the lathe. This is useful for lining-up, and for setting the tailstock over for certain types of taper turning. It will be seen that the tailstock casting is separate from its base, but is located by a tongue in a machined slot. Adjustment is effected by the two screws which have been indicated.

(24) **The Tailstock Barrel.** This component should be a tight, sliding fit in the casting, and consists of a barrel, one end of which bears a square thread, while the other end has an internal taper. Movement of the handwheel (29) causes the barrel

methods allow complete rotation of the top-slide, as the holding-down bolts move in a circular slot. The top-slide moves on "V" slides, in the same manner as the cross-slide, but is entirely detachable, so as to present a flat surface which may be used as a boring table. Here, again, movement is obtained by means of a feed-screw.

(22) **The Tool Post.** This component is discussed more fully in the next chapter. The type shown is quite common on lathes of this sort, and is satisfactory in use.

(23) **The Tailstock Casting.** The underside of this important component should be machined and scraped perfectly flat, and be so designed that it will slide along the lathe ways without any slackness or

Fig. 3B
Modern example of the small screwcutting lathe. The Myford M.L.7 3½-in. lathe, fitted with drive clutch, with deep tray raising-blocks, on pressed-steel stand.

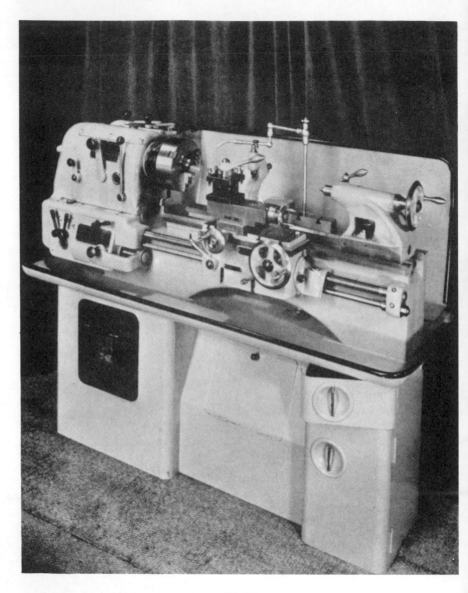

Fig. 3C

The Colchester " Student " 6 in., gap bed, lathe, incorporating all-geared head, screwcutting gearbox, built-in cabinet stand, and many refinements which the higher price allows. Although designed primarily for technical schools, and production work, its compactness and neat layout makes it an ideal machine for those amateurs with good workshop facilities, and to whom price is not a first consideration. (*Courtesy Colchester Lathe Co. Ltd.*)

Fig. 4A

The very well known 'Unimat' many thousands of which are performing satisfactorily in the hands of model makers. (Courtesy E. H. Jeynes, Newcastle on Tyne.)

to move back and forth in the casting. It may be locked in any position by means of the clamping lever (27).

The uses of the tailstock are many. Drill chucks, or drills and reamers may be located in the internal taper, for operation on work held at the headstock. In addition, the tailstock is used for supporting work held in the chuck or faceplate, and for supporting long, slender work between centres. All these operations will be dealt with.

(25) and (26) **Lathe Centres.** These components are detachable, and should plug firmly into the tapers of both head- and tailstock. That in the headstock (26) revolves with the work, and is known as the **live centre.** Its companion, in the tailstock (25), is called the **dead centre,** as this does not revolve, but forms a bearing for the work. For reasons to be explained, the live centre is sometimes left soft, while the dead centre is always of hardened steel. On English and American lathes the angle of the point is always 60 degrees, inclusive; while the taper is usually Morse or some other standard type.

(27) **Tailstock Barrel Clamping Lever.**

(28) **Tailstock Clamping Lever.**

(29) **Tailstock Handwheel.**

Some forms of tailstock have the barrel screw housed internally in the body casting, with an ejection device to push centres or other tools from the taper housing. This type is not usually so solid as that illustrated, where a heavy screw can be employed. The barrel is, in this instance, hollow, so that centres may be knocked out with a brass rod.

(30) **Leadscrew Handwheel.** A useful addition which enables the lathe carriage to be moved along the bed by hand. Some makers provide a graduated index for this wheel, which is particularly useful for such operations as milling in the lathe.

(31) **Tailstock Cross Adjustment.**

(32) **Top-Slide Swivelling Device.**

The size of a centre lathe is, in English practice, always referred to in terms of the distance between the top of the **lathe ways** and the point of the **live centre;** in other words, it indicates the maximum *radius* of work which may be swung over the lathe ways. Thus, a $3\frac{1}{2}$-in. lathe will

Fig. 4B

For those amateurs not unduly governed by price considerations, the new Harrison 4½-in. lathe has many appealing features, including an all-geared headstock providing eight spindle speeds from 21 to 960 r.p.m. Although a full Norton screwcutting gearbox can be provided, the standard machine has a modified gearbox giving three feeds or three threads by the operation of one lever. (*Courtesy T. S. Harrison and Sons Ltd.*)

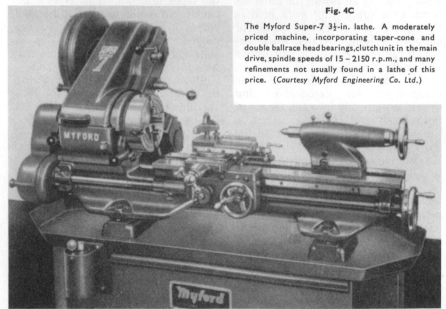

Fig. 4C

The Myford Super-7 3½-in. lathe. A moderately priced machine, incorporating taper-cone and double ballrace head bearings, clutch unit in the main drive, spindle speeds of 15 – 2150 r.p.m., and many refinements not usually found in a lathe of this price. (*Courtesy Myford Engineering Co. Ltd.*)

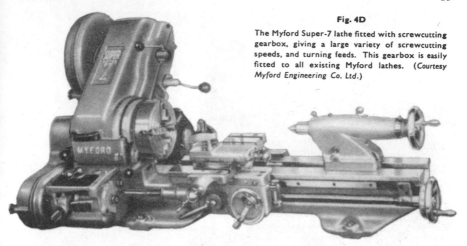

Fig. 4D

The Myford Super-7 lathe fitted with screwcutting gearbox, giving a large variety of screwcutting speeds, and turning feeds. This gearbox is easily fitted to all existing Myford lathes. (*Courtesy Myford Engineering Co. Ltd.*)

take work of 7 in. diameter. American lathes, and some Continental ones, have their sizes designated by the maximum *diameter* which may be swung over the lathe ways. An American 7-in. lathe, therefore, is of equivalent size to an English 3½-in. machine. The swing in the gap is not considered.

Geared-head Lathes

Modern lathes, in the higher-price range, now have **geared-heads,** incorporating a gearbox, which makes available a series of spindle speeds without changing the belt from one pulley to another. The arrangement is often extended to include another gearbox yielding a range of screwcutting gears.

Fig. 4E

The Myford MO 10 Screwcutting Lathe having a centre height of 3¼ inches, and admitting 13 inches between centres. Careful design has provided a sturdy machine at a most competitive price. (*Courtesy Myford Ltd.*)

The 'Emcomat 7' a precision 3½ inch bench lathe with a precision vertical milling attachment. (Courtesy E. H. Jeynes, Newcastle on Tyne.)

As an instance of the heights to which such refinements can rise, the writer worked for a long period on a 10-in. all-geared toolroom lathe, giving 48 speeds, a full range of feeds, a full range of English and American screw pitches, a full range of metric pitches, a full range of diametral pitches, and a full range of module pitches. There were fourteen levers on the gearbox, including those for double-pitching and fast reverse! Such machines will not be featured in these pages, because the higher prices put them beyond the average amateur.

CHAPTER 2

CHOOSING A LATHE

AS the novice is now familiar with the general characteristics of the small lathe, we may turn our attention to certain features which may be considered as advantageous or essential to the amateur.

Mention has been made in the last chapter of the " plain lathe ", which, as we have seen, is a machine which may or may not be provided with all the features of the screwcutting lathe, with the exception of the leadscrew, and gearing arrangements for backgear and screwcutting. It has been advocated in some quarters that a plain lathe is suitable for general amateur use; it being argued that threads can, in any case, be cut with taps, dies or chasers, so that the expense and complication of the screwcutting lathe is not warranted. These advocates have, obviously, either had no experience of general model engineering, or their efforts have been confined to one certain type of work where taps and dies may suffice. The experience of the vast majority of model engineers will support the statement that, if any one thing can be considered as essential, provision for screwcutting is just that!

Fortunately, the majority of lathe manufacturers realise this point, so that there are few machines now made which are not so equipped. However, the beginner may be offered second-hand lathes of the plain type; or may, on the grounds of expense, otherwise be tempted to purchase one. The advice is—don't; unless it is to be but a temporary stepping-stone to the " real thing ".

This does not mean to say that the plain lathe has no utility under any circumstances. A small plain lathe, up to about 2-in. centre height, can form a useful adjunct to a larger, screwcutting lathe, as it can be used for a variety of small turning jobs, and may even prove to be a tool giving easier production in certain cases. The plain lathe under these circumstances is quite a different matter, and can add considerably to the scope of a small workshop. Nevertheless, for general amateur engineering, the plain lathe should not be selected as the nucleus of an amateur workshop, as its limitation will soon become apparent.

Suitable Sizes

It is obviously impossible here to give a complete treatise on lathe design, or to give step-by-step details of the features of manufacture to be looked for in each part, but certain general observations can be of use, especially to the beginner, who may be puzzled as to the desirability, or even necessity, of certain matters. The utility of many seemingly unimportant details may only become apparent after prolonged experience of the multitude of uses to which the amateur's lathe may be put.

With confidence it may be said that fully 50 per cent. of the work done on the amateur's lathe is really too big for the machine. This, as will be seen later, has a profound influence on amateur technique; at the moment it is important as emphasising two points of lathe selection. In the first place, it is desirable to buy as large a machine as the pocket or the accommodation will allow. Very few amateurs will be able to afford or house anything bigger than a lathe of 5-in. centre height; in fact, one of 3½-in. centre height will be the uttermost limit for the vast majority; while in many cases one of 3-in. capacity will have to suffice. While it is still true that the larger the lathe the better, comfort may be taken from the fact that all these sizes are capable of doing useful work if used intelligently. The keen amateur need not, therefore, be deterred from embarking on the finest of hobbies because circumstances permit only of the smallest machine.

Lathes of 1¾-in. and 2¼-in. centre height are available, and some wonderful and almost unbelievable work has been accomplished on these machines. Nevertheless, as the soundest advice, it may be said that the lathe of 3½-in. centre height meets amateur requirements of cost, size and general usefulness, better than any other, and is certainly the type most often found in amateur workshops.

Whatever size of lathe is chosen, sturdiness of construction should be looked for in the bed, head and tailstock, and these components should be as large and heavy as is compatible with the size of the machine. Fortunately again, modern small lathes have been much improved in these features. Many small lathes—and big ones, too—made prior to the first World War were appallingly flimsy and inadequate.

The amateur will, quite rightly, be particularly concerned over the matter of accuracy. There is no rough-and-ready test for accuracy which can be applied to a lathe in a store or showroom, and the amateur must rely on the reputation and integrity of the manufacturer. Most new lathes are well within the limits of accuracy claimed; especially as modern production methods make for truth and uniformity of product. The amateur is safe in placing his faith in the statements of any reputable lathe manufacturer.

When buying a second-hand lathe, privately, it is quite usual to see the machine in operation, and actual turning tests will usually show up any serious defects. Even this test must be carried out circumspectly, as many factors may combine to give a false impression. An accurate lathe, unskilfully used, will produce ill results; as such matters as turning speed, the shape and sharpness of the tool, " spring " in the work, and other factors must be considered. It is therefore essential that the novice should seek the help of some knowledgeable friend who will undertake to inspect any second-hand machine.

The Gap Bed

One of the first things to which consideration should be given in the selection of a lathe for amateur use is its ability to cope with all types of work. In the course of a model engineering life some surprisingly large work will be encountered. This brings up the question of the **gap bed**, a feature which has been noted in the illustration, Fig. 1. Its obvious utility is that it will allow comparatively large workpieces to be swung. Some small lathes, which are generally intended as an adjunct to a larger machine, have the lathe ways continued to the headstock, so that no gap is provided. The makers claim that this stiffens the lathe bed, and this is doubtless true to some extent, but the weakness, if such it be, does not seem noticeable in a correctly designed gap bed machine. Manufacturers generally see to it that plenty of " meat " is provided at the vital points. As the amateur usually has not access to a larger lathe, the gap bed must be considered essential.

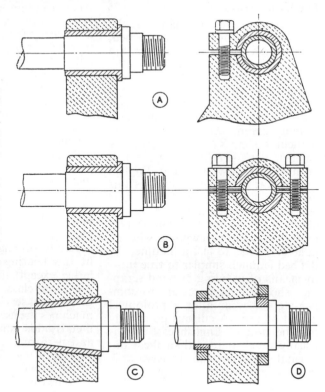

Fig. 6

Some types of head bearings associated with the small lathe. (A) The half-split bearing; (B) split parallel bearing; (C) taper bearing; (D) parallel-bore external cone bearing. The type (A) is that most often found on the cheapest class of lathe, and proves quite satisfactory in use. The bearing (B) is probably that most widely used on medium-priced machines, and meets most amateur needs. Taper bearings (C) and (D) are usually associated only with the higher-priced " precision " type of centre lathe.

The Backgear

Another necessity for the amateur lathe is the **backgear**. This is a necessary complement to the screw-cutting lathe, and no modern machine divorces the two. Some old lathes were, however, made without back gear, and they should be avoided. A great deal of amateur turning should be done in backgear, and much of a lathe's usefulness is lost without it.

The Hollow Mandrel

In very early lathes the mandrel, or **lathe spindle,** was often made solid, but the limitations of this were soon apparent, and very early gave way to the modern, hollow type. The advan-

tage of being able to accommodate long work in the hollow mandrel, while the portion to be turned is gripped in the lathe chuck, is obvious. The amateur will, therefore, do well to see that his lathe has the largest possible clearance hole in the lathe spindle. Some lathes fail badly in this respect, and it may not be considered unreasonable for the amateur to expect a clearance of around $\frac{5}{8}$ in. in the mandrel of any $3\frac{1}{2}$-in. lathe. A large clearance hole is also a pretty good guarantee that the spindle itself is of ample proportions. Another incidental good effect is that large lathe centres may be used; it being possible to accommodate the No. 2 Morse taper size in place of the much lighter No. 1 Morse.

The Lathe Ways

As we have seen in Chapter 1, the machined portions of the lathe bed, upon which the carriage moves, are known as the **ways**. Variations in the sectional shape of lathe ways are numerous, especially in American machines, where sloping ways, and raised " Vees " are often employed. Various claims are made for these particular shapes, yet, for ordinary amateur use, there does not seem to be much wrong with the old, English type of **flat bed**. Not only does this bed wear extremely well, but it is easier to make accurately at a reasonable cost. Also, and this is important from the amateur viewpoint, where a lathe often has to last a lifetime, the flat bed is much simpler to true up— by means of grinding or hand-scraping—should it be necessary to compensate for wear after a prolonged period of use. A curious point may here be noted. English cast-iron is usually much harder than the Continental or American variety, and, in consequence, wears longer.

Head Bearings

This is one of those matters which can be touched upon only lightly here, as the types of mandrel bearings are legion. They do, however, fall roughly into groups, certain of which are used extensively in the type of lathe under discussion.

A bearing which the amateur is likely to encounter, especially on the cheaper class of lathes, is that shown at (A) in Fig. 6. It consists of a bronze bush, split along one side, and held in a circular housing in the head casting, which is also split along the side. The tightness of the bearing may be adjusted by means of a nipping screw. This bearing is capable of long and satisfactory service, but presents difficulties if the lathe has to be re-aligned to compensate for wear.

Also, a failing which has sometimes been encountered is that there exists a tendency for the cast-iron housing to crack at a point opposite to the adjusting screw. Great care, therefore, should be exercised when adjusting head bearings of this design. Nevertheless, many thousands of such lathes have done excellent service in the model engineering cause for many years.

At (B) in Fig. 6 is shown the **split-parallel bearing,** where the adjustment is carried out by means of two screws which clamp down a cast-iron cap. The bearing itself is a split bush, and solidity is obtained by means of packing-shims of thin brass foil. If correctly shimmed and scraped to a fit this bearing is excellent on any lathe except those of the super-precision class, and is capable of giving long service. In some modern machines the use of new type bearing-metals adds considerably to the life and performance. Quite a satisfactory bearing for those amateurs whose expenditure must be limited.

Some form of **taper bearing,** such as is fitted to almost all high-class " professional " lathes, is also to be met with in the more expensive machines for amateur use. Generally speaking, the high initial cost of these lathes puts them beyond the reach of most amateurs, but, where cost is of no consideration, taper bearings are to be recommended. That shown at (C) is, probably, the most mechanically simple type; yet it is usually found only on lathes of the very highest class. In practice, the rear bearing has its taper in the reverse direction to that of the front; thus, thrust requirements are self-contained. A very excellent bearing indeed, but one calling for the highest grade in materials, manufacture and fitting; hence, it is by no means cheap.

The bearing known as the " parallel-bore external cone " is shown at

(D) in Fig. 6. This is an extremely good type, wherein the bushes are slit three ways, from end to end, and are adjusted in the housings by means of screwed ring-nuts. These nuts must have **square threads**, otherwise they exercise a " closing " effect on the bushes when they are tightened. This is a most excellent form of bearing, unfortunately somewhat expensive to produce accurately, but, when well made from good materials, having an almost indefinite life.

This summary of the bearings most likely to be encountered may well end with a word on **ball-bearing** and **roller-bearing** headstocks. The general consensus of opinion seems to be that such headstocks are productive of " chatter " on the work. Fundamentally, there seems no reason why this type of bearing should not be excellent in every way. Without doubt, however, this system calls for scrupulous care in design and fitting, and it seems probable that any failures in the past may be attributed to shortcomings in either of these.

It becomes apparent, therefore, that the matter of lathe headstock bearings is governed, like so many other things in life, by the length of one's purse.

Power or Treadle Drive

It will become evident by now that the choice of an amateur's lathe does, in fact, depend largely upon what one is prepared to spend on one's hobby, but, were this the only governing factor, this chapter might just as well not have been written. Important as the financial aspect is, there is sometimes so little difference in the cost of alternative fitments that the prospective mechanic really may be said to have an unfettered choice. In the matter of power drive this would really seem to be so as the cost of a suitable electric motor and counter-shaft is usually about on a par with that of an efficient stand and treadle. Power drive, by means of an electric motor, has so many advantages that the motor may be considered an essential and integral part of the machine. These advantages can hardly be over-emphasised, and the addition of an electric motor, to a machine which has previously been foot-operated, may well revolutionise one's whole outlook on model engineering. Not only is accurate work performed more easily, but many jobs, hitherto shirked because of the considerable amount of physical energy involved, may be undertaken with pleasure and profit. A power-driven lathe, properly installed, is infinitely to be preferred to any foot-driven arrangement.

The Lathe Stand

Most small lathes may be purchased either separately as a bench lathe, or mounted on a stand. While it cannot be denied that the provision of a suitable stand adds greatly to the ease with which a lathe may be installed, the considerable cost may well cause the model mechanic to think twice. Generally, it may be taken that where financial considerations are important—as they usually are—a lathe stand may be dispensed with.

These remarks apply, however, only where great care is exercised in setting up a lathe on the bench. Uneven bolting, or an uneven bench surface, may seriously distort the lathe bed. The matter is dealt with in the following chapter, but unless the instructions are carefully carried out it is much better for the amateur to obtain a correctly machined lathe stand in the first place. It must be fully realised that a comparatively light bench lathe cannot be bolted down satisfactorily to any sort of bench surface, and that much of the inaccuracy often attributed to the cheaper lathes, and the expensive ones too for that matter, is due to this error.

Drives

The modern tendency towards building the small lathe as a self-contained unit, complete with electric motor, is a step in the right direction, and automatically solves one of the amateur's problems. Such machine units are desirable in every way.

It may well be, however, that alternative arrangements are necessary, as quite often a good lathe may be purchased separately, and an electric motor obtained later. Suitable methods of installation will be discussed, but as the question is intimately bound up with the driving features of the lathe itself, a word may well be inserted here.

Only two methods of lathe drive are commonly used: the **flat belt,** and the **" V " belt drive.** The latter is sometimes called the **" V " rope drive.** As the names imply, the difference centres around the shape of the driving pulleys. In the first instance, the crowns of the pulleys are flat (they are slightly " domed ", in reality) so that only a flat belt may be utilised. In the second, the pulleys have a " V "-shaped groove cut into them, and a belt of similar section must be used. Both methods have advantages and disadvantages, yet the balance is mostly in favour of the " V " belt.

A much more positive drive may be had from the " V " rope, and the annoyance of belt-slip is almost eliminated. The arrangement is also much neater, as the belts can be of short length without perceptible inefficiency. The rope takes the form of an endless belt, thus obviating the use of belt-fasteners—that great weakness of belt drives—making for trouble-free operation and silent running. Noise is of great importance in the home workshop!

The disadvantages of the " V " rope are not serious, and may be confined to two instances. First, the belt being endless, it is necessary to dismantle the lathe head, and sometimes the countershaft, to fit or replace the belt, but as these ropes will wear for many years, this objection is not of great importance. To overcome this difficulty, some amateurs advocate the use of a detachable " V " belt—known as the **Whittle** type. These belts seem satisfactory, although the use of any type of fasteners has its weakness. It may, however, often be more desirable to use a detachable belt than to disturb the bearings of a lathe which is running perfectly.

The second disadvantage of the " V " belt is that it is more difficult to slip the belt from one pulley to another for speed changing purposes. This trouble may be obviated by the use of a proper countershaft, whereby the belt tension may be relaxed by the movement of a lever. Such countershafts are on the market.

The Flat Belt

Driving by means of a flat belt is one of the earliest systems of machine drive, and has held its own because of its simplicity in operation, fitting, and manufacture, yet it is generally considered, today, to be somewhat old-fashioned. One of its chief drawbacks is that the ordinary leather or fabric belt is not suitable for short drives; that is, the pulleys upon which the belt runs must be some considerable distance apart before power can be transmitted without undue slip. Short drives necessitate that the belts be extremely tight upon the pulleys, a condition not easy to maintain, and one which causes considerable strain and wear on the pulley shafts. Unfortunately, long belt drives are not easy to obtain with convenience and safety in the home workshop.

Belt fasteners also present a problem to the amateur. Although the usual types of belt fasteners are quite satisfactory in professional workshops and factories—where noise is of little consequence—the use of commercial fasteners in the home workshop results in undue noise as the fasteners pass over the pulleys, in some cases being responsible for almost half the noise of operation. Where the workshop occupies a room in a dwelling-house, this objection can be serious. Quieter methods of belt joining, such as lacing with brass or copper wire, usually mean frequent breakages and repairs.

The advantages of flat belt drive are usually associated with the **overhead line-shaft,** where several machines are operated from one source of power. This is dealt with in the next chapter; meanwhile it can be said here that the flat belt recommends itself for this purpose because of the ease with which it may be slipped from one pulley to another for the purpose of stopping one machine in the line, whilst allowing others to run.

The advent of endless, flat belts woven in nylon or similar modern materials has, to some extent, reinstated the flat belt for certain purposes, mostly connected with very high-speed operation. The weight and comparative inflexibility of the " V " rope makes it unsuitable for use at the extremely high speeds required for such machines as grinders, and small production lathes and capstans. On the other hand, the great strength, lightness and flexibility of the new woven belts enables them to perform under conditions that would wreck the ordinary "V" rope in a few minutes.

Toolposts
One of the things which conduces

to the convenient operation and, in some ways, the utility of the amateur's lathe, is the manner in which the cutting tool is secured to the top slide.

Before detailing some desirable types, it may be well to mention a toolpost which is probably the least desirable from the amateur's viewpoint. This is the post known as the **American Type,** a drawing of which is given in Fig. 7. As may be seen, the lathe tool is gripped, by means of a bolt, in a slotted post; the action of tightening the bolt locking, at the same time, the post to the topslide. The tool rests on a metal packing piece with a curved underside—called a " boat "—and this in turn rests in a shallow, saucer-like washer. The

Fig. 7

American type toolpost, not generally ideal for amateur use.

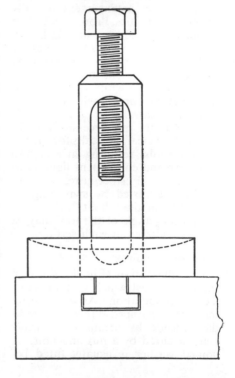

object of the arrangement is to allow the tool to be swivelled to the right or left; a tilting movement may also be given to the tool, thus allowing the tool-tip to be adjusted to the correct cutting height.

On the face of it it would appear an ideal arrangement, as the necessity for adjusting the tool to height by means of packing strips is eliminated. In practice, however, this toolpost has some serious snags; the chief one being that, owing to the manner in which the post must be secured, the cutting tool occupies a position some distance from the leading edge of the topslide, and it is, therefore, difficult to take cuts close up to the lathe chuck without the danger of the jaws or workpiece hitting the projecting end of the topslide.

The trouble can be somewhat overcome by using specially forged tools or a curved tool-holder, but, in spite of this, the arrangement usually presents difficulties. Proof may be had by inspecting almost any lathe on which this toolpost has been used for any length of time. The battered condition of the end of the topslide will usually bear witness to many unfortunate encounters with the revolving chuck jaws.

In addition, this necessity for obtaining tool clearance calls for the use of long tools, resulting in excessive overhang and consequent liability to " chatter ". Furthermore, as tool height is adjusted by swivelling on the radius of the " boat ", the effective cutting angle of the tool may be seriously altered at each setting.

A Popular Toolpost

The illustration (Fig. 8) shows a simple toolpost which is quite satisfactory in operation. As will be seen, the tool is clamped directly down to the topslide by means of a heavy plate, secured by a nut and bolt. A domed washer is usually fitted beneath the nut; its object being to

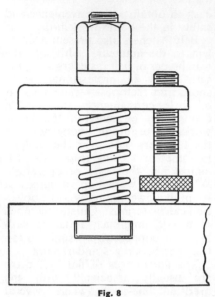

Fig. 8

A popular type of toolpost, which fulfils amateur requirements.

prevent side-strain on the bolt due to uneven clamping. A finger screw, carrying a knurled disc, is provided as an adjustable packing-stop, while a stout spring prevents the clamping plate from falling when the tool is released.

This toolpost is infinitely to be preferred to the American type. The disadvantages are that the top of the slide is liable to become dented and damaged, after prolonged use, by the pressure of the tools and packing stop; also, if it is desired to alter the angle of the tools in the horizontal plane, the height packing becomes disturbed, and the whole tool must be reset in position.

The Box Toolpost

A somewhat better arrangement is provided by the toolpost illustrated in Fig. 9, known as the **box type.** In this the tool is held in the toolpost itself, which can be detached from the lathe with the tool *in situ*. The angle of the tool, in the horizontal plane, can, therefore, be altered without in any other way disturbing it, which is a great convenience. The topslide is not injured by this type of toolpost.

The Four-way Toolpost

The four-way toolpost is undoubtedly the ideal type. It has none of the evils of the American post, nor does it deface the topslide; yet it has all the merits of the other types. In addition, tool changing— an irksome job—is reduced to a minimum, as four tools of different shapes can be accommodated. Certain tools, such as the parting-off tool, can remain almost permanently in position.

Most four-way toolposts are provided with a spring-and-plunger locating device in the base, so that a

tool which has been swung out of operation may be re-located at any time. The arrangement is useful when turning a number of duplicate parts calling for the accurate resetting of a number of tools. Some patterns of locating toolposts have an exceptionally thick and heavy base, which makes it necessary to remove the topslide in order that the tools may be located low enough for correct operation. Other toolposts, however, have the locking mechanism in the base of the turret itself, so that the height is not increased. They may be used, therefore, in exactly the same way as an ordinary post, and are much to be preferred.

The Slotted Cross-Slide

One of the essential characteristics of the successful turner is a scrupulous attention to detail, and this practice may well be extended to the choice of the lathe itself. Details, which to the novice may seem unimportant, can contribute very greatly to the ease of manipulation and the versatility of the amateur's machine.

A typical instance is provided by the cross-slide of the small lathe. On a great number of these machines this component is provided with a series of " T "-shaped slots, enabling vertical slides, angle plates, and milling spindles to be bolted into place on the carriage. Thus, milling operations, and certain types of boring, may be readily undertaken, and the scope of the lathe is increased out of all proportion to this seemingly insignificant addition. Some makers also slot the topslide of the machine, but a slotted cross-slide is really all that is necessary.

So essential is this feature—which, by the way, is rarely found on large " professional " lathes—that quite a considerable business has arisen in the supply of slotted slides to those unfortunates whose lathes do not

Fig. 9
The box toolpost, having some advantages over those shown in Figs. 7 and 8.

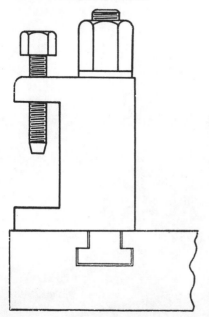

possess them; the owners finding it worth while to spend several pounds to supply a deficiency which should not have existed in the first place. Many American machines are notorious in this respect.

The Topslide

In a commendable endeavour to cheapen a lathe, some manufacturers list their products minus a topslide, the lathe being supplied either with or without this accessory. Some provision for swivelling the cross-slide itself is usually provided, so that taper turning and such like may be undertaken. Where extreme financial considerations are important the topslide may, possibly, be dispensed with, and good and useful work may still be done. The versatility of the lathe will, naturally, be curtailed, especially during such operations as screwcutting, in certain methods of taper turning, and in repetition work. This will become evident later.

The Index Dial

Another apparently small matter which needs the amateur's attention is the provision of **graduated index dials** to the cross-slide, topslide, and sometimes the hand-wheel on the leadscrew. The importance of these refinements is in the order given above, but a graduated index to the cross-slide may be considered an essential. This dial should be graduated to show movement of the cross-slide in thousandths of an inch. With this fitting, accurate work can be done more quickly and with greater certainty; tool settings can be readily duplicated, and the graduated dial is useful for taper turning and for screwcutting.

It must be remembered when turning to size by means of the index dial

Fig. 10

The ideal toolposts for the amateur's lathe. The four-way toolpost saves repeated tool changes, and is a most convenient time-saver. (*Photo by courtesy Myford Engineering Co., Ltd.*)

that a movement of, say, 0·001 in. on the index scale will reduce the diameter of the work by 0·002 in.; in other words, the diameter of the work is always reduced twice the amount registered on the dial. This is because the dial-index shows the amount which the tool is advanced into the radius of the work, whereas the tool removes material from the diameter. We all know, of course, that the radius is always half the diameter.

Fig. 12
A useful aid to screwcutting: the thread dial indicator.
(*Courtesy Myford Eng. Co., Ltd.*)

Fig. 11
Tumbler reverse gearing for instantaneous reversal of leadscrew rotation. (*Courtesy Myford Eng. Co., Ltd.*)

Tumbler Reverse

The mechanics of the tumbler reverse gear have been explained in Chapter 1, and it may be considered a highly desirable, but not essential feature. Its uses are found in reversing the direction of travel of the lathe carriage along the bed, a condition which may be desirable in plain turning, screwcutting, in cutting left-hand threads, and for certain types of boring.

Thread Dial-Indicator

A large number of lathes may be provided—usually at a small extra cost—with a thread dial-indicator, which may be attached to the side of the lathe saddle. The mechanism may be engaged at will with the leadscrew, and provides a simple method of " striking " or " picking-up " the thread when screwcutting. Here again, this accessory and its operation will be fully described in a later chapter, but as it may be said to form a part of the lathe mechanism, it may be mentioned here as a useful, but not indispensable, adjunct.

Rack and Pinion Feed

Some of the older types of lathe, and some of the simpler new ones, do not have provision for releasing the lathe carriage from the leadscrew, which are, therefore, permanently coupled together. No rack and pinion are provided for movement of the carriage along the lathe bed, a result which must be attained by winding the carriage along by a hand-wheel on the end of the lead screw.

The arrangement is not so bad as it may sound, although the writer has always found it to be a little tedious. Its main disadvantage seems to be that one is inclined to move the carriage only the minimum distance from the chuck when it is necessary to have clearance for such operations as filing, or tapping and threading work in the lathe. This tends to cramp free movement, and can be dangerous to the hands owing to the proximity of sharp lathe tools. The failing is one of human nature rather than of lathe design, yet, however good one's intentions may be, the interest and eagerness to get to the job will cause any but the superman to fail occasionally. If possible obtain a lathe with a split or half-nut arrangement, and a rack feed.

It may be remarked that some small lathes, so equipped, have the hand-wheel directly geared to an inverted rack. This is inclined to be awkward, as it is then necessary to turn the hand-wheel in a clockwise direction to feed towards the headstock. The movement is not natural, and a better arrangement is that in which the hand-wheel is coupled to the rack through an intermediate gear; thus the carriage moves in the direction in which the wheel is turned. It is small matters such as this which count for so much in working comfort and convenience.

Set-over Tailstock

In some of the simpler and cheaper lathes one sometimes finds that the tailstock is made as one solid casting, so that it cannot be set-over or relined with the headstock should occasion arise. This is a grave disadvantage, as owing to its mobility the tailstock rarely remains truly lined with the head over any long period. True turning " between centres " cannot be done under these conditions. Furthermore, the lathe cannot be used for turning long tapers between centres; both these operations will be described later, when the novice will appreciate the force of these remarks.

Summary

It will be appreciated that much of the foregoing applies mainly to the older types of second-hand lathes, many thousands of which change hands in the amateur market each year. Nevertheless, we may see, in a general way, the usual features over which the amateur may exercise a choice. They may be enumerated as follows:

1. Choose the largest and heaviest lathe—other things being equal—that you can afford or accommodate.

2. From the considerations of cost and workshop facilities the $3\frac{1}{2}$-in. centre lathe will fill most amateur requirements.

3. **Some Essential Features**
    (a) Screwcutting gear.
    (b) Backgear.
    (c) Gap bed.
    (d) Set-over tailstock.
    (e) Slotted cross-slide.
    (f) Graduated index to cross-slide.

4. **Highly Desirable Features**
    (a) Power drive.
    (b) " V " Belts.
    (c) Four-way Toolpost.
    (d) Independent topslide.
    (e) Large clearance hole in mandrel.
    (f) Tumbler reverse.
    (g) Rack feed with intermediate gearing.

5. **Some Desirable Features**
    (a) Thread dial-indicator.
    (b) Lathe stand.

CHAPTER 3

INSTALLING THE LATHE

ONE of the highlights of a model engineering life is the acquisition and installation of the lathe. Few other possessions can impart that thrilling anticipation of joys to come, or give such genuine promise of many happy hours.

When, for the first time, this important event occurs, the primary consideration must be the workshop in which our future friend and companion is to be housed. He is worthy of a good home. The model mechanic is here likely to be confronted with the serious question—indoor or outdoor workshop? A good many of us, unfortunately, will have the matter settled for us by circumstances; lack of space precluding an indoor workshop. Where, however, a choice can be made, it cannot be too strongly urged that an indoor workshop be chosen. This, for preference, should be a room on the ground floor, but an upstairs workshop is quite a feasible proposition, and the writer has used such a shop for many years, without undue annoyance to the "domestic powers", or, almost as important, the neighbours. While it cannot be denied that an indoor workshop is bound to make a little mess however careful one may be, it must be taken for granted that a little give-and-take in domestic arrangements exists, and that one's womenfolk have, at least, a certain interest in one's hobbies and pleasures. It should, in any case, be made a penal offence not to disclose that one is a model engineer, before marriage!

The advantages of the indoor workshop centre around one matter —damp. Only by extreme precautions can this enemy be kept within bounds in the outdoor workshop. It is to be understood, of course, that by "outdoor workshop" is meant the usual " portable " type of wooden structure, sold for this purpose. If a proper brick-built workshop can be constructed, this is an entirely different matter, which may be equal in all respects to the indoor variety. Few of us can contemplate such luxury, so that the term " outside workshop " invariably means the wooden building.

Some years ago the writer was forced by circumstances to own such a workshop, and, through lack of precaution, most of his tools—including the lathe—were ruined. The great trouble was to maintain a fairly even temperature. Business requirements necessitated that the workshop be left unattended for some days at a time, and, in the winter especially, it was found that on turning on the electric fire for heating purposes prior to starting work, the condensation of moisture in the air presented a grave problem. As the air heated up, the moisture condensed on the cold metal of tools and machinery, which would in consequence, literally be running with water in a short time. This had disastrous results, as it was impossible to wipe every drop of moisture away, so that rust was inevitable. The cure lay, of course, in providing some constant form of heating—not an easy thing to do with economy.

If an outdoor workshop is inevitable, some precautions must be taken. The matter may be helped somewhat by providing the shop with a double " skin "; that is to say, with an inner lining of wood or " wall-board ", with an air space between the outer and inner shells. Combined with good-fitting doors and windows, this can help a lot.

Constant heating does provide a problem. Electric heating is expensive but does the job perfectly. A more economical method of maintaining some semblance of even temperature is provided by one of the small, paraffin oil heater-lamps, which are sold under the name of " radiator lamps ", and which are designed to keep the engines and radiators of motor cars warm during cold weather. Such lamps burn for several days on one filling of oil, and while the heat generated is not great, it is constant, and sufficient for any but extreme conditions.

Small tools should be kept in closed cupboards or boxes, and may be smeared with some rust-preventing compound, several of which are on the market. Finally, the more one uses an outdoor workshop the better.

The Bench

Whether your workshop be indoors or out, the first consideration must be the bench upon which the lathe is to rest. Those that purchase the lathe complete with the stand will not be concerned with this matter, but for others the question of the bench is of utmost importance.

The first requirement is rigidity. The supports must be of sturdy proportions—at least 3 in. by 3 in. if in wood—with a heavy top of 2-in. planking. It is surprising how stiff and heavy a lathe bench must be if vibration is to be kept to a minimum. The bench must be well braced and free from " shake ", as any swaying of the bench will be fatal to good lathe work. Probably the finest type of bench is that constructed from 2-in. angle iron, with a top of 2-in. planking. Angle iron will probably be as cheap to buy as the sound and heavy wood necessary, and may, for those used to metal work, be easier to make successfully. Making good joints in wood is not an easy job for the inexperienced.

In Fig. 13 is indicated a simple but efficient bench framework, made from 2-in. by $\frac{1}{4}$-in. angle iron with

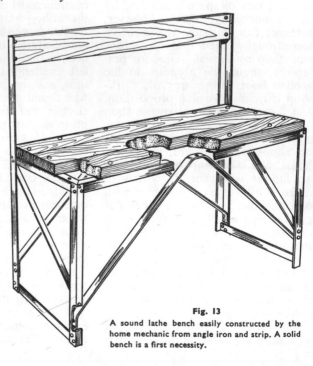

Fig. 13

A sound lathe bench easily constructed by the home mechanic from angle iron and strip. A solid bench is a first necessity.

bracings of 1½-in. by ¼-in. flat iron strip. It is an advantage to carry the rear legs upwards, some two feet above the bench top, and to brace this with a length of ¾-in. board, bolted on. To this may be attached shelves to house the chucks and other accessories, while a series of hooks may accommodate the lathe change wheels.

If the bench is made about 6 ft. long, other tools, such as a drill and bench grinder, may be fitted, but care should be taken to place the grinder as far away from the lathe as possible. Grinding grit flies about pretty freely, and is fatal to the lathe ways and slides. If the bench framework is made about 17 in. wide it may then be planked with three lengths of 6 in. by 2 in. wood—oak for preference.

Finding the Lathe Height

The height at which the lathe is placed has a profound effect on comfort and ease of working. Do not place the lathe too low so that excessive stooping is necessary. A comfortable " working height " may be determined by standing upright against a wall with the arms extended downwards. Now bend the forearm upwards at the elbow and make a mark on the wall at the point where the bent elbow lies. It is at this height that the top surface of the topslide should be set. This method is, by the way, also useful in fixing the correct height for the bench vice.

The Lathe Foundation

Assuming that we are making a bench somewhat on the lines of that suggested in Fig. 13, it should be arranged for the top planking to lie 2 in. lower than is necessary to bring the lathe to the correct working height. This is so that the lathe may rest upon two cross-members of 2-in. planking, which should be bolted across the three top planks at the points where the lathe feet will lie. It is then necessary to place a piece of ⅛-in. sheet iron, somewhat larger than the lathe base, on the top of these cross-members. A lathe which is bolted directly down to a wooden bench top is liable to be strained as the feet sink into the wood under the pressure of the holding-down bolts.

It is possible to buy large, flat trays, of substantial gauge sheet iron in a number of suitable sizes. They are stocked by the suppliers of butcher's equipment, and are reasonably priced. They make ideal swarf trays for fitting beneath a lathe, and may replace the sheet iron plate.

Bolting Down the Lathe

It is customary to regard textbook instructions as being aimed at an academic perfection not really necessary for practical purposes, and it may seem that the present details may fall into this class. So many amateurs' lathes have been simply bolted down to a more or less uneven bench, without apparent ill effects, that many an amateur may be tempted to do the same. More particularly will the following instructions be disregarded by the inexperienced; yet, if the instructions are carried out, the amateur will be provided with a visible proof of their necessity.

It has been mentioned that uneven bolting down will pull a light bench lathe badly out of truth. To prevent this it is necessary to actually see what is happening as the holding-down bolts are tightened. There is only one instrument available to the amateur which will do this, and that is a **test dial-indicator**, commonly known as a " clock ".

These instruments are sold at a cost of about £2 or £3, and consist of a clock-like dial, graduated in thousandths of an inch, over which moves an indicator hand. This is actuated by a plunger in the side of the clock, so that any movement of the plunger is registered in thousandths of an inch on the dial. To the amateur this may seem an expensive and pretentious instrument for the home workshop, yet it may safely be said that there is hardly anything which the amateur mechanic čan buy which can prove of more use. For setting-up and checking work on the faceplate or four-jaw chuck; for re-setting work which has been disturbed; for lining-up the tailstock for parallel turning between centres; for setting-up for taper turning; for screwcutting multiple threads; these are but a few of the myriad uses of the " clock ", and many hitherto "impossible jobs " become simplicity itself when reflected in its magic face. Setting up your bench lathe is a case in point. If you cannot buy a "clock" then borrow one. Some member of your model enginering society has one, and would doubtless be willing if not to lend it to you, then to give you a hand in bolting down your lathe.

We now come to the actual bolting-down operation. Place the lathe on the prepared bed, the bolt holes having been marked out and drilled, and place the bolts loosely in position. Take a piece of mild steel bar, about $\frac{3}{4}$ in. in diameter, and as long as will go into the lathe, and grip it tightly in the three-jaw chuck. Now lock the mandrel by engaging the backgears, so that the chuck cannot turn.

The " clock " should now be clamped in the toolpost, and the plunger located at the extreme end of the steel bar; the position of the clock being adjusted by means of the cross-slide until the indicator hand rests on zero. Be sure that the indicator hand is " under tension "; that is, that it will register a plus or minus movement either side of the zero mark if the cross-slide is moved. While the clock is registering in this position the lathe is in an unstressed condition, but immediately the bed is twisted or strained the indicator will move a certain amount. The obvious aim is to tighten the holding-down bolts so that, when finally tight, the indicator needle still remains at zero.

Tightening one bolt will rarely show movement of the indicator, so this should be done; now tighten an opposite bolt and note the movement. As an experiment, all the bolts may be tightened, and, as this is done, the indicator will show a surprising amount of variation. It remains, therefore, to loosen off each bolt, and place large pieces of shim-steel packing under each bolting surface, until all bolts may be fully tightened without movement of the indicator. Complicated as this process may sound, it is really very simple, as the clock will immediately show up any errors of packing, and one can see the situation clearly at any time.

In passing, it may be of interest to note that the writer has checked up the accuracy of several lathes which have been bolted down without these precautions. In every instance the lathe was found to be in a state of strain, in one instance as much as 20 thousandths of an inch!

Fitting-up the Drive

If the lathe has been bought as a unit, complete with motor and countershaft, nothing remains but to connect up the electric wiring. Many, however, will have acquired motorless machines, the motor being purchased separately. The drive will then depend upon the type of pulleys with which the lathe is fitted.

Although the " V " rope drive is much to be preferred, the majority of small lathes have, until recently, been equipped for flat belt, and the odds are that a second-hand machine will be so fitted. Let us therefore, consider this type first.

Mention has been made of the possibility of running several machines from one power source by means of the **line shaft**, and the flat belt lends itself admirably to this purpose. In

Fig. 15 is shown a theoretical overhead line shaft, with **striking gear** for disengaging the drive of one or more machines. As may be seen, the drive is taken by the belt (A) from the motor to the **line shaft,** which may run the whole length of the bench, or even the workshop. The wide pulley (D) is fixed to this line shaft, and drives, by belt (B), the pulley (E) on the **countershaft.** This pulley is also a fixture, but the pulley (F) is not so fixed, but is allowed to run loose on the countershaft, being located by a collar. The three-step pulley (H) is fixed to the countershaft, and matches with a similar pulley (G) on the lathe spindle.

It may thus be seen that while the belt (B) is on pulley (E) the countershaft will be driven, and will turn the lathe spindle *via* belt (C). If, however, the belt (B) is transferred to the loose pulley (F), the countershaft will not revolve, and the drive between motor and lathe will be

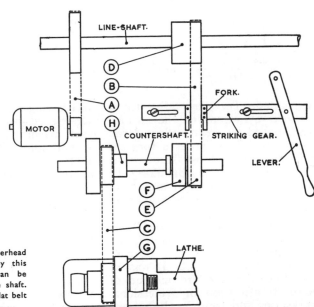

Fig. 15

Theoretical lay-out for overhead countershaft lathe drive. By this method several machines can be driven at will from one line shaft. Suitable only for flat or part-flat belt drive.

Fig. 16

Two useful bearings which are obtainable commercially; the 'Picador' die-cast plummer blocks made in the patterns shown; i.e. the 'Standard' and the 'Tallboy' with centre heights respectively of 1¼† and 3¾†. These bearings have oil-impregnated bushes in sizes suitable for a variety of shaft diameters. The bearings are well made, and accurate in centre height and alignment, which makes them suitable for a number of shaft and countershaft lay-outs.

The range also includes self-aligning bearings, die-cast pulleys, collars and line shafting. There is also available a 'Utility Spindle' comprising a shaft and housing supplied as a unit, with either plain bearings or ballrace bearings for the higher speeds.

interrupted. Transfer of the belt is obtained by means of the **striking gear,** moved by means of the **lever.** The striking gear carries a fork engaging with the " loose " side of the belt (that is the side not taking the pull of the drive) so that movement of the lever pushes the belt on or off the pulleys (E) and (F).

This is the principle of the " fast and loose pulley countershaft ", and any number of these may be connected to the line shaft. It was, at one time, the standard method of power transmission in professional workshops and factories, but, while still having its uses, is rapidly being superseded by the system wherein each machine tool has its own individual motor. Nevertheless, the line shaft can be very useful in the amateur workshop, as, once the somewhat complicated fitting-up has been done, the installation will run for years with little trouble. The striking gear can be made by the amateur himself, while the pulleys, shafting and plummer-blocks (i.e. bearings) are easily obtainable. The chief drawback from the amateur's viewpoint is that the arrangement is somewhat cumbersome, and is apt to be noisy. When only two machines, such as a lathe and a bench grinder, are to be run, the amateur may, perhaps, be content to use the plain lineshaft, unshipping the belts by hand as the necessity arises.

A Clever Alternative Arrangement

Where the motor is required to drive only the lathe, the arrangement shown in the accompanying photograph and drawings forms a simple and speedy method of motorising a small lathe. Very little additional equipment is required; these being a small bench countershaft (obtainable from most good tool dealers), a stout plank of wood, some strip iron, together with some nuts, bolts and coach screws.

The drawings and photograph are practically self-explanatory, and while the arrangement is shown fixed

to a lathe stand, there is no reason why it should not be similarly applied to a bench lathe. In spite of its almost stark simplicity, the original—developed by Mr. H. E. White, of the North London S.M.E.—ran for a prolonged period without trouble.

Without entering fully into the

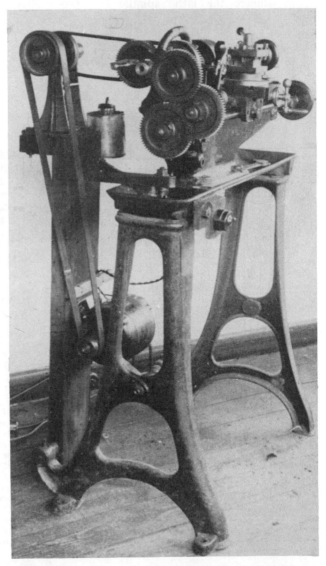

Fig. 17

An ingenious amateur arrangement of a plain countershaft. Although simple in design and materials it has all the requirements of a good lathe drive, i.e., long belt centres and provision for adjustment.

details, which may be gathered from the drawings, the assembly consists of a stout beam which is pivoted at the base to the lathe stand, movement being restricted by an iron stirrup by means of which the beam may be locked in any position, thus adjusting the belt tension. To the top of this beam a small countershaft is fixed, from whence the lathe spindle is driven by a flat or round belt. The motor is bolted low down on the beam, thus providing a long belt drive.

The "V" Belt Drive

The above arrangement is suitable for flat or round belts, as these may be transferred from one range of speed-pulleys to another without alteration of the belt tension. This is not feasible with the "V" belt, and some device must be incorporated which will allow the belt to be slackened and tightened again with the least possible trouble. By fitting a clamping lever in place of the nut on the stirrup a quick belt adjustment could be obtained with the system just detailed, and it would seem that it could be applied to both flat or "V" belts.

The more usual arrangement, however, is to employ a proper "V" rope countershaft, such as that

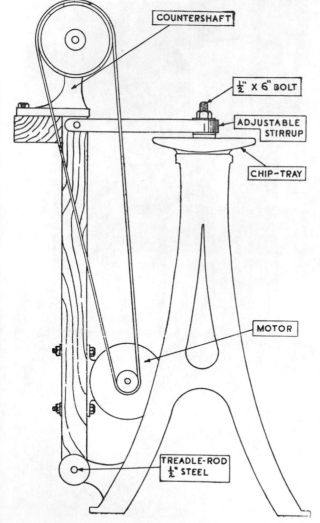

COUNTERSHAFT

½" X 6" BOLT

ADJUSTABLE STIRRUP

CHIP-TRAY

MOTOR

TREADLE-ROD ¼" STEEL

Fig. 18

Side elevation of the drive shown in Fig. 17. A plain countershaft is mounted to the top of a stout wooden beam, hinged on the treadle rod of the lathe stand. Slotted holes in the beam provide for adjustment of the motor-belt, while the adjustable stirrup takes care of the lathe-belt tension. This serviceable set-up can be constructed by any amateur in a couple of hours from easily obtainable and cheap materials.

shown in Fig. 19, and this is certainly the most straightforward way. Alternatively, a home-made countershaft, using plummer-blocks, is quite within the scope of the amateur mechanic. The greatest difficulty would be to provide the instantaneous belt adjustment which is necessary. A modification of Fig. 18, using a shorter wooden beam, is a likely suggestion. Belt adjustment on proprietary countershafts is usually obtained by the movement of eccentrics on a spindle.

Independent Overhead Drives

For the purpose of milling, grinding, or the operation of revolving tools which may be held in the lathe toolpost, some form of **independent overhead drive** is usually required. A grinding attachment, for instance, when clamped to the lathe topslide, must be revolved at a comparatively high speed; yet, at the same time, provision must be made for the drive to be continuous while the grinder is making a back and forth movement along the lathe bed. This rather complicates matters, as an overhead pulley, fixed in one position, would not allow the driving belt to follow the movements of the grinder beneath.

The situation is best met by the use of the **revolving roller,** which is illustrated in Fig. 20. Here, a wooden roller about 18 in. long is mounted —preferably on ball races—in a position above the lathe, and may be driven either from a separate motor or from an additional pulley on the shaft of the lathe motor itself. The simplest method, and one which is quite efficient in practice is to take the overhead drive from the large pulley on the lathe mandrel.

When doing cylindrical grinding, where the job in the chuck must revolve as well as the grinding wheel, the lathe spindle is revolved by

Fig. 19
Plain countershaft and adjustable motor mount giving a range of six speeds. (*Courtesy Myford Eng. Co., Ltd.*)

slipping the motor belt on to the slow speed pulleys; thus, the work revolves slowly in comparison to the grinding wheel, which may, of course, be geared to run at high speed from the large lathe pulley. At times, however, it is necessary to have the work stationary, as in some types of milling and when using a drilling spindle. For this purpose the lathe pulleys may be disconnected from the lathe spindle by releasing the backgear locking-pin, leaving the backgears disengaged. By doing this, the lathe pulleys will revolve independently of the mandrel which may be locked by engaging a gear train—leaving the leadscrew free—and wedging two of the gears with a slip of brass. Wedging the gears in this manner can do them no harm, as the strain involved is very small indeed. When operated in this way, use can be made of the high and low change speed pulleys on the lathe by driving the lathe pulleys on the middle gear, and taking the overhead drive from either the large or the small pulley. In Fig. 20, which should make the arrangement plain, the motor countershaft has been omitted for the sake of clarity, and the drive shown in dotted line.

By this means, drive may be provided to any toolpost attachment; the belt, which may be flat or of round section such as is used on sewing machines, following the movement of the lathe saddle by progressing back and forth along the overhead roller. While overhead drive is a most useful addition, and adds enormously to the utility of the amateur's lathe, it is difficult, if not impossible, to obtain sufficiently high speeds for such processes as grinding, and an independent motor drive is necessary.

Lathe Speeds

It will be found that a good range of **low spindle speeds** is of more use to the amateur mechanic than a range of high speeds. The main reason for this is, as already stated, that a great deal of amateur lathe work is really too big for the machine employed, so that quite a good part of it must be performed at low turning speed if " chatter " and like troubles are to be avoided.

The small electric motors most often used for the purpose (usually $\frac{1}{4}$ or $\frac{1}{3}$ h.p.) are of the **split phase** type, with a speed of about 1,450 r.p.m. This " open " speed is too high for amateur purposes, as excessive vibration is likely to occur with the average home installation. Nor is such a speed often desirable, except, perhaps, for certain kinds of small brass work.

A maximum spindle speed of approximately 700 r.p.m. will be found most suitable for average purposes, and this can be achieved by gearing down the countershaft at a ratio of 4–1 to the motor speed,

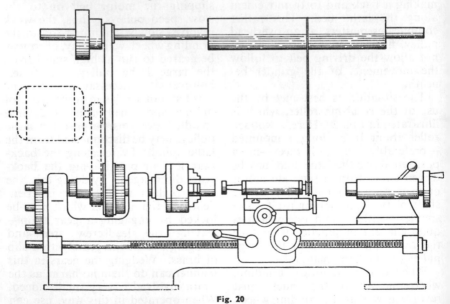

Fig. 20

most useful arrangement is the overhead drive, whereby milling spindles and drilling attachments may be operated from the toolpost. This drawing illustrates a method of driving from the lathe pulleys.

using, say, a pulley of $2\frac{1}{2}$ in. diameter on the motor shaft and one of 10 in. diameter on the countershaft. This will give a countershaft speed of around 360 r.p.m.

The three-step pulleys most often found on small lathes give a step-up of 2–1 on the large lathe pulley; the middle pulley is even-geared to the countershaft, while the small pulley gives a step-down of 2–1. Thus the " open " spindle speeds (that is, not using backgear) will be, in round figures: top gear, 720 r.p.m.; middle gear, 360 r.p.m., and low gear, 180 r.p.m.

The ratio of step-down given by the average backgear is 5–1, so that by dividing the above speeds by five, we arrive at speeds of 144, 72, and 36 r.p.m. These speeds are highly satisfactory, and form an almost ideal combination.

Electrical Wiring

It must be admitted that the electrical installation of the average home workshop does, more often than not, leave much to be desired. In an understandable eagerness to " see the wheels go round ", temporary wiring hook-ups, often from the house lighting circuits, are perpetrated, and do, alas! only too often remain as permanencies. These may continue to function indefinitely without undue trouble, and the amateur is apt to add other machines, such as a driller or grinder, to the existing arrangements, until the workshop presents an ideal set-up for a spot of arson!

No electric motor above $\frac{1}{10}$ h.p. should ever be connected to the house lighting curcuit.

The wise amateur mechanic will, therefore, ensure that a proper 3-plug, earthed power point is fitted in his workshop, from whence he may wire up his machinery with a heavy cable. If this cable is secured to the benches and walls of the workshop, so that it is out of the way of damage, and cannot chafe, metal conduit may be dispensed with, although, of course, conduit tubing is the ideal.

A point often neglected is the provision of an **earthing lead** to all machines, and it is quite a common occurrence, especially in damp weather, for the operator to experience an electric shock, of more or less severity, whenever the metal portion of a machine is touched. Apart from being extremely disconcerting, this can be dangerous, as it may cause the operator to " jump " on contact. Sudden, uncontrolled movements such as this should never be made near revolving machinery!

Public authorities have varying local regulations covering electrical installations, but all insist that an adequate earthing system be provided. In most instances it is sufficient to connect the earthing wire to the ordinary, " third-pin ", earthing point provided in the house wiring; in others, the earthing wire may be connected directly to a **mains water pipe.** Do not earth to a gas main; it is illegal.

Switching

It is highly desirable that some switching method be used which permits of instantaneous reversal of the motor rotation. Electric motors vary to some extent in the manner in which this may be done; yet, generally speaking, the majority call for the reversal of the field and/or armature connections, depending on the type of motor used. This may sound very technical, but in practice the operation is extremely simple.

The majority of the small motors which the amateur is likely to use are of the **split-phase, induction type.** On these an inspection box may usually be found, containing four terminals to which wires from the windings are connected. By reversing two of the wires upon their respective terminals a contrary rotation may be obtained.

The upper drawing in Fig. 21 depicts such a terminal arrangement. The lead marked (C) is normally connected to the terminal (A), and the lead (D) to terminal (B). If, however, (C) is placed on terminal (B), and (D) on (A), the direction of rotation will be reversed. The terminals marked (S) (S) receive the electric supply, and are not changed over. They are, of course, connected to the on-off switch.

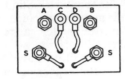

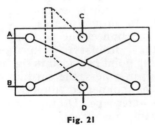

Fig. 21

Theoretical drawing of switching for the reversal of motor rotation. The upper sketch shows the usual arrangement of leads and terminals in a split-phase induction type A.C. motor.

The lower drawing shows a theoretical **double - pole double - throw switch,** indicating the wiring of the motor leads. The manner in which the leads are reversed is obvious.

The foregoing details, which apply only to alternating current motors, will explain the principles of reverse switching, but it must be remembered that there are a variety of motor types, so that Fig. 21 can only outline broad principles. **It is advisable to contact the makers of any electric motor which is to be switched for reverse operation.**

Special reversing switches which, besides providing reversing arrangements, embody an on-and-off switch also, may be purchased quite cheaply. They form the ideal method of lathe control, being simple to fit, and positive in action. They are usually totally enclosed so that swarf cannot enter and cause a short circuit.

It is important to bear in mind that before throwing over a reversing switch the current to the motor must be cut; that is to say, a **plain** reversing switch must not be suddenly operated while the motor is running, but the current must first be cut off by means of the on-off switch. When this is done the reversing switch may then be thrown over. The advantages of the commercial type of reversing switch is that the switch lever occupies a neutral position midway between the reversing contacts, so that the current is cut off, and reversing effected, by the one operation.

The great advantage of being able to reverse the direction of motor rotation in some simple way will become apparent in later chapters.

It is, of course, possible to reverse the direction of lathe rotation by means of an auxiliary **crossed belt** on a countershaft lay-out. While this is sometimes used in professional practice it is rather too complicated for amateur set-ups, as some form of reversing clutch, operated by a hanging lever, must be incorporated in the overhead drive. In these days of universal television and radio, the amateur will, of course, be certain that his electrical equipment will not cause interference. The usual induction type motor will not cause any trouble, but " brush " motors—such as are often used in the popular, electric hand-drills—should be adequately suppressed.

CHAPTER 4

LATHE ACCESSORIES

ACCESSORIES for the lathe are legion. It is quite possible, in fact, to parallel the case of those famous miniature cameras where the cost of the accessories may easily amount to twice that of the cameras themselves! No such absurdity will be advocated here, and this chapter will be devoted to the lathe equipment without which turning—in the usual sense of the word—cannot be accomplished.

Some accessories will not be mentioned at all at this point, as they will be met later in those pages devoted to the special purposes for which these accessories are designed. At the moment we are concerned with that minimum of equipment necessary to an intelligent and versatile use of the amateur's machine.

The Three-jaw, Self-centring Chuck

Methods of holding work in the lathe will, naturally, claim prior attention, and for this purpose there is nothing so universally used as the **self-centring chuck.** Few other methods have so wide an application, or can provide such easy operation.

There are several types of self-centring chuck on the market, but that most commonly used is the " geared scroll " type. In this the three chuck jaws are operated by a revolving scroll in the body of the chuck, through internal gearing operated by a detachable key. As the scroll is turned, all the chuck jaws move together an identical amount, so that any symmetrical body held in the jaws is automatically centred in the chuck.

It is usual to purchase these chucks with two sets of jaws—known as **inside** and **outside jaws.** These should always be obtained, as the scope of the chuck is much increased, and larger work may be safely gripped.

Three-jaw chucks are sold in various sizes, but one larger than 6 in. in diameter is usually beyond the scope of the amateur's lathe. For the 3½-in. lathe a chuck of 4 in. diameter is most usual; while the 3-in. lathe may be best suited by a chuck of 3 in. diameter. Some of the smaller chucks are operated by a knurled ring on the chuck body, but for sizes of 3 in. or over, those requiring a separate key are the most suitable.

Fig. 22
The three-jaw chuck showing key and " outside " jaws.

The Four-jaw Independent Chuck

This is another indispensable accessory, which is used for holding work of irregular shape, or for turning work " off centre ". In this case each jaw is operated independently by a separate screw. The same jaws may also be reversed for holding large work, so that another set is not required.

Independent chucks may often be used of larger diameter than that of the self-centring type, as they are usually of less depth, or thickness, with consequent less overhang. Thus quite a large independent chuck may revolve in the lathe gap, whereas one of self-centring type would foul the lathe ways. A diameter of 6 in. is useful for a $3\frac{1}{2}$-in. centre lathe, and one of 4 in. diameter for a machine of 3 in. centre height.

Work may be held very firmly in an independent chuck, so that large work, where the cutting strains are apt to be great, should always be held in the four-jaw chuck in preference to the self-centring type.

Lathe Collets

Collets, or **split chucks,** as they are sometimes called, formed one of the first methods of holding work in the centre lathe, and are, in fact, still used to the exclusion of almost all other devices, in the small watchmakers' lathes of to-day.

As will be seen in Fig. 24, collets

Fig. 24

Home-made collet adapter and collets; quite suitable for amateur construction.

are hollow pieces of metal, split in three places, with a steep taper turned on one end. The collet fits into an adapter in the lathe spindle; the adapter having an internal taper corresponding to that of the collet itself. Thus, if the collet is drawn into the adapter, the tapers cause the collet to close along the slits, so that a workpiece may be gripped. A separate collet is necessary for each diameter of work.

Some method of forcing the collet into the adapter is necessary, and two systems are commonly employed. In the one used mostly in the larger lathes, an external thread is provided on the inner end of the collet (usually a " buttress thread ", see Chapter 12) which engages with the internal thread of a hollow drawbar. This passes through the hollow lathe mandrel, and is operated by a hand wheel. The system is shown in Fig. 25.

The limitation of this system is that it allows only comparatively small collets to be used, as the diameter is limited by the drawbar. In large lathes having a hollow mandrel of 1 in. or more clearance this restriction is not, naturally, so severe; but in the smaller machines, with clearances of $\frac{1}{2}$ in. or $\frac{5}{8}$ in., it is a grave

Fig. 23

The four-jaw independent chuck, with a workpiece offset for boring. Note the lower jaw reversed.

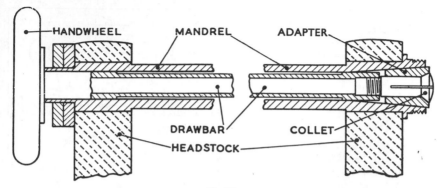

HANDWHEEL MANDREL ADAPTER

DRAWBAR COLLET

HEADSTOCK

Fig. 25

Sectional drawing of collet operated by a drawbar. Maximum size of collets is restricted in the small lathe.

handicap and limits the size of the collets to about $\frac{1}{4}$ in.

To overcome this restriction of size the second method is used extensively. It is illustrated in Fig. 26, and a drawing given in Fig. 27. It will be seen that the adapter is, in this case, screwed on to the nose of the lathe, and is bored to accommodate the collet. A threaded cap (B) screws over the nose of the adapter, thus forcing the collet into the taper. By this method the size of the rod to be held is limited only by the bore of the lathe spindle; while, for short

work which need not protrude into the mandrel, even larger sizes may be used. This is undoubtedly one of the best methods for the amateur's lathe.

A third system is also used. Here the outside of the collet is turned to fit the internal taper of the lathe mandrel itself, and the retaining cap screws directly on to the spindle thread. This is an excellent method which has been ingeniously adapted, commercially, to provide a self-extracting collet, taking work which is much larger than that possible with the draw-bar type.

Fig. 26

The home-made collet adapter shown with collet in position and retaining cap screwed on. The adapter screws on the lathe nose, and allows work to be held, the size of which is limited only by the mandrel bore. This invaluable accessory is quite simple to make by anyone prepared to work to average limits of accuracy. As the adapter and the collets are bored off the mandrel nose truth is not difficult to maintain.

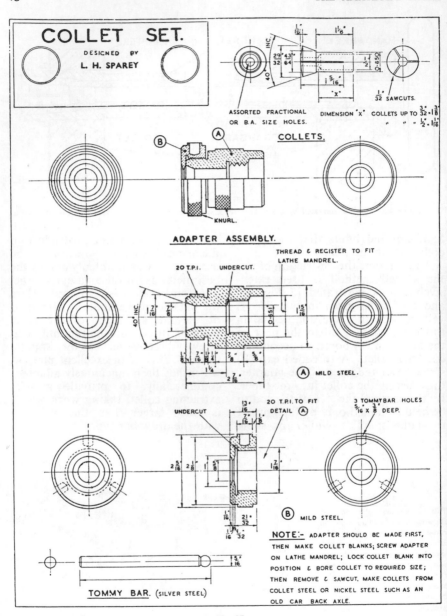

Fig. 27

Reduced drawing of home-made collet set, where the simplicity of the arrangement is well shown. It is advisable to bore the smaller-sized collets first, so that they may be opened out to a larger size if the initial drilling runs out of truth. Suggested sizes are from $\frac{1}{32}$ in. to $\frac{1}{2}$ in. in steps of $\frac{1}{32}$ in. B.A. sizes are also to be recommended.

Fig. 28

Collets which fit directly into the taper of the lathe mandrel, shown with cap and extractor. Allows maximum size of work to be held. (*Courtesy Myford Eng. Co., Ltd.*)

The utility of collets lies mainly in their ability to centre symmetrical work—such as mild and silver steel rods—accurately and instantly, which can be an asset of untold worth. In addition, rod of square, hexagon, or like section, may be held and centred with similar facility. Also, as collets are not likely to damage any work held, they are invaluable for gripping finished work or screw threads.

While the beginner may be content to leave the acquisition of collets to a later time, concentrating on the necessities rather than the refinements of lathe equipment, it should be remembered that it is just such refinements which add so greatly to the convenience and pleasure of the amateur mechanic, so that a collet set will be noted and **underlined** for some future time.

The Angle Plate

A great deal of lathe work cannot be held in a chuck of any sort, either because it is too large, or too irregular to be gripped satisfactorily. One also encounters work which requires two or more machining operations at right angles one to another—such as the cylinder bore and crankcase bore of a small petrol engine. In these cases it is usually necessary to mount the job on an **angle plate** which is then bolted to the faceplate of the lathe.

Fig. 30 shows two angle plates such as are commonly used in the home workshop. The left-hand angle plate is of the ordinary type; that is, having two faces machined at a right angle to each other, and containing slots to which the workpiece may be bolted. This type of plate is quite cheap, and the amateur may well provide himself with at least two sizes—say, 3 in. and 6 in.—this measurement being that of the longest edge. Such angle plates, as will be seen later, have numerous applications.

The angle plate on the right-hand side of the picture is a most useful accessory, and though more expensive than the plain type, will fully justify its cost as an auxiliary form of mounting. It is known as the

Fig. 29

Photograph depicting lathe mandrel cut away showing the collets pictured in Fig. 28 *in situ.* (*Courtesy Myford Eng. Co., Ltd.*)

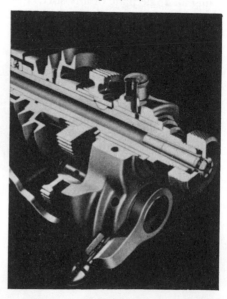

Fig. 30

Ordinary angle plate (*left*) and a faceplate " V "
block, or " Keats " angle plate (*right*).

" Keats " Angle Plate, and has
numerous applications, ranging from
the turning of small crankshafts to
repetition jig work—a most worth-
while accessory which will increase
the amateur's scope enormously.

Faceplate Dogs

Quite often a job must be bolted
directly to the faceplate, without
using an angle plate of any sort. For
this purpose **faceplate dogs** are
usually required. These are small
clamping plates suitably designed to
withstand the pull of the clamping
bolts. They may take various forms,
one of which may be seen in the
photograph (Fig. 31).

Considering their small cost, a surprising number of quite seasoned
amateurs have never experienced the
convenience of using proper faceplate dogs, being content to use strips
of mild steel drilled to take the bolt.
While these may suffice in an emergency, they are too prone to bend
under strain, with consequent loosening of the work on the faceplate—an
event which can be disastrous not
only to the workpiece but to the lathe
itself. A large job, suddenly becoming loose, may strike the lathe bed or

topslide, and some damage is sure to
result. Therefore, good, strong faceplate dogs are a necessity.

Arising out of this matter is that
of the **holding-down bolts** themselves.
Every amateur should possess a good
assortment of these, ranging from
1 in. to 8 or 9 in. in length. Good,
bright steel engineer's bolts and nuts
should be purchased, having a dia-
meter of $\frac{5}{16}$ or $\frac{3}{8}$ in. (some of each is
advisable) with B.S.F. threads. Bolts
with specially designed heads for the
purpose can be bought quite cheaply.
They are worth the money, as nothing is more annoying or so unwork-
manlike as the necessity to search
through boxes of odds and ends in an
effort to find a suitable clamping
bolt.

Lathe Centres

Every new lathe is provided with
at least one pair of lathe centres, and
these should be guarded and cher-
ished as vital parts, on which the
accuracy of a great deal of work will
depend. Too often one sees these
valuable accessories lying carelessly
about the workbench, and—one
shudders to say it—used, or rather
misused, for such horrible purposes
as centre punching! In the best professional engineering circles lathe
centres are appreciated for what they
are—precision fitments, and many
toolroom turners have their own set
of centres which only they use.

Turning between centres is the
oldest manner of performing work
in the lathe, and is still unrivalled for
many purposes where accuracy is
essential. It will be understood that
when working in this manner the
centre which is housed in the lathe
mandrel **revolves with the work,** while
the centre in the tailstock acts as a
bearing upon which the work revolves. The head-centre is, therefore,
known as the **live-centre,** while its

Fig. 31
Faceplate dogs used to clamp workpiece to an angle plate.

companion is called the **dead-centre.** While the dead-centre is always of hardened steel, the live-centre is often left soft, so that it may be trued-up in running position should the necessity arise. Care must be taken to see that the centres always occupy their correct places, as any attempt to revolve work on the soft, live-centre will result in damage to the point. Therefore, make some form of mark on the live-centre, as often the two look exactly alike, and cannot otherwise be readily distinguished.

Several other types of centre exist; notably the **half-centre,** shown at (3) in Fig. 33, which is useful for facing the end of a shaft, as it allows the tool to cut to the centre of the work —a necessary requirement.

While all the centres depicted have their uses, it is not to be laid down here that the amateur must possess them all. The **fluted-centre** (4), and the **prong-centre** (7), for wood turning, are, however, well worth having.

The other types may be added as the workshop grows.

Lathe Carriers

When turning between centres it is

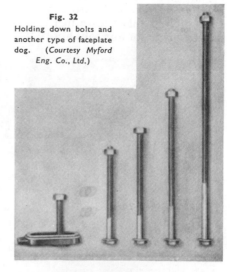

Fig. 32
Holding down bolts and another type of faceplate dog. (*Courtesy Myford Eng. Co., Ltd.*)

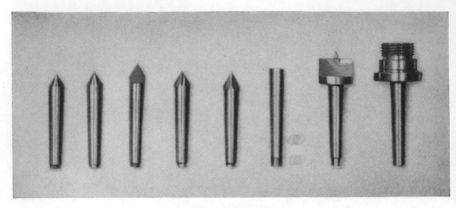

Fig. 33

An assortment of lathe centres.   Reading left to right: (1) and (2) plain centres;   (3) half-centre;   (4) counter-sink centre for centring shafts, etc.;   (5) square centre;   (6) female centre;   (7) wood-turning, or prong, centre; (8) screwed centre, having screw and register duplicating that on lathe mandrel.   (*Courtesy Myford Eng. Co., Ltd.*)

necessary to have some form of clamp which may be affixed to the job to take the drive. The photograph (Fig. 34) shows a number of lathe carriers used for this purpose. These indispensable accessories are made in a variety of sizes, ranging from about 1 in. in length to those capable of accommodating a shaft of 6 in. diameter. The amateur will do well to obtain several lathe carriers, the largest of which should fit a shaft of 2-in. diameter. Improvised carriers, such as that shown in Fig. 35, may be made for any jobs above this size, and it is hardly worth while for the model engineer to purchase the large sizes as they are not often required in the home workshop.

Fixed and Travelling Steadies

For certain types of turning on long work, of a diameter too great to be accommodated in the lathe mandrel, a **fixed steady** is essential. As an example, let us take the operation of boring a recess in the end of a 12-in. length of 2-in. diameter mild steel bar. Obviously, the steel bar will not enter the lathe mandrel, and if gripped in the chuck, the excessive overhang would make work impossible. Some means of supporting the overhanging end of the job is essential, and for this purpose

Fig. 34
Selection of lathe carriers for taking the drive when turning between centres.

a fixed steady is used. It also has a most useful application in centring the ends of long shafts, and suchlike work, some of which will be treated in detail later.

Most lathe manufacturers supply these steadies specially designed for their products, and the amateur is advised to obtain the **fixed steady** at least.

Temporary steadies can be rigged up, however, and, while not having the adaptability or convenience of the

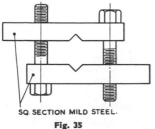

SQ. SECTION MILD STEEL.

Fig. 35
Home-made lathe carrier.

proper job, may be used as a means of overcoming a difficulty. The drawing to the right of Fig. 37, shows a temporary fixed steady which may be made from a piece of 1½-in. wood. When the block has been drilled, and the bolt and lock-ing-plate fitted, it should be bolted in-to position on the lathe bed, and the hole to accommo-date the work drilled and bored in position off the headstock.

Fig. 36
Fixed steady (left) for sup-porting work with long overhang. (Right) travelling steady.

The **travelling steady** is not so often required as is the fixed steady, but it is useful for supporting long, slender work, which is apt to " spring " under the pressure of the cutting tool. The steady is clamped to the carriage of the lathe, behind the work, and travels with the car-riage along the lathe bed.

The temporary travelling steady illustrated is also constructed of hardwood. When made it should be clamped into position on the lathe carriage, and the radius in the cor-ner bored out *in situ*. The appliance consists of a piece of hardwood, about 2 in. by 2 in., drilled through its length, with a long bolt fitted to clamp it to the lathe carriage. A smaller piece of hardwood screwed to the top of the post forms the lip.

Another makeshift fixed steady can be obtained by using the tailstock casting for the purpose. It is, how-ever, necessary to remove the tail-stock barrel. Prior to this, a bronze bush should be turned to be a tight fit in the barrel housing of the cast-ing, and bored to a running fit on the shaft to be held. The photograph, Fig. 38, shows this set-up in use on a 3½-in. lathe. The system is sound for diameters less than that of the tail-

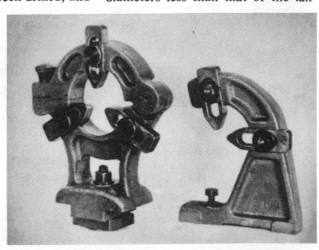

stock barrel, but cannot, of course, be used for larger work. Like most makeshift expedients, however, it entails a fair amount of trouble, and the amateur will be wise to obtain a proper fixed steady in the first place.

Drill Chucks

An absolute necessity for the amateur turner is a good drill chuck. These may be had in a variety of types, but whatever kind is selected it must possess a tapered shank which will fit the tailstock barrel of the lathe. The novice is advised to buy the best chuck he can afford, as a bad drill chuck can be an unmitigated nuisance. Such chucks are easily strained, so that not only is the drill held unsecurely, but, more important still, it will not line up with the axis of the lathe. It will be found impossible to drill a true and central hole under these conditions.

For use on small lathes a drill chuck of a capacity of $\frac{3}{8}$ in. is all that is required. Drills larger than this should be provided with taper shanks

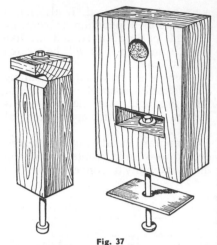

Fig. 37

Temporary fixed steady (*right*), and travelling steady (*left*) made from hardwood.

which will fit the tailstock barrel, as these are much more satisfactory in the large sizes. Only a heavy drill chuck can handle a $\frac{1}{2}$-in. drill satisfactorily.

An extremely good type of chuck

Fig. 38

The tailstock casting used as a temporary steady for small work.

for amateur use is that known as the " Jacobs ", shown in Fig. 39 (right). These chucks are well made and hardened, so that they will give long and satisfactory service. The jaws are operated by turning the knurled body, but the final tightening is done by means of a detachable key.

To the left of this same photograph will be seen a two-jaw chuck, one of the best known types of which is the " Little Giant ". They are well named, for few small chucks can exert such a tight grip on the drill, so that it does not tend to turn under the stress of drilling. A very sturdy and satisfactory pattern.

The central chuck shown in the picture is known as the " keyless "

fessional, that any accessory for this purpose is an essential part of the workshop equipment.

The photograph in Fig. 40 will show the usual appearance of these most useful tools, while the drawing in Fig. 41 gives details sufficient for amateur construction. Such die-holders can, of course, be purchased, and are inexpensive. It will be noted that the body of the dieholder, which slides along the shank, is " double-ended "; that is, one end is bored for dies of 1-in. diameter, while the other end accommodates the $\frac{13}{16}$-in. dies. The taper shank may be replaced by a parallel shank, which may be held in the drill chuck, but the taper is a far better proposition.

Fig. 39

Some types of tailstock drill chucks. (*Left to right*) A two-jaw chuck; a low-priced three-jaw chuck; the well-known Jacobs drill chuck. The first- and last-named are particularly sound types.

type. Here, the jaws are operated by turning the chuck body by means of a knurled hand grip. Most of the cheaper chucks are of this pattern. While being satisfactory if carefully handled, they do not seem to keep their truth for any length of time. They are widely used, however, in amateur workshops owing to their low initial cost.

The Tailstock Dieholder

The cutting of small threads with taps and dies is such a vital part of engineering, both amateur and pro-

Fig. 40

Home-made tailstock die-holder, reversible to take the 1-in. and the $\frac{13}{16}$-in. round dies.

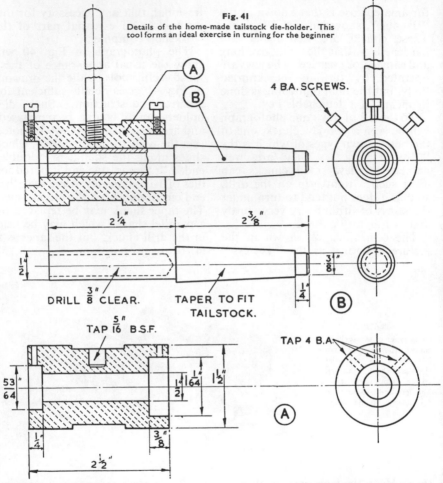

Fig. 41

Details of the home-made tailstock die-holder. This tool forms an ideal exercise in turning for the beginner

A

B

4 B.A. SCREWS.

2¼"

2⅜"

½"

DRILL ⅜" CLEAR.

TAP ⁵⁄₁₆" B.S.F.

TAPER TO FIT TAILSTOCK.

3⁄8"

1⁄4"

B

53⁄64"

1⁄64" 1½"

1⁄2"

1⁄4"

3⁄8"

2½"

TAP 4 B.A.

A

Special Accessories

In addition to the necessary equipment just detailed, there are numerous special lathe accessories available. Some of these will be encountered later, but a few may be mentioned here as being concerned only with turning operations.

Fig. 42 shows a photograph of a most useful piece of equipment. It is known as a **turret tool holder,** and its purpose is to hold a selection of six tools, which may be operated from the tailstock. The disc, carrying the tools, may be rotated by hand, and automatically centres each tool as it is presented for operation.

The amateur will encounter a surprising number of jobs calling for the frequent repetition of a sequence of operations. Normally, each tool must be separately handled and secured in the drill chuck; then removed and replaced by another. This is irksome and time wasting, especially when, as frequently happens, these operations must be repeated a hundred times or more. The tailstock turret tool holder solves the problem, and is a valuable

Fig. 42

One of the most useful accessories for the turner—a tailstock turret tool holder —suitable for amateur production in the home workshop. The tools shown are: centring drill, pilot drill, tapping drill, taper tap, plug tap, while the sixth location holds a tailstock die-holder. Each tool may be presented in quick succession to the work, and locates accurately, thus saving endless changing of tools for sequence operations.

acquisition. A much-reduced drawing is given on page 59, but full-sized blueprints are available, so that the amateur may construct for himself this most valuable accessory.

In a rather different class is the gadget shown in Fig. 44, with a drawing on page 60. This tool is called a **running centre,** and it is intended to replace the ordinary centre in the

Fig. 44

Another useful home-made accessory. The running centre, invaluable for centre turning, spinning, and such-like operations.

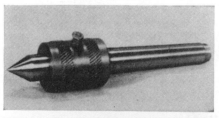

tailstock when turning work between centres. As may be seen from the drawing, the actual centre runs on ball races within a housing, so that the extremely fine adjustment of the tailstock required when turning between centres is obviated. This is also a tool suitable for amateur manufacture.

The running centre also has uses in metal spinning and for turning blank discs, operations which will be dealt with in due course.

Other special accessories, designed as an aid to turning operations, exist. Such appliances as **taper-turning attachments,** or **ball-turning attachments,** are often used in professional workshops, but as they have no special application to amateur use they will be omitted here.

Four-way Toolpost for Amateur Construction

In Fig. 10 is shown a commercial four-way toolpost, which incorporates a ratchet device in the base for relocating the tool. While this device is useful for repetition work, it has little utility value for the amateur, who is concerned mostly

Fig. 44A

A simple and efficient four-way toolpost which may be made by the amateur. The measurements given in Fig. 44B are those suitable for the Myford range of 3½-in. lathes, but the toolpost may be easily adapted to other makes of machine by altering the thickness of the baseplate, to give suitable tool height.

with one-off jobs. Figs. 44A and 44B show a four-way toolpost suitable for amateur construction, which omits any locating device, and which makes use of fabrication in its manufacture. Commercial toolposts are invariably milled from the solid, but there is little difference in strength between the two types.

The illustrations are self-explanatory, as it is just a simple matter of bolting three pieces of mild-steel plate together. It may be helpful to suggest, however, that the plates may first be roughly cut to shape, marked out, and then squared-up on the lathe, in the manner shown in Fig. 89. The slight recess on the underside of the baseplate is desirable, as it enables the toolpost to sit snugly upon the topslide.

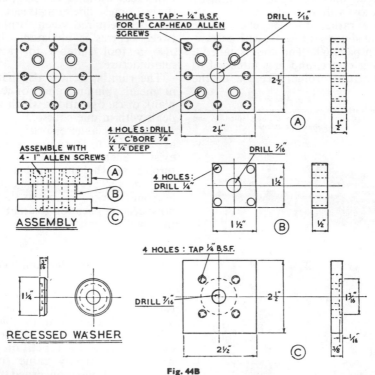

Fig. 44B
Constructional drawing for the mild-steel four-way toolpost shown in Fig. 44A.

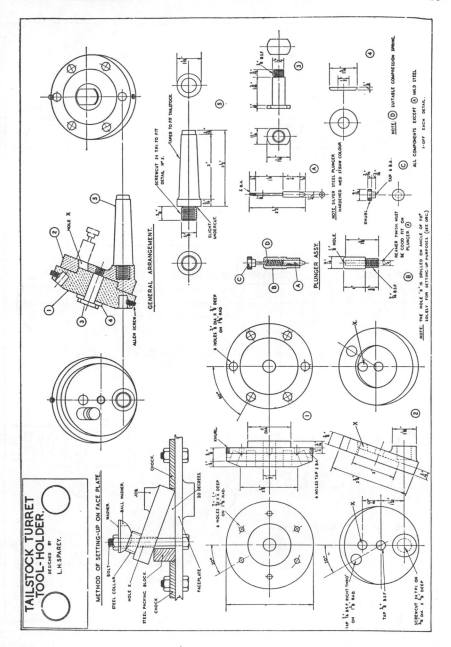

Fig. 43

Reduced drawing of the tailstock turret tool holder shown at Fig. 42. The locations for the tools are bored off the headstock after the whole tool has been completed and assembled. This nsures accurate positioning tools as they are swung into place.

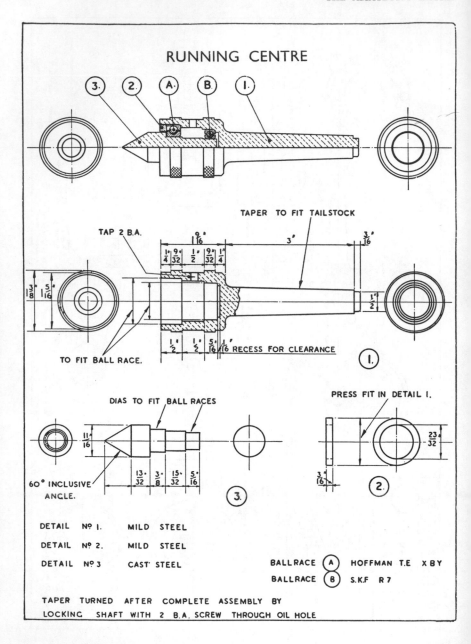

Fig. 45

Constructional drawing for the running centre. When completely made and assembled, the centre spigot is
locked by a screw in the oil-hole, the component plugged into the mandrel, and the centre point turned true.
The locking screw is then, of course, removed.

CHAPTER 5

MEASURING EQUIPMENT

IN the professional engineering world the standard of accuracy has, in recent years, risen enormously. Whereas, a few years ago limits of one-thousandth of an inch were considered satisfactory, the modern toolmaker must be prepared to work to a tenth of this amount. Nor is this by any means the limit in man's achievements in this direction, as certain of his products—notably the famous Johansson Slip Gauges—are guaranteed accurate to within a few millionths of an inch.

Fortunately, the model mechanic need not concern himself with microscopical measurements of this order; nor can it be said that the standard of the amateur's accuracy has kept pace with that of his professional brother. This is by no means a reflection on the skill of the model engineer—the discrepancy is solely due to new and improved equipment available to the professional. By and large, it may be said that the equipment of the model engineer of to-day is exactly that of his father before him. Here and there, perhaps, a little improvement in machine design, but, fundamentally, the accuracy of the amateur still depends upon the quality of his hand and eye, rather than upon the precision of his tools.

It has often been said that the accuracy to which one can work is limited by that of one's measuring equipment; but many experienced model engineers would, with every justification, dispute this statement. When making "one-off" jobs, with which the amateur is mostly concerned, it is possible so to fit one part

to another that the degree of accuracy between the two is of the very highest. The writer would, in fact, defy any model engineer, possessing the usual amateur equipment, to make and fit the piston and cylinder of, say, a model "Diesel" engine, purely by independent measurement of each component alone, and arrive at that degree of fit and accuracy which this job would demand! This does not imply that the micrometer and the vernier have not a highly necessary place in the model engineer's outfit, but is given as an example of one of the many cases where the amateur's inch cannot be measured with the professional's yardstick.

Far from implying that the micrometer is superfluous, it should, indeed, be one of the first things for the amateur to obtain, for lathe work without this necessary instrument is unthinkable. It is the writer's fear that he will be accused, not of advocating too little measuring equipment, but too much; his strong advocacy of such instruments as the **test dial-indicator,** for instance, having induced a belief among his model engineering friends that he possesses a "high-brow attitude" to these things.

The Micrometer

Be this as it may, the **micrometer** is an absolute necessity for intelligent engineering. Invented in 1848 by the Frenchman, Jean Palmer, the micrometer has spread throughout the world, so that to-day it is the standard engineering measuring instrument.

61

At one time the Americans undoubtedly made the finest micrometers, and their products are still, very justly, held in highest esteem; such names as Starrett, Brown and Sharpe, and Lufkin being household engineering words. In recent years, however, certain British firms, notably Messrs. Moore and Wright, have steadily crept to the top, so that to-day their products may be classed as quite equal to the American instruments. Furthermore, the price is somewhat lower.

The principle of the micrometer is based upon the movement obtained by turning an accurately cut screw thread. The drawing in Fig. 47 will explain the matter more fully. First, we have the **frame** (A), through which screws the **spindle** (B), which is secured to the **thimble** (C) at the point (D). On the frame is the **anvil** (E).

The **sleeve** (F) is graduated in divisions, each representing twenty-five thousandths ($\frac{1}{40}$) in. These divisions are further subdivided into groups of four; these being indicated by longer lines, each representing one hundred thousandths ($\frac{1}{10}$) in. and being marked, progressively, from 0 to 10 inclusive.

The spindle (B) carries a fine thread of a pitch of 40 threads per inch, which turns in an internal nut in the frame (A). It is thus obvious that if the thimble is revolved one complete turn it will have moved the spindle (B) the pitch of one thread ($\frac{1}{40}$ = twenty-five thousandths in.) to or from the anvil (E). On the bevel of the thimble (C) are 25 divisions, numbered in groups of five, from 0 to 25, inclusive.

Let us now set the micrometer so that it is completely closed; that is, with the spindle (B) closely touching

Fig. 46

(*Top*) 0·1-in. Starrett micrometer. (*Lower*) Brown & Sharpe 0·2-in.; the anvil may be replaced by one of longer length ,and the instrument set to a check gauge.

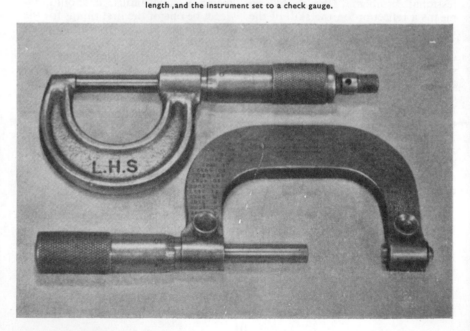

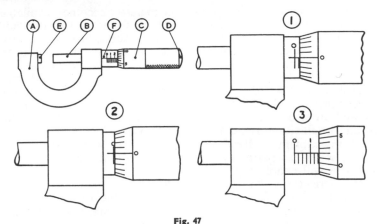

Fig. 47

Diagram illustrating method of reading a micrometer. The matter is fully explained in the text.

the anvil (E). In this position the division line marked 0 on the thimble will be registering with the division line 0 on the sleeve, and will appear as is shown in the sketch marked 2 in the drawing. Now we will turn the spindle (B) one complete revolution. The division 0 on the thimble will again rest on a line on the sleeve, but will have moved backwards the pitch of one thread (twenty-five thousandths of an inch, = ·025 in.) so that the bevel of the thimble (C) will coincide with one division on the sleeve. This position is shown in the drawing (1), which shows that the micrometer has been opened twenty-five thousandths of an inch (·025 in.). Were the spindle turned four complete revolutions, the bevel of the thimble would, of course, rest on the division on the sleeve marked 1; so that this would indicate that the micrometer had been opened one hundred thousandths of an inch (·100 in.).

We thus see that one complete revolution of the thimble moves the spindle (which is connected to it) longitudinally twenty-five thousandths of an inch (·025 in.). If, therefore, the thimble is turned one twenty-fifth of a revolution, the spindle will move, longitudinally, one thousandth of an inch (·001 in.). As the thimble bears twenty-five divisions on the bevel, a turn of one division moves the spindle ·001 in.

In order, therefore, to read the micrometer, it is necessary only to multiply the number of vertical divisions visible on the sleeve by 25, and to add to this the number of divisions on the thimble from 0 to the line which coincides with the horizontal line on the sleeve.

As an example, let us take the drawing (3) in Fig. 47. Here we see that the instrument has been opened so that one large division of ·100 in. (one hundred thousandths of an inch) is completely exposed. In addition, two of the smaller divisions —each of twenty-five thousandths (·025) of an inch—are also visible, so that the total of complete divisions exposed on the sleeve amounts to one hundred and fifty thousandths (·150) of an inch. We must, however, add to this the number of single thousandths on the bevel of the thimble which coincide with the horizontal line on the sleeve. In the drawing we see that the second thimble division occupies this position, so that we must add two thousandths (·002) of an inch to the amount. The micrometer reads, therefore, ·152 in. (one hundred and fifty-two thousandths); that is, $100 + 25 + 25 + 2 = 152$.

All technical explanations are tedious, and are usually complicated out of all proportion to the thing which is being explained. Reading a micrometer is no exception, as very little practice will enable the model mechanic to read his " mike " as easily as he does his newspaper, and with, probably, more profit to himself!

Micrometers are made in a variety of sizes, from $\frac{1}{2}$ in. to 12 in.; and indeed, to several feet for special purposes. Luckily, the model engineer need not concern himself with these, as a **one-inch micrometer** is usually all that is required. If, at some future time, a **two-inch**

micrometer becomes available, this will be found a valuable addition.

As to the choice of a micrometer. there is nothing to choose between any good make. One point, however, may be noted. Select a " mike " in which the frame thins down considerably at the anvil. Some micrometer frames have an ugly lump at this point, which prevents the instrument from being used to measure small, shouldered work.

The Vernier Caliper Gauge

This is the oldest known instrument for precision measurement, having been invented by Pierre Vernier, another French scientist, in the early seventeenth century. In spite of the vernier being over 300 years old, it is still a hale and hearty veteran, and is used extensively for numerous purposes to-day. The photograph (Fig. 48) shows a typical modern **vernier caliper gauge.**

Fig. 48

(*Top*) Slide or Columbus gauge, reading in fractional measurements. (*Lower*) A vernier caliper or slide gauge reading to one thousandth in. This instrument also has vernier depth gauge attachment.

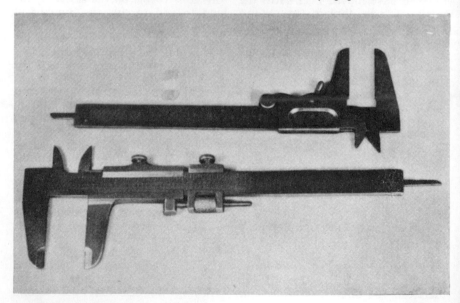

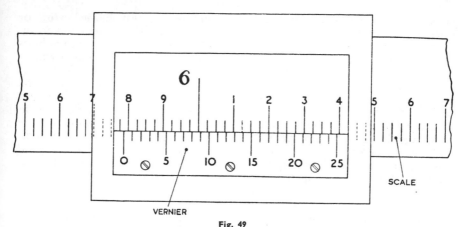

Fig. 49

Diagram illustrating method of reading a vernier. Note that the 18th division on the vernier scale coincides with a mark on the scale. (See text.)

The system upon which the vernier operates is a most ingenious one, and depends upon the difference in graduation between two scales of equal length. As may be seen in Fig. 49, the scale of the instrument is graduated in $\frac{1}{40}$ ($\cdot$025) of an inch; and every fourth division, representing $\frac{1}{10}$ ($\cdot$100) of an inch, is numbered. Ten of these longer divisions do, of course, represent one inch, which is marked accordingly on the scale, in the same manner as on an ordinary rule.

On the scale is a sliding frame (connected to the moving jaw of the instrument) bearing a vernier plate with a space divided into 25 parts; these are subdivided into groups of five, and are numbered 0, 5, 10, 15, 20 and 25.

The 24 divisions on the scale occupy the same space as the 25 divisions on the vernier, so that the difference in width between one division on the scale and one division on the vernier is $\frac{1}{25}$ of $\frac{1}{40}$ of an inch; that is $\frac{1}{1000}$ ($\cdot$001) in. If we close the jaws of the vernier right up, so that the 0 division on the scale corresponds with the 0 division on the

vernier, the next lines will not coincide by $\frac{1}{1000}$ of an inch, and the next lines by two thousandths of an inch ($\cdot$002 in.), and so on throughout the vernier scale, so that the tenth lines on scale and vernier are ten thousandths ($\cdot$010) in. apart.

The vernier is read as follows: count the number of full inch (1$\cdot$000 in.) spaces, and the number of full twenty-fifth in. ($\cdot$025 in.) spaces which lie between the 0 mark on the scale and the 0 mark on the vernier. In the drawing, Fig. 49, this shows as five 1-in. divisions, seven $\frac{1}{10}$ in. divisions, and three $\frac{1}{25}$-in. divisions; which total 5$\cdot$775 in. To read the odd thousandths of an inch it is necessary to count the number of divisions on the vernier scale from 0 to another line on the vernier scale which coincides exactly with a line on the scale. In the drawing, it will be found that the eighteenth line on the vernier is exactly opposite to a line on the scale, and this denotes that eighteen thousandths ($\cdot$018 in.) must be added to the sum of the full divisions on the scale. The vernier thus reads, 5$\cdot$793 in.; that is, 5 + $\cdot$700 + $\cdot$075 + 18 = 5$\cdot$793 in., and the

E

jaws of the instrument have been opened this amount.

In counting the final odd thousandths the actual numbers on the scale are ignored, and counting is confined to the spaces on the **vernier.** Briefly, add up the full spaces on the scale and then add the number of divisions indicated on the vernier.

All vernier calipers are provided with inside and outside jaws. On the type shown in the photograph the reading obtained is that for both outside and inside jaws, but in some verniers a simple calculation is necessary when reading with the inside jaws, as allowance has to be made for the width of these. The combined width of these jaws is made some standard amount—usually ½ in.—so that in taking inside measurements this amount must be added to the apparent reading on the scales. Some verniers have scales on both sides of the blade, one of which compensates for the jaw widths, so a direct reading may be had in both instances. It will be noted that the vernier shown in Fig. 48 also has a depth gauge provided. This is an extremely handy addition, but the vernier must be exceedingly well made if all readings from inside and outside jaws and the depth gauge are to be identical.

The amateur should note that the vernier caliper gauge is a delicate instrument, and should be treated as such. It should be housed in a fitted, wooden box and always replaced immediately after use. If a vernier is dropped or accidentally knocked off the bench it can irreparably affect its accuracy. Furthermore, it should never be strained when in use. Close the jaws lightly upon the object to be measured. Unlike a micrometer, a vernier cannot be reset for accuracy when once deranged.

The Test Dial-Indicator

In Chapter 3 one important application of the **test dial-indicator,** or "clock", as it is generally known, has been given in the instance of bolting down a lathe truly to its bench.

Were this its only application it would probably "be worth the money", but far from being the case, the clock has innumerable uses in lathe work. A description of the working principles of the dial-indicator has been given, and its usual appearance may be gathered from Fig. 50. In this instance, the clock is shown mounted, with a special fitting, on a base (all, by the way, made in an amateur workshop), but the absence of these accessories does not seriously limit its uses in lathe work.

The main function of the test dial-indicator is to check the position of one object in relationship to another. Thus, it may be used for centring work in the 4-jaw chuck or on the faceplate; the clock being held in the toolpost with the plunger against

Fig. 50

Test dial-indicator set. All fittings, except the "clock", were made in the author's home workshop, on a 3½-in. lathe.

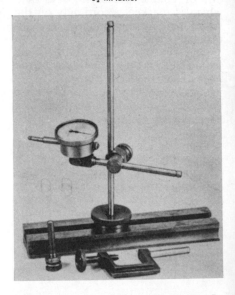

Fig. 51
Scribing block made by the author on a 3½-in. lathe.

the work, somewhat in the manner shown in Fig. 14. The workpiece may thus be moved until the indicator needle is stationary, denoting that the outside diameter of the work is running truly.

Similarly, the clock may be used to check that the face of a piece of work is truly " square " with the axis of the lathe mandrel, in which case the plunger is located against the face of the work instead of against the side. These operations are invaluable when it is necessary to replace turned work in the lathe for subsequent operations, such as occurs when reversing a job in the chuck.

Many other uses of the clock will become apparent in later chapters, and to anticipate here would only serve to upset continuity. When the last page of this book is reached, the

value of the test dial-indicator may well be left to the reader's own judgment.

The Scribing Block

The photograph (Fig. 51) shows the **scribing block.** Strictly speaking, this tool has no direct bearing on lathe work as such, except that it is necessary for marking out work for turning operations. It is inserted here because such a tool must not be overlooked by the amateur, and because it can form an ideal base to which a test dial-indicator may be attached. An exploded view of a universal clamp suitable for securing the clock to the post of the scribing block is given in Fig. 52. It is constructed entirely of mild steel, to measurements most suitable for the tool in question.

We shall meet the scribing block again in its correct context.

Calipers

Tools which have become intimately bound up with lathe work are the **inside** and **outside calipers,** specimens of which may be seen in Fig. 53. Calipers are probably older than engineering itself, and, considering their simplicity, remarkably accurate measurements may be taken with them. Calipers are really only instruments of comparison, as they do not give a direct reading of measurement. Thus, the size of a

Fig. 52
Exploded view of an easily made universal clamp for attaching " clock " to scribing block pillar.

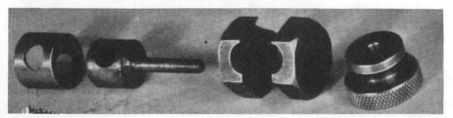

shaft may be taken with the outside calipers, the setting transferred to the inside calipers, and then compared with a hole in which the shaft is to fit. Alternatively, and by far the better way for small work, is to measure the shaft with the micrometer or vernier, and set the inside calipers to these instruments. Conversely, the size of a hole may be taken with the calipers, and then compared with the reading of a micrometer or rule.

The older type of calipers, which were set by tapping, have, of recent years given way to the type wherein adjustment is obtained by a screw and nut. These are much to be preferred by the amateur, as speedy and accurate setting of the older type takes almost a lifetime to acquire!

Because outside measurements are so much easier to take with micrometer or vernier, the amateur will not so often use the **outside** calipers, except for large diameters. This is far from being so with the **inside** calipers, where direct measurement is difficult to obtain, and they are still the standard instrument for inside work. The amateur must early acquire the knack of use.

Difference in size of ·001 (one thousandth) of an inch can easily be detected with calipers. They should be held lightly, at the extreme end, and the tips moved about lightly in the hole, and adjusted so that they are truly registering the full diameter. It will be understood that unless the calipers are really only touching the bore at its full diameter a smaller reading will be recorded. This is probably the most difficult part of the operation to perform exactly, and some practice will be required. It should be quite possible to find the diameter of any hole to within ·001 inch.

The caliper tips should **not** be a tight " scrape " fit in the bore to be measured, but a faint, " sliding " feel should be obtained. This will come with practice. As an aid to this, the novice is recommended to practise with the inside calipers, using the

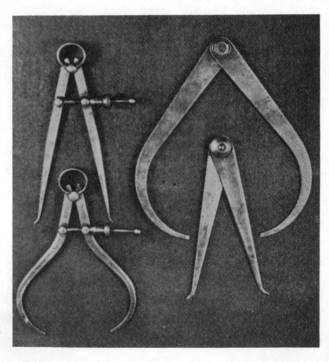

Fig. 53

Some examples of calipers. (*Left top*) Spring-bow inside calipers; (*Lower left*) spring-bow outside calipers; (*Top right*) plain outside calipers; (*Lower right*) plain inside calipers. The latter types must be set by tapping. Tapping on the sides closes them, while tapping on the base of the joint opens them.

micrometer as a test piece. Set the micrometer to, say, a measurement of ·750 in. Now caliper the gap, getting the finest " feel " that one possibly can. Then open the micrometer one thousandth of an inch, to ·751 in.; at this setting it should not be possible to feel contact between the calipers and the micrometer. Try it; it's quite easy.

Calipers should never be used to check work when it is revolving. Apart from the fact that one cannot obtain an accurate reading this way, there is danger that the calipers may catch on the work, thus bending or destroying them altogether. In fact, no measurements with any kind of instrument should ever be taken while the work is in movement.

The Slide Gauge

This instrument (Fig. 48) is very like a vernier caliper gauge in appearance, except that the vernier attachment reading to ·001 in. is not fitted, and all readings are, therefore, only fractional. The slide gauge, or **Columbus gauge,** as it is often called, is quite a cheap tool, costing but a few shillings. Nevertheless, it is an extremely useful one, as it may be used for taking outside diameters, to which inside calipers may be set for a corresponding bore. One of its most useful purposes is in checking work at the roughing-out stage. Most slide gauges have inside and outside jaws.

Combination Sets and Protractors

An instrument much used professionally, and one of equal use to the amateur, is the combination set.

The tool consists essentially of a stout steel blade, graduated in fractional inch rulings. Down the centre of one side of this blade runs a shallow channel, which serves to locate several fittings which may be clamped into place. The fittings comprise a spirit level, a 45-deg. set

Fig. 54

combination protractor set, comprising a centring square, a protractor, a 90-deg. square, a 45-deg. square a spirit level, and a steel rule.

Fig. 55
A simple type of plain gauge for measuring depths, lengths of shoulders, etc.

square, and a 90-deg. set square; in addition, there are a protractor head, and a centring square. While primarily useful for marking out purposes, the tool has applications in turning practice; notably for checking taper work in the lathe, and for setting the topslide to a correct angle. Quite often, the degree markings on the swivelling topslide on some of the cheaper lathes are not accurate enough for certainty. As the combination set has many other uses, it is a great convenience to possess one.

Depth Gauges

The simple type of depth gauge, shown in Fig. 55, presents a convenient method of measuring the depth of bored holes, the length of turned shoulders, and such like. Such instruments, in the plain type, are quite inexpensive, and should be in every amateur kit.

More elaborate depth gauges, having vernier scales, are obtainable, but these are so much more expensive that they are not often found in the home workshop. Nor are they often required for the type of work generally encountered.

The Centre Finder

Here is a very valuable tool, which is used for setting up a centre dot which must run truly on a piece of

work in the lathe. In principle it consists of a thin, pointed rod which is universally swivelled on a bar held in the toolpost; the swivel being much nearer to one end of the rod than the other. Advantage is taken of the lever action; so that any movement of the tip of the shorter portion is greatly exaggerated at the tip of the longer.

In practice, the workpiece is centred roughly by eye in the 4-jaw chuck or on the faceplate; then the point of the short lever is located in the centre dot, and the lathe revolved by hand. The tip of the longer lever will describe a wide circle, dependent upon the amount that the centre dot is " running out ", but, of course, very much exaggerated. The workpiece is then adjusted until the tip of the longer lever shows no movement.

Work may be centred quickly by this method, as the longer lever indicates the direction in which the dot is off-set. In cases where a number of holes, for instance, must be bored at specified points on a job, the positions may be marked out and indicated by centre dots, each of which may, in turn, be accurately located in the lathe.

While the photograph shows a somewhat elaborate example, embodying a spring-loaded lever to retain the point in the centre dot,

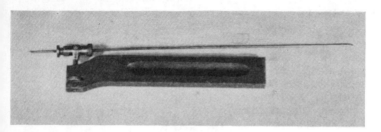

Fig. 56

A centre finder, a most useful tool, made in the author's home workshop. The lever arm is spring loaded, and is adjustable for height setting.

quite an efficient centre finder may be made by the home mechanic in the manner shown in Fig. 57. This drawing will give a general idea of the arrangement; no measurements are given, as these are unimportant, and the amateur will, in any case, make the size most suited to his machine. As will be seen, it consists of a steel ring, into which two 4-B.A. silver steel rods are screwed. The shorter rod protrudes into the inside of the ring for a short distance, and the pointed end shown in dotted line, locates in a centre-drill hole in the bar. The bar and rod are not fixed together in any way, but are, in practice, held by the pressure of the point in the workpiece. When drilling the fulcrum hole in the bar, this should be held in the toolpost and drilled with a centre-drill in the chuck. In this way the indicator rod will lie at centre height, so that the position of the tip of the longer end may be compared with that of a lathe centre held in the tailstock, and the centring of work thus facilitated.

Telescopic Inside Gauges

A useful little instrument, costing

Fig. 57

An efficient and simple centre-finder which will do all that the amateur requires.

but a few shillings, is depicted in Fig. 58, and is known as the telescopic inside gauge. One limb of the cross-piece telescopes into the other, and is spring-loaded to keep it always at maximum length. The sliding member can, however, be instantly locked into any position by a slight turn of the milled head of the handle.

To use the instrument to measure the diameter of a hole, the telescopic

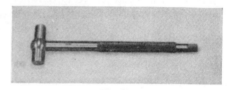

Fig. 58

Telescopic inside gauge for measuring small bores. Extremely accurate and easy to use.

head is compressed and locked; it is then inserted into the hole, and the lock released, so that the plunger expands across the hole. It is then locked again by a turn of the milled head, and withdrawn, when the measurement may be taken with a micrometer.

These instruments are made in various ranges, dealing with holes from $\frac{1}{2}$ in. to 6 in. in diameter. Two sizes are of particular use to the home mechanic—the $\frac{1}{2}$ in. to $\frac{3}{4}$ in. and the $\frac{3}{4}$ in. to $1\frac{1}{4}$ in. Measurements are extremely accurate, and the tool is easier to use, and more reliable, than the ordinary leg calipers in inexperienced hands.

Parallels and " V " Blocks

The illustration (Fig. 59) shows examples of these indispensable tools. They are included in " measuring instruments " because they are intimately connected with measuring operations. Chapter 16 deals more fully with this aspect; meanwhile " V " blocks and parallels are of great use for packing work accurately on the faceplate or cross-slide. Hardened **strip-parallels** are somewhat costly, as they must be accurately ground all over, but the amateur may obtain a good substitute almost " for nothing "! These are the outer and inner rings of large ballraces—old ones will do—which may be obtained from any car breakers. These rings are hardened and ground to precision limits, and can be used for most of the purposes for which strip-parallels are suitable. Ring parallels may, in fact, have somewhat wider application. Every serious amateur should avail himself of this tip.

Inside Micrometers

A brief mention of inside micro-

Fig. 59

(*Left*) " V " blocks and clamp; (*right*) Ballrace rings used as circular parallels; (*lower*) a pair of hardened and ground strip parallels.

meters may be made here. They consist of hardened steel rods, which may be expanded by the action of a fine screw thread, operating a scale arrangement similar to that of the orthodox micrometer. They have limited appeal to the amateur, as their construction makes them usable only in holes of 2 in. or more diameter, so that they have a restricted application for most " model " work.

The Steel Rule

This chapter may well close with a reference to the humble steel rule —the most used measuring tool of them all.

The amateur will require two sizes: the 6 in. and the 12 in. The thin, flexible type will be found to be more versatile than the stiff sort, as they may be bent to measure into awkward and restricted places. The 6-in. rule, No. 34C, made by Messrs. Rabone & Sons, of Birmingham, is an ideal tool, having both English and metric graduations. Similar rules by Starrett and others are equally good—it is the type which is important.

Engineers' rules may be had in various markings, and there are, probably, a dozen or so variations of scales. The No. C34, however, covers most requirements.

To-day, rules are obtainable in stainless steel, and these are to be preferred to the ordinary steel type. As, of course, they neither stain nor rust, the scales are always clearly visible.

When setting-off from a steel rule, it is not generally advisable to use the extreme end of the rule which gets damaged and worn down in use. Start the measurement from one of the inner inch markings, as this is more likely to give correct results.

There are, of course, other measuring accessories necessary to a universal use of the amateur's lathe. These have not been overlooked, but will be met in their proper context later.

CHAPTER 6

LATHE TOOLS

A FEW years ago it was customary for textbooks on lathe operation to devote a great deal of space to the subject of lathe tools. Some dozens of different types were illustrated and described, together with pages of instructions on cutting angles, rakes, and such matters.

This policy will not be followed here. Not that the question of lathe tools is not as important now as then, but modern experience has shown that a great number of the old tools are redundant, and that quite as good work may be done with only a few of the accepted types. This discovery was made in professional workshops and factories as the result of the modern tendency to supply machinists with standard tools, ready ground to shape on special jigs. Under these circumstances it is, naturally, desirable to keep the number of tool types down to a minimum; a policy which has been followed with every success. The amateur who takes this tip from professional experience will find that he, too, can get along quite nicely with just a few patterns.

In the drawings, angles and clearances will be given in the usual way, but it is appreciated that the model mechanic will not be able to conform to these angles exactly, as, to do so consistently, he would require grinding jigs of his own. The angles, therefore, are given more as a guide than as laws to be strictly followed. A degree or two one way or another will make no perceptible difference to the amateur, as he is not concerned with the removal of the maximum amount of metal in the shortest possible time.

The purists will, undoubtedly decry this heresy, but I leave it to any professional turner to say how often the correct " textbook " angles are adhered to, even in the most high-class workshop where jig grinding is not employed. It will be agreed that each turner grinds his tools to his own fancy, and few indeed conform exactly to standard types. These remarks do not, of course, apply to screwcutting tools, where the correct angle **must** be obtained.

The Grinding Head

Before proceeding to actual tools, a few words about the grinder upon which they will be shaped may be helpful.

In the first place, a good bench grinder is necessary. The proprietary double-ended bench grinder, with wheels of about 6 in. diameter, is rather an expensive item, but is, without doubt, the ideal. Most amateurs will, however, have to rest content with some sort of grinding head with an auxiliary drive from some existing motor or line shaft. Small grinding or polishing heads may be bought quite cheaply, and will do a satisfactory job. The main disadvantage is that they are generally of light construction, so that only small wheels—about 3 or 4 in. in diameter—may be used. This necessitates high speed; somewhere around 3,000 r.p.m. for satisfactory results. Some sort of tool rest must also be provided. Whatever grinder is used, the tool rest must be set as close to the stone as is possible. Large gaps are dangerous as the tools may get jammed between the stone and the rest.

Do not run a high-speed grinder without a guard! A sudden jam may cause the grinding wheel to burst. The results can be appalling! Guards of sheet iron are easy to make and fit, and should be one of the amateur's first jobs. Also, **never clamp up a grinding wheel on its spindle without placing thick paper discs between the grinding wheel and the clamping washers.** The wheel is almost sure to burst, sooner or later, if you neglect this. If you are not prepared to adhere to these common-sense rules, then it is better to abandon the idea of a home workshop, and to live a safe and quiet life in some other sphere.

How to Grind Tools

Only the man who likes doing things the hard way will ever work

Fig. 61

Small head for auxiliary drive. Although only small wheels may be used, this forms a satisfactory grinding head for amateur uses, at a low cost.

with blunt tools. Always see to it that tools are as sharp as they can possibly be, and give them a slight "touch-up" on the grinder whenever a suspicion of dullness appears. Frequent **light grinding** is better than

Fig. 60

This small bench grinder has wheels of 6-in. diameter, and is an ideal tool for the home workshop.

occasional **heavy grinding,** both from the points of view of tool life and ease of working.

During grinding operations keep a can of cold water at hand, and frequently dip the tool to prevent heating. Tools which are heated up and "blued" are useless. Nothing is so conducive to this as heavy grinding pressure on the tool, so do not force the tool on to the wheel. Hold it lightly but firmly, and let the portion to be ground "float" against the stone. When once the angle of the tool has been formed it will take up its own position against the wheel if allowed to float in this manner. This avoids "double angles" on the tool faces. The tools should also be kept moving across the face of the grindstone; if held in one place any irregularities of the wheel will be duplicated on the tool, and the stone itself is liable to become ribbed.

Never grind a tool in a haphazard manner; have some definite shape in view, and work carefully to this end. Happy-go-lucky grinding methods account for most of the weird looking tools—with as many facets as a diamond—which one so often sees in the amateur workshop.

Do not grind a good tool into another shape just to meet the need of the moment. High-speed steel is reasonably cheap in the amateurs' sizes, so that a separate piece for each requirement can be used. If you neglect this rule you will finish up with a collection of odds and ends which are of no use to anyone.

Finally, remember that grinding hardened steel is a slow process, and that any attempt to hurry the job can only result in disappointment. Take your time, and approach the job in that frame of mind wherein you realise that the correct shaping of the tool is a necessary and vital part of "doing the job".

High-Speed Steel

Following the modern tendency the amateur will do well to confine himself to **high-speed steel** only. **High carbon steel,** or **tool steel,** as it is still called, is obsolete for anything but makeshift turning purposes. There is a prevalent misconception among amateurs that carbon steel gives a better finish than does high-speed steel. This is not so; the tips of carbon steel tools soon wear off, thus causing a rubbing action which can, under certain circumstances, give a polished finish.

The enemy of all lathe tools is heat. High-speed steel will stand almost three to four times the heat that carbon steel will stand, without ill effect. It is, in fact, a remarkable substance. Under test, using a lathe of 18-in. centres, specially constructed by Messrs. Armstrong Whitworth, it was found possible to take huge cuts—" swarf " of $1\frac{1}{4}$ in. wide and $\frac{1}{4}$ in. thick being removed at a speed of 32 ft. per minute, using ordinary high-speed steel. This should be good enough for the amateur. High-speed steel bits are usually purchased in a hardened state, thus saving much trouble.

Cemented Carbide Tools

Following their expanding use in industry, the throw-away-tip cemented carbide tools, Figs. 61a & b have been specially developed for use on small lathes. The renewable tips have six cutting edges which may be used in succession as others become dulled or broken. They are not unduly expensive to replace.

Although one of the hardest known substances, cemented carbide is somewhat brittle, and should not be subjected to heavy blows such as might be imparted when turning irregular castings. Cemented carbide must be ground on a special wheel—usually green in colour.

Fig. 62

All tools that the amateur requires for general work. (A) Knife tool for steel, etc.; (B) corner tool for steel, etc.; (C) round-nosed tool for steel, etc.; (D) knife tool for brass; (E) round-nosed tool for brass; (F) parting tool for steel, etc. Many tools of old-fashioned shape have become redundant.

Fig. 61a

The Myford 'Hoybide' tool, with cemented carbide throw-away-tip.

Fig. 61b.

Showing the holder and throw-away-tip of the 'Hoybide' tool. They will turn hard steels at high speed without a coolant.

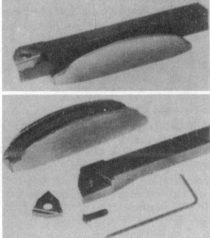

The Knife Tool

The picture (A in Fig. 62) shows what may almost be called the universal turning tool for steel. Knife tools will yield remarkably heavy cuts for roughing out work; they will also, if correctly set, produce a good finish. They are much to be preferred to the round-nosed tool usually recommended for amateur use on steel, as these invariably produce " chatter " on a light lathe. A good knife tool will do 80 per cent. of all amateur turning.

As will be seen in Fig. 64 at (A) they may be formed from a piece of square section high-speed steel— about $\frac{3}{8}$ in. or $\frac{1}{2}$ in. across flats— with a pronounced cutting angle. Front and side clearances need be very small. Use this tool at dead-centre height, and keep it sharp.

For finishing cuts the tool should be set as in Fig. 63; that is, with the front edge almost parallel to the axis of the work. This will cause a " rubbing " action, which, in conjunction with slow turning speed, fine feed, and plenty of lubricant (see Chapter 10) will produce an extremely high finish on steel work. The knife tool

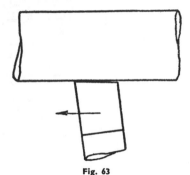

Fig. 63
Setting a steel-turning knife tool to rub, for high finish.

is also excellent for turning aluminium, dural, and like metals, and is equally good for ebonite, fibre, wood and similar materials.

The illustration shows a right-handed tool used for cutting towards the chuck. A left-handed knife tool, though not often required, may form a useful addition to the kit.

The Corner Tool

Although the knife tool may be used for almost every steel turning purpose, a tool of more " delicate " shape is often an advantage for fine work, especially that which has many steps or shoulders. Such a tool may be seen at (B) in Fig. 62, with a sketch at (B) in Fig. 64. Fundamentally, it is a knife tool, having the same pronounced cutting angle, some top rake, and similar clearances. The tip, however, is shaped to a more acute point, making it particularly convenient for working into a corner.

Round-nosed Tool for Steel

The orthodox round-nosed tool for steel, as usually recommended, is too broad for use on a small lathe, and " chatter " on the work takes place. A round-nosed tool, ground somewhat on the lines of that shown at (C) in Fig. 62, and at (C) in Fig.

64, can, however, be used. As will be noted, the tool is ground to a taper, with a radius of about $\frac{1}{16}$ in. at the extreme tip. It is of use in finishing shouldered work where a small radius is required in the corner, when, for reasons of strength, a square corner is not permissible.

Universal Brass Tool

This follows the lines of the steel knife tool except, as may be seen at (D) and (D) in the illustrations, little or no cutting angle is incorporated. Here again, the tool is very satisfactory for roughing-out, and also for obtaining a good finish on hard brass. In this instance, however, setting the tool to give a rubbing action is not permissible, as " chatter " will result. For finishing, the extreme tip of the tool is slightly rounded-off by two or three strokes with an oil slip-stone.

Round-nosed Tool for Brass

We see at (E) and (E) in the illustrations, that the lines of the steel tool are again followed, except that only a small cutting angle is used. The radius of the tip may be greater —about $\frac{1}{8}$ in. The uses are similar to those of the steel-cutting counterpart.

Parting-off Tools

Parting-off tools are often called the " amateur's nightmare ", and it is certainly true that more good work is ruined at the parting-off stage than at any other. The reasons for this are numerous, and some will be dealt with in Chapter 10. Not the least of the troubles encountered are due to incorrect grinding of the parting tool; lack of clearance being the chief error.

At (F) and (F) in the illustrations a parting-off tool for steel is shown. It will be observed that the blade is ground with **back clearance** (that is, the tip is wider than the rear of the

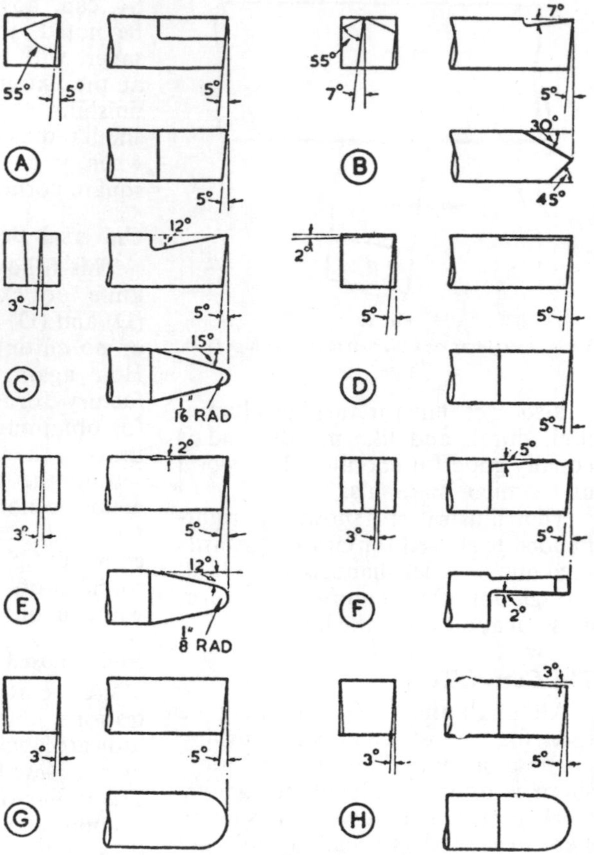

Fig. 64

Diagram showing approximate angles of the tools shown in Fig. 62. Very rarely will the amateur be able to grind to exact angles without special grinding jigs, but experience shows that slight variations make little or no difference in general practice. Theoretically correct angles are, however, important when utmost cutting efficiency is required.

blade) and that side clearance is also given. These clearances should not be excessive, as this weakens the tool greatly. Also, excessive front clearance takes away support from the cutting edge.

If the top is ground to a large radius (Fig. 65) the swarf will tend to come away in a long ribbon, and will not curl tightly and jam in the cut. It may be desirable to place the cutting edge a trifle

Fig. 65

Diagram showing parting tool set below centre (exaggerated).

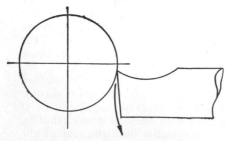

below lathe-centre height; the reason being that if the tool has any tendency to " dig in ", the blade will be flexed downwards away from the work, as shown in dotted line. If, however, the tool is placed above centre height, as is sometimes advised, the tool tends to dig into the work still more if it is flexed by the cutting pressure.

The parting-off tool for brass differs only by reason of having no top rake and no lip, but is similar in other ways to the steel-cutting blade.

Special parting-off blades may be bought at most good tool shops. They are extremely economical, as the side clearance is already ground in, and very little of the tool need be ground away for back clearance. They require, however, to be held in a special tool holder, which is sold for the purpose. This is necessary as it is important that the blade be held truly vertical in the tool post.

A cleaner " part off " is sometimes obtained if the cutting edge is ground at a slight angle, as shown at (F) in Fig. 64. It must not be overdone, however, as this angle virtually increases the width of the cutting edge, which is not an advantage. Parting-off blades for the small lathe should not exceed ⅛ in. in width.

Form Tools

As the name implies, these are tools which are ground to some desired shape, so that the reverse of this shape is imparted to the work. The most common form is that shown at (G) in Fig. 64, which is used for turning large concave radii. Their uses are somewhat limited in the small lathe as considerable cutting strain is imposed by a form tool of any size. For steel work the top of the tool should be flat, as any rake will cause the tool to dig in. Slowest backgear, fine feed, and plenty of " suds " are the requirements.

Form tools for brass should have a negative rake as shown in the sketch (H) in Fig. 64; they provide one of the rare cases where a cutting lubricant should be used for brass work.

Tool Holders

Fig. 66 shows a popular type of tool bit-holder much favoured by professional engineers. Loose cutting bits of high-speed steel may be firmly held, and may be used until ground away to the last half-inch.

While extremely efficient in the large sizes, those suitable for the amateurs' lathes are much smaller, and tool bits of about $\frac{3}{16}$ in., square

Fig. 66
Armstrong tool holder with removable high-speed cutter bit.

section, must be used. This makes them rather flimsy, so that they are mainly suitable for light work.

These tool holders are, by the way, almost the only pattern suitable for use in the American toolpost described in Chapter 2.

Boring Tools

The **single-point boring tool** is so universally used that it deserves a few special words. It is usually made from a length of round high-speed steel, which may be purchased soft. One end is heated to white heat, knocked over at a right-angle, and then ground to shape. The tip is again brought to a white heat, and hardened by plunging into a bath of **whale oil,** moving the tool about meanwhile. Failing whale oil, the writer has had good results from a bath of **soluble oil,** as used as a cutting lubricant (Chapter 10). The soluble oil should be mixed with water so that it is rather thick—about equal proportions of each. High-speed steel may also be hardened in a blast of cold air such as from the nozzle of a spray gun. Unlike carbon steel it requires no tempering operation.

The photograph (Fig. 67 (A)) shows a forged boring tool, while the drawing at (A) in Fig. 68 gives further particulars. It will be seen that for steel the top rake is again maintained.

Similar boring tools may be made with the tip rounded off as shown at (B) in Fig. 68. If used with plenty of

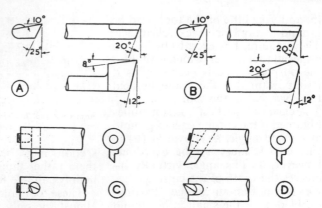

Fig. 68
Diagram showing approximate angles for steel boring tools. (A) pointed tool; (B) round-nosed tool; (C) boring tool holder with adjustable cutter; (D) boring tool holder with cutter set at an angle for blind holes. Here again, exact precision of angles is unimportant for general work.

lubricant, and slow speed and feed, these give a good finish on mild steel. For harder steels it is better to remove the pointed tip of the tool (A) by a few light rubs with a slip stone for finishing purposes.

The shanks of boring tools should be as sturdy as is compatible with the size, but a little " spring " in the shank is desirable, as this, strange as it may seem, can be a great help in boring holes to exact size. Advantage can then be taken of the " spring " in the tool to remove very fine cuts, too small to be easily set by movement of the cross-slide.

Tipped Tools

To save the expense of the long pieces of high-speed steel required for the forged tool, it is customary to braze tips of high-speed steel to shanks of round mild steel.

The mild steel is filed to half its diameter for a distance of about $\frac{3}{8}$ in. at one end. A suitable piece of high-speed steel is then bound into position with iron wire, and the whole brazed up. While still at white heat the bit is plunged into whale oil or soluble oil, and then ground in the ordinary way.

Such tools form, probably, the ideal type for the amateur; they are economical, and easily made, so that a variety of types and sizes may always be on hand. The writer has used this type of tool for many years to the exclusion of almost all others.

The Boring Tool Holder

A useful form of boring tool holder may be made as shown in Figs. 67 and 68 (C). It consists of a length of round mild steel through which a hole is drilled at one end to take a removable cutter bit. This is secured by an Allen screw through the end of the bar. Suitable bits may be made from broken centre drills, or from the **shanks** of ordinary twist drills. These latter are usually soft and must be hardened, but care must be taken to distinguish between high-speed and carbon-steel drills. Carbon steel should be avoided for cutter bits.

Fig. 67
Internal tools. (A) forged boring tool; (B) tipped tool with high-speed bit brazed on; (C) boring tool holder with removable cutter; (D) tipped tool for internal screwcutting.

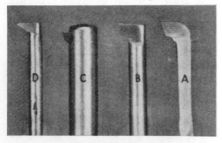

Such boring-tool holders may be made in a variety of sizes, but their use in the very small sizes is somewhat restricted. Also, the tool holder shown in Fig. 67 is suitable only for holes which go right through the job, as clearance for the end of the bar must be had. By boring the tool hole at an angle, as shown in Fig. 68 (D), the tip of the cutter bit precedes the end of the bar, and this difficulty is overcome.

The Boring Bar

Boring bars, sometimes called " fly-cutter bars ", such as that shown in Fig. 69 in the illustrations, form a most useful tool for the amateur mechanic. They are made from a length of mild steel bar, centred at each end, with a cutter bit located in a hole, and secured with an Allen screw.

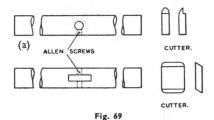

(a) ALLEN SCREWS   CUTTER.

CUTTER.

Fig. 69

Boring bars with removable cutters. At (A) is shown a fly-cutter, while (B) indicates a cutter giving high finish.

They are driven between the lathe centres, or one end may be held in a three-jaw chuck; they are used for boring large work which may be clamped to the cross-slide table. They should be made in a variety of sizes, and form an excellent method of boring holes parallel and true. Care should be taken to ensure that the bar is truly centred at each end, otherwise the cutting tool will " swing " as it revolves, and setting the tool to a definite size of cut will become more difficult. The bits for

this tool may also be made from broken centre drills and twist drills. We shall meet the **boring bar** again later, when its setting and operation will be more fully described. It also has definite uses for milling in the lathe.

Boring Tool " V " Blocks

The most convenient method of holding round-shank boring tools in the toolpost is by means of the boring-tool " V " block, shown in Fig. 70. It consists of a flat strip of

Fig 70

" V " block for holding boring tool in toolpost.

mild steel, about 2 in. long, down one side of which a long " V " groove is cut. Great accuracy is not essential, so that the amateur may well make such a tool with hacksaw and file.

External Screwcutting Tools

The fundamental requirements of a screwcutting tool are accuracy of shape and ample clearances. They may be ground up from the usual type of high-speed tool bit which may be clamped directly in the toolpost, or they may be in the form of detachable bits held in a special tool holder. The photograph (Fig. 71) shows both examples.

It will be appreciated that accuracy of form is of vital importance, especially if the thread to be cut must mate with one already existing. Screw threads of the " V " form fall into two general types—the **Whitworth** form, which has an inclusive angle of 55 degrees, and the **Metric** and **American** forms, which have an inclusive angle of 60 deg. The photograph (Fig. 73) depicts two **threading-tool form gauges,** to which screwing tools may be accurately ground.

Fig. 71

Spring threading tool holder with removable bit; made in the author's workshop. Below is shown a threading tool ground from high-speed steel.

There exists more or less complicated formula for determining the correct side slope and side clearances for threading tools (especially for those of square or acme form), so that the skirt of the tool may conform to the helix angle of the thread being cut, and which does, of course, vary with each pitch. As has been pointed out before, such formula is of little use to the amateur mechanic, as, without special jig equipment, it is extremely difficult to grind, or even to determine, the angles which any hand-ground tool possesses. In view of this, no such formula will be given. Those interested will find that such things occupy a great deal of space in professional treatise and in "amateur textbooks" moulded upon them, and they may always be found there if wanted.

Fig. 72

Diagram of external " V "-thread tool. The thread angle is important.

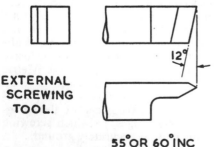

EXTERNAL
SCREWING
TOOL.

12°

55° OR 60° INC

The ordinary amateur will be content to fix the clearance angles by trial and error methods, and may take comfort from the fact that he is following 50 per cent. of professional **practice**. Clearance angles on " V " threads only become of importance when large and deep threads are being tackled; work which the amateur does not often encounter. If, therefore, the model mechanic shapes his threading tools with plenty of clearance, somewhat after the manner shown in Fig. 72, he will find no trouble.

Grinding tools to the correct " V " form by means of the gauge is another matter, but is quite a simple operation. When grinding, the tool should be frequently offered to the gauge and held against the light, until it conforms exactly. Finally, the extreme tip of the tool should be slightly rounded with a slipstone. In order to maintain the correct form of the tool, however, it is necessary that the top of the tool be flat, as any rake may alter the effective cutting form. As screwcutting is always done at extremely low turning speed this disadvantage will not be apparent on steel work.

The Spring Tool Holder

In the picture (Fig. 71) may be seen a home-made version of a screwing-tool holder which greatly helps towards the production of clean, well-finished threads. This tool, it will be noticed, is so fashioned that a certain amount of spring is imparted to the cutter. The utility of this tool is beyond question, and certain well-informed persons have gone so far as to say that it is the only tool by which perfect threads may be cut in the lathe. This is doubtless an exaggeration, but a short experience of its merits will convince the turner that there may be a certain degree of truth in the

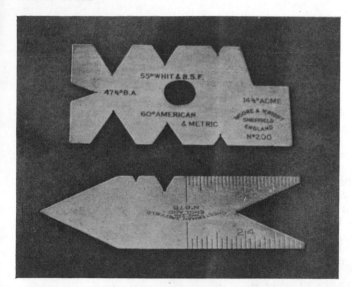

Fig. 73
Threading-tool templates. The lower is only of Whitworth form, but the upper provides for Whitworth, B.A., American and Continental, and Acme forms.

the tool will not foul the threaded bore. No top rake is used.

Knurling Tools

Knurling is carried out by means of hardened wheels which carry a series of shallow, diagonal teeth; those of one wheel slanting in the opposite direction from those on the other. The knurling shown in Fig. 42 is obtained by using one wheel only, while that shown in Fig. 24 is obtained by superimposing the cut of one wheel upon that of the other. As knurling is done by forcing the wheels into the work, considerable strain can be imposed on the lathe, especially when a knurling tool is used which presents both wheels to the work at the same time. A single knurl-holder, a home-made example of which is depicted in Fig. 75, is the best proposition, as the wheels may be used consecutively, and far less strain is imposed. Considerable care should always be exercised, and the knurls fed in slowly, with constant pauses to allow them to cut.

statement. Construction is evident from the photograph, and shows that it is a tool eminently suitable for amateur manufacture.

In use, advantage is taken of the " spring " of the tool by occasionally traversing the thread at the same lathe setting, so that a fine, polishing cut is given. This will produce perfect work.

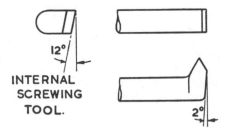

Fig. 74
Diagram of internal threading-tool showing clearances.

Internal Threading Tools

These are simply internal boring tools, the tips of which have been ground to the correct " V " form. Front and side clearances are comparatively large, so that the skirt of

Fig. 75
Knurling tool holder made by the author.

CHAPTER 7

DRILLS AND REAMERS

DRILLS are of so much importance in lathe work that they may quite legitimately be classed as lathe tools. They are, in fact, one of the most extensively used tools in our equipment; yet in very few cases are they exploited to the full extent of their usefulness. The reason for this is that for different purposes drills must be ground in different ways, and few of us have troubled to find out exactly what these ways are. It is sometimes said that a very good idea of the quality of an engineer may be had by noting the manner in which he grinds a drill, and this statement is very largely true because the difference between good and bad work is mainly a matter of suchlike details.

When a drill is not ground correctly it not only does not do its job, but can, at times, be very dangerous. Most model makers will have noticed the tendency for a drill to " grab ", especially when breaking through. This is particularly noticeable when working on brass or sheet metal, where there is a tendency for the work to run up the flutes of the drill, and this has been known to swing round a heavy machine vice, badly cutting the operator's hand in the process. In addition, a good drill may often be ruined for future use by using it in a blunt condition, thus causing it to *rub* instead of *cut*, with a consequent heating up of the drill and loss of hardness. In this softer condition the drill will lose its side clearance, and will bind badly in all future work.

Backing-off

Good grinding is chiefly a matter of obtaining the correct clearance or " backing-off ", as it is called, and this clearance should vary according to the material to be drilled. Unless one knows how, it is a difficult matter to judge by eye just how much clearance a drill has, as there is nothing against which the angle may be compared by just looking at it. In our picture (Fig. 76) is shown a simple method by which the clearance may be very accurately gauged. The appliance consists merely of a piece of tubing, of a diameter slightly smaller than that of the drill to be judged, with the end turned square in the lathe. The tip of the drill is entered into the bore of the tubing, when the amount of clearance which the drill has may be easily seen. Even in our picture it

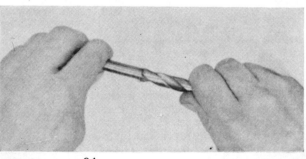

Fig. 76
How to gauge the backing-off on a drill, by comparison with the squared end of a piece of tubing.

may be noted that the drill in question has but a small clearance; in fact, it has been ground up for the special purpose of drilling holes in thin sheet metal. Most of us are aware that this is usually a difficult drilling operation, especially if the drill is of large size, as there is a tendency for the drill not to cut a round hole, but to leave an irregularly shaped hole with a series of flats around the edge. The secret is to have the very minimum of backing-off on the drill tip; in fact, when held against the tubing the clearance should be hardly perceptible. In this manner it is possible to drill holes of 1 in. or more diameter through thin sheet metal cleanly and truly. It must be remembered, however, that a small central hole should first be put through the work, as the points of large drills cannot cut very well. In fact, for all drilling operations it is advisable to start with a small drill first and work upwards to size.

General Purpose Drill

The photograph (Fig. 77) shows a few drills ground for special purposes, and will give a good idea of just how versatile a humble drill can be. At (A) we see a drill correctly ground for general work; that is, for use with mild or alloy steels, cast iron or aluminium, and such-like materials. As may be seen, a fair amount of clearance is allowable, with the point not too steeply angled. It is not proposed to give the actual degrees of the angles in figures, as these can very rarely be worked to in amateur practice—except with new drills just purchased.

Plastics Drill

The picture (B) shows a drill specially ground for ebonite, bakelite or other plastics. The steep angle of the point will be noted, also the large amount of clearance. High-speed drills should always be used when drilling this type of material, as it has a very abrasive action, and carbon-steel drills will quickly be blunted. High drilling speed should also be used, and no lubricant applied.

Countersink Drill

The drill shown at (C) is one ground up as a countersink; that is, with the point at an angle of 90 degs. This is correct for English countersinks, and is probably the only one

Fig. 77

Some ways in which twist drills may be ground. (A) general-purpose drill; (B) drill for plastics and ebonite; (C) countersink drill; (D) twist drill sharpened for wood boring; (E) flat-bottomed drill or end mill.

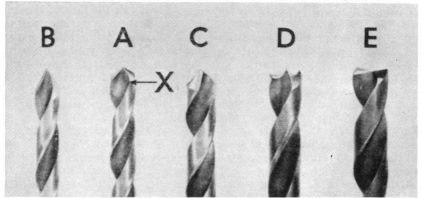

Fig. 78
Ensuring the correct 45-deg.
angle for a countersink drill
by means of set-square.

which the amateur
will be interested
in. Our picture (Fig.
78) shows how this
angle may be
measured against an
ordinary set-square.
With countersinks it
is important that the
angle should be
correct, as nothing
looks worse or more
"amateurish" than
screws which do not seat nicely
into their countersinks. A little
trouble in this direction is, therefore,
well repaid. In this instance, the
drill should have the minimum of
backing, and a short drill (one which
has been broken and reground will
do nicely) should be used. These
two precautions, coupled with low
speed, will prevent the "chatter" so
often experienced when counter-
sinking.

Wood Drill

Returning to Fig. 77, our attention
goes to the drill marked (D). This
drill has been sharpened for use
with wood, and will be found better
than the orthodox spoon-and-bit
type. In fact, engineers' twist drills
have largely superseded these in
woodworking factories, owing to
their cheapness, the ease with which
they may be reground, and the
beautiful clean holes, without any
"rags", which may be made with
them when run at a high speed.

Reference to the picture will show
that the drill is ground with a central
point, plenty of backing-off, and
that the edges of the drill protrude
above the general level of the cutting
faces. In spite of their somewhat
complicated appearance these drills
are quite simple to grind up.

Flat Bottom Drill

Although the drills shown in our
picture by no means exhaust the
possibilities, we now may note the
last drill shown at (E). This is
known as a flat-bottom drill, a name
which indicates that its purpose is
to finish holes requiring a flat bottom
rather than the tapered bottom which
the ordinary drill will leave. This
type of drill cannot be used alone,
but must always follow a hole made
by an orthodox drill of identical
size. Owing to the lack of any pilot
on the drill-tip it is essential that
flat-bottomed drills must have a
clearance hole in which to operate.
As may be seen, the two cutting
faces are ground square across the
drill end, and that each face has a
medium amount of backing-off. In
passing, it may be remarked that
this type of drill is, in effect, an
end-mill, and may be used quite
successfully for this purpose. It will
be appreciated that drills may be
ground to almost any shape at the
cutting faces, such as that known

as a "rose drill", which is shaped to give a hole with a rounded bottom.

Drilling Holes to Correct Size

One of the greatest difficulties which the model engineer encounters is that of drills cutting oversize, but this need hold no fears if he knows how to counteract it. The chief reasons for drills behaving in this unkindly fashion may be summarised as follows. Forcing a drill instead of allowing it to cut naturally; too much backing-off; drill tip ground out-of-centre; no small pilot hole for the drill to follow; failure to withdraw the drill occasionally to clear the swarf.

The first fault needs little enlarging upon, beyond saying that if a drill is forced the tips of the cutting edge will tend to "grab", thus expanding the drill by the flexing of the flutes. The second fault, that is, too much backing-off, is easily remedied, especially if checked by the means already detailed. Thirdly, if the drill tip is ground out-of-centre, that is, if one cutting edge is longer than another, the drill will tend to an eccentric motion, which will, of course, enlarge the hole. Lastly, failure to clear the swarf will wedge the drill against the sides of the hole, thus tending to cut big, besides causing the risk of the drill jamming as the flutes become packed with cuttings.

Many amateurs will find difficulty in believing that it is possible to cut a hole so close on size that it is almost impossible to force the drill into it afterwards, but it can be done, and this is the way to do it. First drill the pilot hole with a drill considerably smaller than the finished size required, then follow with a series of drills, gradually increasing in diameter. When you have reached the drill which is just one size smaller than the finishing drill, lightly stone the tips of the cutting edges with a fine oilstone, just removing the sharp points. Now run the drill through. Taking the finishing drill, again stone the tips, and very slowly drill through, using the correct lubricant for the metal in hand. (This will be detailed later.) The resultant hole will be dead to size. The object of stoning the drill tip is to prevent the drill from "grabbing" in any way, thus obviating the danger of the drill expanding on the flutes. Also a reamering action is obtained. A word of warning, however. Never stone the **points** of a drill when operating on copper or phosphor-bronze, as these metals always tend to bind, and a stoned drill will probably become immovably fixed in the work.

Drilling Bronze and Copper

This leads us to the correct method of drilling these two metals, and the following hints also apply to brass. Use a drill with a small amount of backing-off, and not too steep a point. Now, with a fine oilstone flatten slightly the whole of the cutting edge, thus giving it a small negative rake. This is exactly the same procedure as is done with turning tools intended for bronze, copper or brass. Please note that the **actual corners of the cutting edges** (as indicated at (X) in Fig. 77) **are not stoned off,** as this will make the drill bind in the hole as before mentioned.

Home-made Drills

Twist drills are such familiar tools that the amateur forgets that several other types of drill exist, and can be of the utmost usefulness. Model engineers do not often possess a range of drills in the large sizes above about $\frac{1}{2}$ in., but this need not worry them if they are prepared to make the type of drill shown in Fig. 79.

Fig. 79
Home-made drill or spoon-
bit. A fast-cutting drill easily
made by the amateur.

This is known as a "flat" or "tool-post" drill, and was the approved type used by the old-time engineers before twist drills were on the market. These drills can be made from flat cast-steel or silver-steel stock, or old files can be utilised. The shape is well shown in the illustration, where it will be seen that the end of the material is splayed-out by bringing to a red heat and hammering. The drill is then ground; the correct backing-off clearance being given as in the case of twist drills.

Flat drills have several advantages apart from the ease with which they may be made. Particularly is this so when large holes must be drilled for such things as bronze bushes prior to finish-turning the bores. Such drills will never jam-up in the job, and are fast cutting. In addition, large twist drills are awkward to use with a drill-chuck in the tailstock of the small type of lathe which most amateurs possess, owing to the inability to hold the drill firmly. The drill consequently turns when pressure is exerted. The flat drill, on the other hand, is clamped in the toolpost of the lathe, and cannot turn under any circumstances. When hardening these drills, if of cast-steel stock or old files, they should be tempered to a medium straw colour. Drills of silver steel, however, should be lowered to a dark straw colour, as this material is rather brittle.

Extension Drills

It is not generally appreciated that the shanks of drills, even high-speed

steel ones, are left soft, so they may, in consequence, be turned down quite easily to fit small drill chucks. This must not be overdone, however, owing to the tendency to twist in the drill-chuck. Another advantage of the soft shanks is that they may be turned down for insertion into a piece of drilled rod to make extension drills. These are necessary when a very deep hole is required. Turn back the shank of the drill for about an inch. Now take a piece of mild steel of a diameter smaller than that of the drill, and drill a hole in the end to be a snug fit over the reduced shank of the drill, which may now be inserted into the hole. The joint may now be brazed or silver-soldered, and cleaned up in the lathe. To prevent the brazing heat from softening the drill it is an old dodge to insert it in a potato during the brazing operation. Do not use silver steel as an extension, as this is liable to harden up and become brittle.

Lubricants

Correct lubrication when drilling is as important as it is when turning, and does, in fact, follow the same principles. Therefore, drill mild and alloy steels with lard-oil or soluble oil, or, failing these, soap-suds or even lubricating oil. Hard brass and cast iron are best worked dry, while for soft brass or copper use lard-oil or "suds". For aluminium and its alloys paraffin should be used.

All the above are what may be termed " orthodox lubricants ", but there are now upon the market special cutting compounds, in the form of a paste, made especially for such processes as drilling, reamering and tapping. Such a compound, which is remarkably effective, is that marketed under the trade name of " Trefolex ".

Finally, it may be said that a full set of fractional, letter and number drills can be one of the most useful outfits that a model engineer can possess. Also, drill stands for these have a practical value far beyond their modest cost, as there is hardly anything so annoying or time-wasting as a search for a particular drill among a jumbled mass.

Reamers

One of the most useful and speedy methods of finishing holes to correct diameter, especially those of small size, is by means of the reamer. Generally speaking, commercially made reamers may be divided into two types—spiral-fluted and straight-fluted—which may again be sub-divided into **hand reamers** and **machine reamers**. Both types are shown in Fig. 80, where it will be seen that the machine reamer has shorter flutes and a longer shank than has the hand reamer. Our picture does, in fact, show a machine reamer embodying a taper shank for use in a tailstock, but quite often machine reamers have plain, parallel shanks.

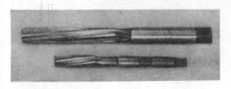

Fig. 80
(*Top*) Spiral fluted hand reamer; (*lower*) spiral fluted machine reamer with taper shank.

For amateur use the hand reamer is the most useful, as this may be used equally well for reamering in the lathe. Those with spiral flutes are the best, as they do not tend to expand on the flutes with the cutting pressure to the same extent as do the straight-fluted kind.

Home-made Reamers

Fluted reamers are comparatively expensive tools, and a collection of all necessary sizes would cost a considerable sum. Fortunately, sizes up to about ⅜ in. can be made quite easily from silver-steel rod of the required size. Two methods may be employed. In the one, the silver steel is filed to exactly half its diameter for a length of about 2 in., with the tip rounded off to form an entry. The second method is the easier one, as the silver steel is filed diagonally across its diameter, as may be seen in Fig. 81. Filing silver steel rod to exactly half its diameter is not a simple job; and as the diagonal reamers seem to perform equally well, they are to be recommended. The finished reamer should be hard-ended and tempered to a dark straw colour.

Using Reamers

Reamers are intended purely as **finishing tools,** so that very little metal should be left in the hole for the reamer to take out. A maximum of from 3 to 5 thousandths of an inch on the diameter of the hole is ample allowance. If the original hole is made smaller than this amount, the reamer will be excessively strained, and it is highly unlikely that the finished hole will be either round or to size. In addition, there is a grave danger of the reamer jamming, and, possibly, breaking.

When using reamers by hand, a strong tap-wrench should be employed, and the cut applied steadily and evenly, without any rocking or side strain. Both in cutting and in

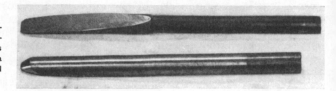

withdrawing the tool it should be rotated in the cutting direction; that is, a reamer should never be turned backwards when withdrawing it. Flutes should be cleared frequently of chips, and a cutting lubricant—such as **lard oil**—should be used on steels and aluminium alloys. If a particularly high finish is required on brass or cast iron, a little **soluble oil** lubricant may be used, but this has a tendency to cause the reamer to jam, especially if the reamer is old and the cutting edges are beginning to dull.

Reaming in the Lathe

Reamers may be used in the lathe by holding them in a chuck in the tailstock, in exactly the same manner as with a drill. For perfect results,

however, it is essential that both the chuck and the tailstock be dead in line with the lathe mandrel. If the reamer is straining the slightest amount out of line the resultant hole cannot be true.

For this reason it is usually much better to use the **floating reamer** system, the set-up of which may be seen in Fig. 82. Here it will be noted that the point of the reamer—which is always a few "thous." undersize—is entered into the hole, while the shank of the reamer is supported by a lathe centre in the tailstock. A large tap-wrench, which is held by hand, serves to prevent the reamer from turning. In the photograph the operator has not been shown for the sake of clarity.

Slowest backgear should be used,

Fig. 82
Putting through a "floating reamer". Pressure is applied from the tailstock, and the reamer steadied by hand.
It is important that the reamer be continually engaged on the back centre during the whole operation.

and a steady pressure applied by the tailstock handwheel. It is essential that the point of the lathe centre should be kept constantly engaged in the centre hole of the reamer, and the reamer should be pulled, hard, backwards against the cutting pressure, so that it cannot become disengaged. The work must be kept constantly revolving, both for cutting and withdrawing, and on no account must the back support of the tailstock be lost during the whole operation.

Contrary to general opinion, reamering holes truly and dead to size is not a simple operation, and the use of a "floating reamer" gives the inexperienced mechanic the best chance of success. The essentials are: the reamer must remove the smallest amount of metal possible; slow turning speed and feed; reamer shank must never become disengaged from the tailstock support; lathe rotation must not be stopped or reversed during the whole process.

Taper Reamers

These are usually made to some standard angle of taper, such as Morse or Brown and Sharpe in the larger sizes, and standard taper-pin angles in the smaller. Taper reamers should always be used by hand, and the very minimum depth of cut applied. They should be frequently withdrawn to clear the chips, and well lubricated during use.

Small taper reamers, one of which

Fig. 83
Taper reamers.   (Top) Commercial hand reamer.
(Lower) Home-made taper reamer.

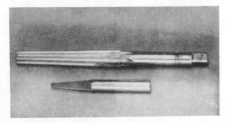

may be seen in Fig. 83, may also be made from silver steel rod, which is turned to the required taper and filed to exactly half its diameter. Harden and temper to dark straw colour.

Words of Warning

Although not, strictly speaking, lathe work, it is felt that a few words of caution on the use of the drilling machine may not be out of place in this book, as most amateurs will possess a drilling machine in addition to the lathe. Also, where no drilling machine is available, the lathe itself will be called upon to perform all drilling functions, so that the following remarks may apply with equal force to the lathe in this instance.

An analysis of the accidents in a large London engineering works showed that forty per cent. of all casualties were caused by the drilling machines! The most prolific cause of trouble was the practice of holding work by hand on the drilling table, so that the work was spun round, out of the hand, by the revolving drill. This is particularly likely to happen as the drill breaks through the work, as the sudden release of resistance causes the drill to snatch forward and bind on the cutting lips.

Particular care is necessary when drilling thin sheet metal, and the drill should be ground with the minimum of backing-off as advised earlier on.

Drills are also particularly liable to snatch when drilling brass, and, here again, the cause is usually too much backing-off. When using drills on brass work it is highly necessary that the sharp cutting edges be flatted off slightly with a slip oilstone, and that excessive feed pressure be not applied.

In addition to the correct grinding

Fig. 83A

Set-up for drilling holes with extreme accuracy, using turned discs as drilling jigs. The versatility of this method is described in the text.

of drills, the best precaution against accident is to remember always that the human hand makes a very poor machine vice. Not only is its gripping power insufficient to cope with the strains from a power-driven machine, but it is subject to injuries to which a machine vice proper is not liable.

Drilling Holes in Correct Positions

When locating holes with dividers, rule, and punch-dot an accuracy greater than about ·005 in. cannot be relied upon, an error which often cannot be tolerated. In addition, it is almost impossible to mark-off holes positioned at odd decimal places of an inch. For instance, while it may be fairly simple to

mark-off holes spaced at a distance of 1 in., it is an entirely different matter if the spacing is to be, say, ·982 in.

There is a system, based on the use of the lathe, by which holes may be drilled in a drilling machine to an accuracy of ·001 in. or even better. The system, moreover, is extremely simple, and consists, briefly, of the use of turned, steel discs, which are used as drilling jigs.

The method is illustrated in Fig. 83B, and for the sake of continuity it has been assumed that the distance required is our hypothetical one of ·982 in. As a first step, two steel discs, with a thickness of about $\frac{1}{4}$ in., should be turned to exactly ·982 in. in diameter, and a hole, slightly smaller than that required in the finished job, should be drilled, from the lathe tailstock, exactly in the centre of each disc.

The discs are then located upon the workpiece, with their edges in close contact, so the centre holes are spaced exactly ·982 in. apart. The discs are secured with toolmakers clamps, as shown in Fig. 83A. The correct size of drill is now selected, and the holes drilled, using the discs as drilling jigs. As the drilling proceeds, the holes in the discs will be slightly " opened out ", and a great accuracy of location will be attained on the job.

The system is extremely versatile, and the drawing, marked A in Fig.

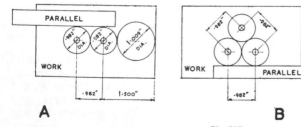

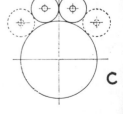

Fig. 83B

Drilling holes in correct positions using turned discs as drilling jigs.

83B, indicates how a correct distance may be set-off from an edge
by using another disc turned to its
appropriate diameter. The use of a
parallel to line-up the drilling discs
is also shown.

The figure marked B in the drawing demonstrates how holes may be
drilled in a triangular form, and it
will be appreciated that considerable accuracy can be attained in this
somewhat difficult operation. Similarly, of course, holes located on
an accurate square or rectangle may
be just as easily obtained; in fact,

the limitations are governed solely
by ones skill as a turner, and by ones
mathematical ability. For instance,
we show at C in Fig. 83B the method
of spacing holes around a given
circumference. It will be noted that
two of the discs have been drawn
in dotted line, which indicates that
only two discs may be used, as each
may be rolled around the central
disc as the drilling proceeds.

If, therefore, one is able to work
out the diameters and chords necessary, a complete circle of any number
of holes cannot be drilled.

CHAPTER 8

HOLDING WORK IN THE LATHE

THE importance of holding work for operation in the lathe is so great that it may be said to constitute half the art of turning. No matter what shape or size a job may be—provided it is within the capacity of the machine— there exists somewhere a method of holding it for machining operations, and the successful turner, be he professional or amateur, is the one who has the knowledge or knack of determining the best method of doing so. To the inexperienced many jobs look, on the face of it, impossible to hold satisfactorily, yet, so many cunning methods may be employed that the impossible does not really exist.

General Observations

The first essential of any setting-up job is that it be held so securely that there is not the slightest chance of the work becoming detached during the most severe machining operations. If you are not absolutely satisfied that, under no conditions, can the job move or work loose, then your set-up is wrong, and other methods must be sought. Any job which detaches itself during machining is extremely dangerous, and may not only spoil the work, damage the lathe, and injure the workman, but is such a sign of inefficiency that the blow to one's pride should be the severest damage of all.

Notes on Chucks

A great deal of lathe work will be done in the self-centring and four-jaw independent chucks, and any

care taken in their use and maintenance will pay good dividends.

Much annoyance and damage can be caused by swarf, chips and dirt entering the threads of the chuck-back, thus causing jamming on the lathe spindle nose. Never force a chuck which appears to be tight on the mandril thread, but always look for the cause of the trouble. A simple tool for cleaning the chuck threads may be made from a piece

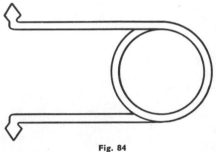

Fig. 84
Tool made from spring wire for cleaning the threads in chuck back-plates.

of stout steel wire, in the manner shown in Fig. 84. This tool should be used frequently, and the mandrel thread cleaned with rag.

Fig. 85
Correct method of parking chucks. If these are stood the other way up, dirt and swarf fall into the threads, and the registers may also be damaged.

The most contributory cause of the above trouble is that, when removed from the lathe, chucks are often stood upon the registers, with the jaws facing upwards. If parked in this way dirt and swarf will fall downwards into the threads; also, the registers may be damaged. Always park chucks as shown in Fig. 85, that is, resting on the jaws with the thread and register uppermost.

Screwing Chucks on the Lathe Spindle

Never, under any circumstances, screw the chuck (or faceplate for that matter) to the lathe spindle under power; that is, by holding the chuck stationary and revolving the mandrel by the power drive. If you do, you will probably find that the chuck or faceplate is immovably fixed to the lathe nose!

Lathe chucks which have become jammed in this way are most difficult things to get off, and usually necessitate the removal of the lathe spindle. The writer has, in fact, known cases where the chuckback has had to be completely turned away, as it was found impossible otherwise to remove it without damage to the precious lathe spindle.

When heavy cuts have been taken it is probable that the chuck will be pretty tightly screwed on the mandrel and some form of lever may have to be used, as the chuck cannot be gripped tightly enough by hand. A brass bar placed between the chuck jaws may be used as a lever for this purpose, with the mandrel locked by engagement of the backgears, leaving the bullwheel pin still in engagement. On no account use the chuck key, located in one of the adjustment holes, for this purpose, especially with four-jaw chucks. The square recess on the adjustment screws will most likely be broken if you do. Removing jammed chucks is a wretched business at the best of times, and probably the safest way is to engage slow backgear, place a piece of hardwood on the rear lathe-way so that a chuck jaw may strike it, and to revolve the mandrel in reverse. Even so, great care is necessary, as the back gears may be stripped in the process. The wise machinist sees to it that the chuck never becomes jammed!

The Chuck Board

Damage is often caused to the chuck, and more particularly to the lathe bed, by the chuck suddenly falling off as it is unscrewed from the mandrel, as, with a good fitting thread, little or no warning is given that the chuck is about to disengage. To prevent this senseless and irreparable damage a chuck board should be one of the first things which the amateur mechanic should make. As may be seen in Fig. 86, it consists simply of a suitable piece of wood with two battens screwed to it so as to fit snugly across the lathe bed.

This board should also be employed when any sawing has to be done on pieces held in the chuck jaws. Quite often, as the hacksaw cuts through, the impetus of the stroke causes the saw to strike the latheways beneath, and damage results.

Don't Strain the Chuck

It has already been pointed out that the self-centring chuck is easily strained by misuse. Even our sturdy friend, the four-jaw, independent chuck, can be damaged by ignorance or foolishness. A prolific cause of trouble is the practice of holding large work which necessitates the chuck jaws being too far extended from the body, so that only a small portion of the gear scroll or adjusting screws is employed. If the job necessitates this, then it is too big for the chuck in use, and other methods of holding must be found.

Supporting by Back Centre

A thing carefully to be watched by the turner is the danger of work being forced out of the chuck jaws by a sudden jam-up of the cutting tool. Emphasis has already been put on the matter of holding the work firmly, but even an apparently good set-up may prove inadequate under emergency conditions. These are particularly liable to arise when the workpiece protrudes for any considerable distance from the chuck jaws, thus presenting excessive overhang and leverage. In such cases, the outer end of the job should always be supported by the back centre. When this is done we have an almost infallible set-up, which should always be employed if any doubts exist in the mind of the operator.

Removing and Replacing Chuck Jaws

Most self-centring chucks are provided with two sets of steel jaws, one set of which allows larger work to be held. Care must be taken when replacing the jaws, as each one must be fitted into its correct slot in the body, and in the correct sequence. For this reason the jaws and slots are always numbered from 1 to 3.

The correct method of replacing jaws is to enter No. 1 jaw into No. 1 slot, so that it just engages with the internal scroll. Now enter No. 2 jaw in its corresponding slot, and turn the scroll forward until this jaw also engages; and so on for No. 3 jaw. If they are not replaced in this manner one or more of the jaws will be eccentrically located.

Using the Self-centring Chuck

Gripping work in the three-jaw chuck seems such an obviously simple procedure that there may appear to be hardly anything which may be said about it. Like most apparently simple things, however, there is rather more in it than may meet the eye.

In the first place, the small three-jaw chuck is a comparatively delicate component; that is, if its truth is to be maintained. It is easily strained

Fig. 86
A valuable accessory. A chuck board fitted across the lathe bed as a protection against accidental damage.

and "put out of truth", so that half its usefulness is destroyed. A self-centring chuck that really does "self-centre", is such a valuable asset that every precaution should be taken to preserve this virtue. Do not expect it, therefore, to handle in its stride all sorts and conditions of large and heavy work. Work such as this should always be held in the independent chuck, which, by reason of its design, can cope successfully with heavy conditions.

Under no consideration should the jaws of a self-centring chuck be excessively tightened in an endeavour to hold work securely. Such methods as that of using a length of tubing to obtain leverage on the chuck-key will be abhorred by all good craftsmen. Particularly should care be taken when gripping short work by the tips of the jaws, as, whilst being quite legitimate practice, much strain can be caused by unnecessary tightening.

The misuse of the three-jaw chuck for gripping irregular work—such as rough castings—provides a common instance of vandalism. If all the three jaws cannot seat evenly upon the workpiece damage will ensue. Such work should be held in the four-jaw chuck in the first stage, transferring the work to the three-jaw when a suitable holding surface has been turned.

On some three-jaw chucks it will be found that one of the key-sockets bears an identification mark —usually stamped on the chuck body adjacent to the key-socket— by means of which this particular socket may be readily selected. If the chuck is operated from this marked socket, work will be held more truly than would be the case if operated from any of the others.

The reason for this is that, during the final stages of manufacture, the chuck is trued by grinding the jaws

Fig. 87

Holding square stock in the three-jaw chuck. The method is also applicable to the four-jaw chuck.

in situ, and the marked key-socket is the one from which the chuck was operated for this process.

Facing Square Stock

The photograph (Fig. 87) shows how square or rectangular stock may be held for facing in the three-jaw chuck, and depicts a simple and convenient method of chucking an otherwise awkward workpiece. The system may also be employed for turning a flat down one side of a length of round bar, thus forming a "D" section. Other applications will be obvious.

The Four-jaw Independent Chuck

As each jaw may be adjusted independently, this form of chuck is primarily used for gripping work of irregular shape, or that requiring "off-set" turning. Its robust construction also makes it suitable for

G

all types of large and heavy work. At the same time it is sensitive enough to be used when symmetrical work must be set up to run dead truly.

Setting-up in the Four-jaw Chuck

When a workpiece must be set-up in the independent chuck for off-set turning it is customary to mark the point which must run centrally with a centre dot. In this way it is possible to use the centre-finder as described in Chapter 4.

If no centre-finder is available, a quick method of setting the punch

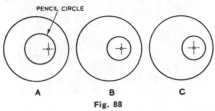

Fig. 88

Method of centring work in the four-jaw chuck with pencil and chalk. A quick method explained in the text.

dot to run truly is shown in the drawing, Fig. 88. The punch dot should be roughly centred in the chuck by eye, and the face of the workpiece lightly rubbed over with chalk. The job should then be revolved in the lathe, and, while it is spinning, a sharp pencil should be held lightly to the chalked face. This will draw a circle on the workface, which will then appear as shown at (A) in the illustration. Here it will be seen that the punch dot

appears off-set in the circle. If the punch dot were in the centre of the circle it would, of course, be truly centred in the lathe, so the chuck jaws are now adjusted to move the punch dot in the direction of the centre of the circle.

Now rechalk the workface, and draw another circle as the lathe revolves. This time the punch dot should be nearer to the centre; somewhat as shown at (B). Again adjust towards the centre of the circle and repeat the process until the punch dot is running truly as at (C). The method is quick and easy, as the amount and direction of movement may be readily seen.

Centring Square Stock

Square section rod cannot of course, be held truly in the three-jaw chuck, so that, apart from collets, the four-jaw chuck presents the obvious method.

In thus setting-up square stock truly, it is simpler first to set up a piece of **round stock** of similar diameter to the across-flats measurement of the square material. Thus, for a piece of $\frac{1}{4}$-in. square steel, a piece of $\frac{1}{4}$-in. diameter round silver

Fig. 89

Holding twin blocks in the four-jaw chuck for identical machining operations.

steel may be used. This may be set to run truly by eye, or by marking with a piece of chalk as it revolves, or, if extreme accuracy is wanted, by the test dial-indicator. The silver steel is then removed by loosening the chuck jaws, and replaced by the square material. This is gripped by *tightening the two jaws which were originally loosened*; the other jaws must not, of course, be touched.

Faceplate Work

No amateur mechanic will get very far with his hobby until he has mastered the technique of setting-up work on the faceplate, which presents probably the most versatile of all chucking methods.

Our illustration (Fig. 90) shows what is, possibly, the most simple form of faceplate mounting, where we see a flat plate set-up for the boring of an off-set hole. The picture is self-explanatory, but is interesting by virtue of the fact that it shows one of the uses for an old ball-race outer-ring, as mentioned in Chapter 5. In an instance of this kind, where the hole to be bored goes right through the workpiece, clearance for the lathe tool must be allowed at the back of the work if damage to the faceplate is to be avoided. Some amateurs clamp the

Fig. 91
The simplest form of faceplate set-up. Machining the tread of a model locomotive wheel. Care is necessary that the work is not strained by excessive pressure on holding bolts.

work to a piece of wood, but as wood is very rarely flat to engineering limits, this practice is bad, as there is no guarantee that the finished hole will be square with the workface.

Another simple faceplate set-up is shown in Fig. 91, where a driving wheel for a model locomotive may be seen bolted—between the wheel spokes—directly to the faceplate for turning the tread, flange and the rim. With such elementary set-ups only one precaution is necessary. Make certain that the shape or

Fig. 90
Old ball-race rings used as parallels for packing work on the faceplate

Fig. 92
Machining the expansion links for a model locomotive. The workpiece is soldered to a flat plate, and bolted at the correct radius of cut on the faceplate.

Fig. 93
(*Below*) Faceplate set-up for machining a hole at an angle to the workface. Note packing blocks and the blocks bolted to faceplate to prevent work slipping. This workpiece is part of the turret, tailstock tool-holder described elsewhere.

nature of the work does not allow it to bend under the pressure of the holding-down clamps, as the nuts are tightened.

More Complicated Set-ups

While the faceplate is valuable for such simple jobs as those above, its real utility is found in the machining of more complicated jobs. As a typical example we may take that shown in Fig. 92, where it was desired to turn a number of semi-circular grooves in the piece of metal which may be seen in a vertical position at the left of the picture. These were required as expansion links for the valve gear of a model locomotive.

The piece of steel was first soft soldered, at a right-angle, to a larger piece, which was then drilled and bolted to the faceplate in the correct position to give the required radius. Slow backgear would be essential for such a job as this, owing to the poor balance and the considerable blow from the intermittent cut. The job forms a good example of the possibilities of the faceplate.

Unusual Faceplate Set-ups

The term "unusual" is here used in the sense that the particular

method of mounting is not at first sight obvious. Only one instance will be given, as these could be multiplied indefinitely, and one case will do as well as many to indicate the lines of thought which the amateur should pursue when faced with an apparent difficulty.

To understand the position, it will be necessary to glance at the casting shown at the top of the picture in Fig. 94. The lower casting we shall meet later on. The illustration shows the body casting of a special dividing head arrangement, and it was desired, as a first step, to machine the bottom face of the casting. Being too large to hold in any type of chuck available, the faceplate was the only alternative, but here again, no ready method of attachment presented itself.

On examining the drawing it was found that oilers had eventually to be fitted to the tops of the cylindrical

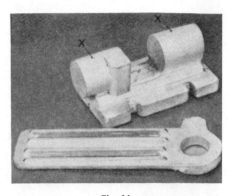

Fig. 94

Examples of components to be machined. Castings or the home-made dividing head also described in this book.

portions, at the points marked (X) (X). Advantage was taken of this fact, and two holes were drilled in the position shown, and tapped $\frac{3}{8}$-in. Whitworth thread. This allowed the casting to be bolted to the faceplate

Fig. 95

An awkward chucking job overcome. The casting has been tapped to receive holding down bolts. This method may often be followed with advantage.

Fig. 96

A familiar set-up to many model engineers. A small crankcase for a petrol engine mounted on the angle plate on the faceplate for machining the cylinder seating.

in the manner shown in Fig. 95, where the operation of facing the bottom is in progress.

The above is a typical example of how intelligent thought will overcome an apparent difficulty. It will often repay the engineer to purposely drill holes in any awkward workpiece solely for the purposes of setting-up. This can usually be done without upsetting either the appearance or utility of the job. In any case, the holes can, if necessary, be filled with metal plugs on completion.

Angle Plate Work

Useful as the faceplate is, its utility can be much increased by the addition of an angle plate. With this accessory it is possible to bolt work at a right-angle to the faceplate, a necessity which often arises. Such an instance is shown in Fig. 96, where we have a set-up for machining the cylinder seating on a small Diesel

engine crankcase. The casting has been bolted down on a previously machined face which must lie at 90 deg. to the cylinder seating. The picture gains additional interest from the fact that it shows the manner in which the set-up is balanced by bolting lathe change wheels to the faceplate to counter the weight of the angle plate and job. Without these counterweights the job would "swing" so badly that work would be impossible at any reasonable speed.

The "Keats", or Faceplate "V" Block

Our picture (Fig. 30) illustrates the faceplate "V" block, one of the most useful accessories that the amateur can possess. As may be gathered from the photograph, the angle plate when bolted to the faceplate presents a sturdy "V" block lying parallel to the lathe axis. Into this "V" all types of round, square, or other material may be securely

Fig. 101

Turning the crankpin on an overhung crankshaft in the "V" block angle plate. These plates also act as turning fixtures for repetition work, and are a valuable accessory for any lathe worker.

clamped, and the reader will quickly see the possibilities which are presented. One of the most useful aspects of the "Keats" plate is that it does, in effect, form a "turning fixture" or faceplate "jig", most useful when a number of duplicate workpieces have to be held. Once one piece has been set to run truly, the location of the "V" block is not altered, so that it is a simple matter to clamp the remaining workpieces into the block. Our illustration (Fig. 101) shows the "Keats" plate used for holding a small crankshaft for the operation of turning the crank-pin.

Work Between Centres

Driving between centres is undoubtedly the oldest form of holding work in the lathe, and is almost the only method used on the primitive types of wood-turning lathe still to be found in out-of-the-way corners of the world—including those of our own islands. In spite of its antiquity it still forms the best, and possibly the only, system for some kinds of work, such as long shafts of any kind. It is a method yielding most accurate results, and is, in fact, chiefly used where precision is required. Although between-centre turning is much used for taper work, this will be considered later, and only parallel turning will be dealt with at the moment.

It is, of course, essential that the work to be turned should have suitable centre holes drilled into the ends, into which the lathe centres may locate. Centre drilling is so

Fig. 97

Another example of angle plate set-up. It should be particularly noted that it is necessary for the inner face of the angle plate to be machined true with the outer faces. Some angle plates are not so finished and are not suitable for the set-up shown.

Fig. 98

A simple angle plate set-up. Boring the hole
in a plummer block.

quite truly when plugged into the lathe mandrel. As quite a small piece of dirt or metal dust on the centre, or in the socket of the mandrel, will cause the centre to run out of true, both should be carefully wiped with clean rag before mating. If truing is necessary, set the top slide over to 30 degrees, check that the point of the turning tool is at dead centre height, and proceed to skim the centre with the lightest of cuts and fine feed. Avoid filing, as this leaves a roughened surface. Clean up the tip of the centre with a fine slip oil-stone.

If the head-centre is not running truly, the finished job will not spin concentrically when turned end-for-end between the centres.

Turning a Parallel Shaft

Assuming for the sake of illustration that we desire to turn a plain, parallel shaft, and that the metal has been suitably centred at the ends, the first consideration must be that

linked up with marking out, however, that it will be dealt with fully in the chapter under that heading.

Truing the Head-Centre

It will be remembered that in Chapter 4 mention was made of the fact that the head-centre was often left soft, so that it could be trued-up if necessary. The first step, there-fore, must be to ascertain that the head-centre is running

Fig. 99

Holding an awkward job. A small engine
connecting rod mounted on a machined
spigot clamped in position on the faceplate.
Note the use of the toolmaker's clamp for
securing the overhung end.

the tailstock-centre is so lined-up with the head-centre that the lathe tool will travel along the bed exactly parallel to the longitudinal axis of the work. Very few amateur type lathes can be depended upon to keep correct alignment between head and tail centres for any length of time; the tailstock leads a hard and active life as it is continually moved along the bed for such operations as drilling. It is almost certain, therefore, that the tailstock will need "lining-up" before accurate work can be turned between centres.

This lining-up is often a puzzle and a trial to the inexperienced amateur, and may be done in two practical ways. The first and quicker of these is by means of a **parallel test bar** and a **test dial-indicator.** The latter we have already spoken about, but for some reason very few amateurs possess a test bar—a most useful · accessory—principally because there is a general idea that they are enormously expensive. This is not so. An accurate test-bar may be made from a 12-in. length of $\frac{3}{4}$-in. diameter, ground, silver steel, which may be purchased quite cheaply from almost any tool store. It may be accurately centred at the ends by a method described in Chapter 9.

The test-bar is, of course, set up between centres, and the "clock" held in the toolpost with its plunger against the bar. The carriage is then wound along the lathe bed from head to tailstock, and any variation in clock reading noted. The tailstock is then set over in the correct direction until no movement is apparent on the indicator from end to end of the bar. The job may now be set up, and a test cut taken, when any small variation from parallel may be corrected.

If no dial-indicator is available, the test-bar may be set approximately correct by clamping a pointed lathe tool in the post. The set-up is then adjusted until the tip of the tool just touches the test-bar at each end. The operation is assisted by placing a piece of white paper on the lathe bed beneath the tool, so that the position of its tip may be more readily seen.

The Trial and Error Method

By this system the material to be turned is set up between centres, with the lathe carrier attached for turning, and a light cut is taken over the whole length of the job. It is necessary that the cut should be taken at fine feed, as a heavy, roughing cut may give a false result owing to the spring of the material. Each end of the job is then measured with a micrometer, and the difference noted. The tailstock must then be set over half the amount of the difference in the correct direction for parallel results. If the job measures too small at the tailstock end it is a sign that the tailstock is too near to the tool, and it must, therefore, be set over in a direction away from it. Conversely, if the job measures large, then the tailstock must be moved towards the tool.

Here again a "clock" is invaluable, as with its aid the tailstock may be adjusted exactly the right amount. Failing a "clock", the tailstock may be set only by guesswork, and the test cut repeated until the micrometer shows that the bar to be turned is parallel.

Adjusting the Lathe Centres

One of the most troublesome things when turning work between centres is to obtain the correct pressure between the lathe centres. The job should revolve freely by hand, without any trace of shake. This condition is easy to determine at first, but, as work proceeds, the material will heat up and expand lengthwise, thus tightening up on the lathe centres. In the early stages of roughing out continual adjustment is necessary, and it is essential that the dead centre be well lubricated. Before the finishing cut is reached the job should have attained a stable heat and expansion point, so that a final centre adjustment can be made. This adjustment should not be left until the final cut, however, and the work should be checked for parallelism after each alteration of the lathe centres. If the centre adjustment has to be altered during the finishing cut it is not probable that the job will be true. A steadier drive may be obtained by lashing the lathe carrier to the driving stub of the driver plate with cord.

Lubricant for Lathe Centres

As a lubricant for the dead centre the usual machine oil may be advantageously replaced by a mixture of white lead and lubricating oil, in equal proportions. This mixture is not so easily pressed out of the centre bearing, and will withstand considerable heat without burning up. The dead centre should, however, be continually watched for signs of overheating or dryness, which will usually make itself known by a loud squeak! This means that immediate attention is necessary, otherwise a burnt-out lathe centre may be the result.

To sum up; no other turning operation requires such constant attention and watchfulness on the part of the operator. Turning long, parallel shafts is probably the most difficult of all lathe undertakings. The work must be constantly checked with the micrometer, and an eye kept always open for anything "going wrong". When you can turn out a 2-ft. shaft, parallel and of a high finish, you may call yourself a turner!

Quite often the amateur must turn wood in the lathe, even if only for such purposes as pattern making,

Fig. 100

Centring a punch dot by means of the centre-finder. The outer end of the rod swings in an exaggerated manner, due to the lever action, when the work is revolved. The work is positioned until the tip of the centre-finder makes no movement when the work is revolved. Checking against the tailstock centre is a great help.

and, being difficult to grip securely in the chuck, between-centre turning must often be used. At the head-stock a wood-turning prong-centre should be used, but there is often a difficulty in supporting at the tail-stock end owing to the centre sinking into the soft wood. If a steel washer is placed over the point of the centre, so as to form a stop, it will prevent this trouble.

Lathe Steadies

This seems the appropriate point to mention the **fixed** and **travelling steadies,** as these are usually associated with long work such as that turned between centres. Our illustration shows (Fig. 102) both these steadies set-up for the cutting of a long leadscrew. For clarity the tool-post has been removed from the lathe.

Take first the fixed steady. As its name implies, this is fixed rigidly to the lathe bed; its object being to support the end of work which protrudes for some distance from the chuck, or to support the middle portion of long work, between centres, where turning is necessary on one end. The usual fixed steady has three movable supports, or jaws, which may be adjusted to grip the diameter of the work involved. These supports should be of bronze or copper, so that the job may not be damaged. In spite of this pre-caution damage sometimes occurs when the jaws have been closed too tightly on the job, or lubrication neglected, so that it is the general practice to leave, where possible, a small roughed-out portion on the work at the point where the steady will bear.

Adjusting the Fixed Steady

When one end of a workpiece is

Fig. 102

The use of the fixed and travelling steadies. Turning a long feedscrew in the lathe. The toolpost has been omitted for the sake of clarity.

gripped in a chuck, with the outer end held in a fixed steady, it is essential that the steady jaws be so adjusted that the job lies parallel with the longitudinal axis of the lathe. If the steady is adjusted so that the workpiece is "out of line" trouble will ensue; such as the freshly-turned portion not being concentric with the rest of the shaft. Mechanical trouble will also be experienced while turning, owing to the wrenching action on the job as it revolves. This will be evidenced by a tendency for the job to work forward out of the chuck jaws, and no matter how tightly these may be secured, the job will gradually work outwards. Much strain is thus imposed on the lathe, steady and workpiece, the gripped end of which will be seriously damaged by the movement in the jaws. Similar trouble will occur if the work is held in a chuck which is out of truth, so that the gripped end of the work follows an eccentric movement instead of spinning truly on its central axis. If the 3-jaw chuck is not true, then the work should be set to run truly in the independent chuck, or held in a collet.

It is a great help if the job can be first centre-drilled at each end, held between centres, and the steady-jaws adjusted in this position. If no centre holes are possible the only satisfactory method of checking the truth of the setting is by means of our old friend, the test dial-indicator. This should be held in the toolpost with the plunger against the work, and the lathe carriage moved along the bed. The steady must then be adjusted so that no movement of the clock needle is perceptible along the whole length of the work. Two such checkings are necessary; one to ascertain that the job is parallel to the front edge of the lathe bed, and one on the top of the job to see that it is lying parallel with the top of the lathe bed. It is obvious that a workpiece may be parallel with the front of the lathe ways, but may, at the same time, be running "up or down hill". If no dial-indicator is available a near approximation to the truth may be found by clamping a lathe tool in the post, registering the tip against one end of the work, traversing the lathe carriage, and adjusting the lathe steady so that the tip of the tool just touches the work at the other end. A similar test must, of course, be again applied to the top of the work.

Beginners are often deceived when setting a fixed steady by the fact that, however much the work may be lying out of parallel with the lathe axis, the end which is gripped by the steady will always appear to be running truly. This is because the steady will always coerce the gripped portion into running truly, so that strain only becomes apparent as the work proceeds. Steady supports must always be kept well lubricated during operation.

It is essential when using the fixed steady to make quite sure that there is no danger of the lathe carriage striking against the steady before the tool has completed its length of cut. Should this happen when in self-act considerable damage may be done, especially to the leadscrew and nut which may both be badly strained. **It is essential before taking a first cut to wind the carriage back and forth by hand to ensure that everything clears.** This advice also applies when using a travelling steady.

Adjusting the Travelling Steady

This steady, being secured to the lathe carriage, moves along the job with the cutting tool, and always presents support in opposition to the cutting pressure. Care in adjustment is necessary, as too hard a

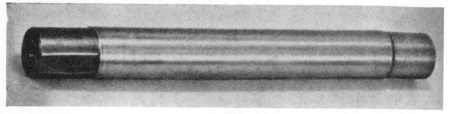

Fig. 103

A plain mandrel. The centre holes are recessed for protection, and the ends carry flats to accommodate the lathe carrier.

pressure may bow slender work inwards at the middle portion. Evidence of this may be seen, when the steady is removed, by a swinging movement of the workpiece when it is revolved; thus showing that it has been bent out of truth. It is the practice, therefore, always to adjust the steady jaws on the work close up to the chuck or lathe centres. If adjustment is attempted at the unsupported middle of the job bending is almost sure to take place, as this is not perceptible to the eye, although evident in the finished product.

Travelling steadies in particular must be kept well lubricated during operations, and frequently checked to see that the setting has not altered owing to wear of the steady supports caused through too tight an adjustment.

Using the Running Centre

In Chapter 4 mention was made of the running centre, where, it will be remembered, the centre point revolved, in ball-races, with the work. While this type of centre will help to overcome many of the troubles so often encountered in between-centre work, it must be remembered that during turning operations the work itself will still heat up and expand lengthwise. While this will not seize-up the centre, it will probably bow the work, often to a considerable extent, so that watchful centre adjustment is still necessary for good results.

Mandrels

It frequently occurs in engineering practice that a job is encountered where external turning is required to be concentric with a bored hole. Usually, both the bore and the outside may be turned at the same setting, but sometimes this is not possible; as in cases where the work must be reversed in the lathe. In such cases a **plain** mandrel is often employed. A picture of a typical plain mandrel may be seen in Fig. 103.

Plain mandrels are simply lengths of round steel bar, centred at each end, and turned with a slight taper, to be a tight, drive fit in the bore of the job in question. The assembly is then set up between the lathe centres, so that any subsequent turning operations are bound to be concentric with the bore. The taper on the mandrel should be small—about ·005 in. to the foot—and the average, or "required", diameter should be somewhere about the centre of the bar. Such mandrels, hardened and ground, may be purchased; these are not necessary in the home workshop, as serviceable mandrels may be made quickly as the need arises. Mild steel is quite suitable, and need not be hardened for amateur use. Such mandrels should, however, be kept as workshop equipment, and a most useful assortment will accumulate in the course of time. It will be seen in the picture that the ends of the mandrel are recessed, as this prevents the centre holes from being damaged by accidental knocks. A flat may also be filed on the end portions so that the lathe carrier may be more easily located.

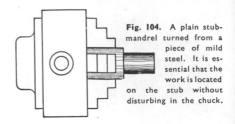

Fig. 104. A plain stub-mandrel turned from a piece of mild steel. It is essential that the work is located on the stub without disturbing in the chuck.

Stub Mandrels

A convenient type of mandrel, suitable for temporary use, may be turned from a piece of mild steel held in the three-jaw chuck, as indicated in Fig. 104. When the mandrel has been turned it is essential that it should not be removed from the chuck when the job is tapped on; it will then be certain to run truly. If too much taper is given to a mandrel it will, however, often be found that the job will tilt over on the excessive taper, and thus be out of truth. For

this reason also, the mandrel should enter the job as far as possible.

Many applications of the mandrel will present themselves to the amateur. As a case in point we give a picture (Fig. 105) of the dividing head casting which was illustrated before. Here, the casting may be seen mounted on a plain, stub mandrel, for the operation of turning a register on one of the bosses.

Expanding Mandrels

In large professional workshops where mandrels are in constant use,

Fig. 105

An awkward job mounted on a long stub-mandrel for turning a register on the end. The picture shows the machining of the dividing head body described elsewhere.

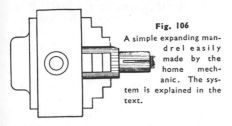

Fig. 106
A simple expanding mandrel easily made by the home mechanic. The system is explained in the text.

an expanding type is often used: the advantage being that they will accommodate themselves to a certain variation in bore diameters. Commercial expanding mandrels are expensive, and unnecessary for the amateur; yet there is one type of easily made, expanding stub mandrel with which every amateur should be familiar. It is shown in the drawing (Fig. 106). A piece of mild steel is chucked in the three-jaw, and a spigot turned to be a good fit in the component to be held. This spigot should now be drilled and tapped to a short depth, but **only a taper tap should be used.** The spigot is now split with a hacksaw, along its length, while still held in the chuck, and an Allen screw inserted in the end. After slipping the job on to the spigot the Allen screw is tightened; this will expand the mandrel owing to the taper thread which has been cut in it, and the job will be held very firmly indeed.

Such mandrels are extremely useful for repetition work, and may be made in quite large sizes—the Allen

screw, of course, being in proportion to the diameter. The spigot should, however, be a really good fit in the job in the first place. They will hold work almost immovably with only a slight turn of the screw; yet a slackening of the screw will release the job instantly.

Expanding mandrels of this sort are handy for holding discs of fair thickness which have a central hole. For similar discs of thin plate, or sheet metal, a better arrangement is provided by a short stub mandrel, turned to a good fit in the disc hole, and threaded for a nut at the outer end. The disc may then be held securely with a large washer.

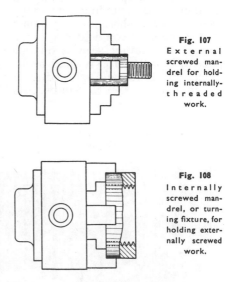

Fig. 107
External screwed mandrel for holding internally-threaded work.

Fig. 108
Internally screwed mandrel, or turning fixture, for holding externally screwed work.

Fig. 109
Diagram explaining the use of spigots specially turned on the work for holding purposes.

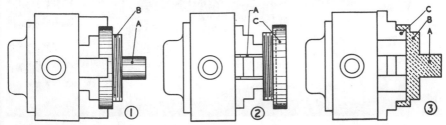

Screwed Mandrels

Work which embodies an internal thread may be securely held without damage in the manner shown in Fig. 107. The method is useful when the job must be reversed in the lathe, and machined truly with the thread and face. The spigot is, of course, turned and screwcut in the lathe without disturbing the mandrel in the chuck. It is desirable that the locating face on the mandrel be of larger diameter than the job, so that a true and firm register be obtained.

Although being more in the nature of a **turning fixture** than a mandrel, the system shown in Fig. 108 may well be introduced here. The method is useful for holding externally screwed work, where direct gripping in the chuck would damage the thread. As may be seen, a suitable piece of brass or steel is faced in the chuck, and bored and screwed to fit the thread on the workpiece. As

with all other similar methods, it is essential that the fixture be not disturbed in the chuck. It is particularly useful for holding screws and suchlike.

Leaving Shanks for Chucking Purposes

When confronted with any job requiring anything other than obviously simple chucking methods, the amateur should make it a practice to run through the sequence of machining operations, mentally, to determine not only the best order, but also whether the machining can be modified so that a later operation may be accomplished more easily.

Such devices can sometimes be employed very profitably, and a typical instance is shown in the drawing in Fig. 109. The job is a screwed cap, recessed on the back face. It will be noted in the left-hand drawing that the job is held in the "outside" jaws of the chuck, and

Fig. 110

Example of an awkward job held safely. The longer portion of the " U "-shaped workpiece must be turned and screwcut. Note the end clamped to an angle plate on the faceplate, and the overhang supported by the tailstock.

that the thread and register (B) have been machined. At the same time the spigot (A) has been turned on. In the second drawing the job has been reversed in the chuck, and is held by the spigot (A), so that the recess (C) may be bored out. When this has been done, the job is again reversed in the chuck, so that the spigot may be turned off. In the last drawing the workpiece has been shown in section, where it will be noted that it has been gripped internally in the recess on the first step of the chuck jaws. Here, again, the amateur will discern a principle having wide applications.

Other chucking methods and set-ups do, of course, exist, but as they are mostly connected with special lathe operations they will be reserved for a later chapter, where some of them will be described in detail.

Toolmakers' Buttons

When two or more bored holes must be located with great accuracy the use of centre-dots may allow too much error, due to the difficulty of placing them in the exact positions. **Toolmakers' buttons** allow work to be positioned on the lathe faceplate with the greatest accuracy.

These buttons are short, steel cylinders, which may be bolted to the work. The diameter of the buttons must be of some set dimension— say, exactly $\frac{1}{2}$-in.— and the end faces must be truly square. The bores must provide ample clearance over the screws.

As an example, we will assume that we wish to bore, in a flat plate, two holes exactly one inch apart, with one hole exactly one inch from the edge. First mark out, with rule and centre-punch, the rough position

of the holes, and drill and tap these points for the holding screws. The buttons are now roughly located, and lightly bolted to the workpiece.

One button must now be located exactly 1 in. from the edge, with a depth gauge, or a test piece located from the edge. We must, of course, allow for the diameter of the button ($\frac{1}{2}$-in.) and half of this amount must be deducted from the test piece. A test piece of $\frac{3}{4}$-in. width, therefore, ensures that the centre-line of the button is exactly 1 in. from the edge. The holding screw is now tightened up.

The second button is located with a micrometer, by measuring across the outsides of the buttons, and tapping until they are the required distance apart. The button diameters must again be considered; so that for a centre distance of 1 in. the micrometer will read $1\frac{1}{2}$ ins.

The buttons now mark the exact positions of the holes, so that the job may be bolted to the faceplate, and the first button set to run truly by means of a dial test-indicator. The button and screw are then removed, and the hole bored. By moving the job on the faceplate, the second button may be clocked, when boring may proceed as before.

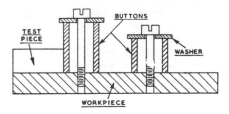

Fig. 111

Diagram illustrating use of toolmakers' buttons. These are shown of unequal lengths to facilitate clocking.

CHAPTER 9

MARKING OUT

MARKING out for engineering purposes is such an important art that whole volumes have been written about it. Nevertheless, a few well-defined rules and methods should enable the amateur to cope successfully with most of the jobs he is likely to encounter. Engineering of any sort may truly be called applied common sense, and in no branch may this description be more aptly used than in marking out.

Marking Out Tools

The tools required are of the simplest and may be found in every model engineer's kit. A good steel rule, a try-square, dividers, a pair of odd-leg calipers, a scribing block, a hammer and a punch. In addition, a surface plate—or other level surface—parallels, and "V" blocks are required. Most of these we have met before.

The Surface Plate

A great number of marking out processes call for a flat and true surface upon which to support the work and tools. In many cases, the bed of the lathe itself may be used for the purpose, but this is not entirely satisfactory owing to the restricted width of the lathe ways.

Proper surface plates of cast iron, ground or hand-scraped to precision flatness, may be purchased, but are rather expensive in the useful sizes. Glass surface plates are also obtainable. Our photograph (Fig. 112) shows an amateur-made surface plate, constructed from a piece of ground plate glass, mounted on a piece of thick felt in a wooden, tray-like box. The edges of the box should be slightly lower than the surface of the glass plate. A similar tray should be used as a cover, as it is essential that the plate be guarded against damage. Such ground and polished plate glass is obtainable from all good-class glaziers. A useful size is 12 in. by 9 in., and such a sheet, in $\frac{3}{8}$ in. or $\frac{1}{2}$ in. thickness, costs but a few shillings.

Fig. 113
A small commercial surface plate of cast iron, hand-scraped to a flat surface.

Odd-leg Calipers and Dividers

To the left of Fig. 114 is shown the odd-leg calipers so useful for marking out processes. It will be noted that while one leg is curved in the

Fig. 112
Home-made surface plate. A sheet of ground plate glass, costing two or three shillings, mounted in a shallow wooden tray. A piece of thick felt supports the glass, and a cover should be provided.

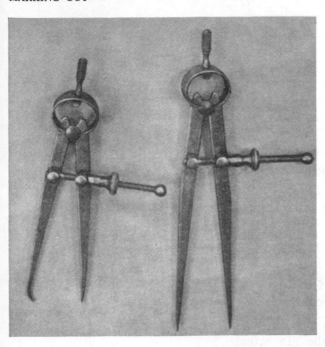

shown in Fig. 116. The bar to be centred is held at one end in a true chuck or collet, while the outer end is supported, at the extreme tip, in a fixed steady. While thus mounted, the end is faced off square, and the material centred with a centre-drill held in the tailstock chuck. Where extreme accuracy is required—as in the case of the silver steel **test bar** mentioned in the previous chapter—

manner of the ordinary outside calipers, the other leg forms a scribing point.

In this same picture may be seen a pair of dividers, which are essential for setting-off distances, and for describing circles.

Centring Round Bars

The accurate centring of the ends of round bars, for subsequent mounting between lathe centres, is one of the most frequently met jobs in engineering practice. Several methods exist, and it is proposed to deal with the simplest and most accurate first. This is undoubtedly the system employing the **fixed steady**, as

the drilled centre hole may be turned true, off the lathe top-slide. This should be set over to an angle of 30 deg,, and a fine-pointed tool, such as shown in Fig. 117, used.

It sometimes happens that the job to be centred is of such length that it will only just enter between the lathe centres, so that there is insufficient room for the drill chuck and drill, or for turning operations. In such instances a short centre drill with a taper shank—such as is shown in Fig. 33 in Chapter 4—

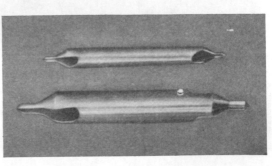

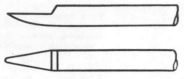

Fig. 117

Tool for truing centres on workpiece. When used in conjunction with the fixed steady as shown in Fig. 115 forms an extremely accurate method of centring.

may be used, in conjunction with the fixed steady set-up.

Nothing bespeaks the inexperienced turner more than large centre holes. They should be made as small as is consistent with a firm support of the job. There is nothing uglier than huge centre holes in the ends of a small shaft.

Centring by Marking Out

In most of the books on lathe operation much is made of the methods of centring plain, round work out of the lathe. In actual amateur practice such a necessity is rarely encountered, as, by the method just described, any work which will go into the lathe may be centred in it. However, as some model engineers do not possess a lathe steady, a few examples may be lightly sketched here.

With Odd-leg Calipers

Probably the simplest method, apart from centring in the lathe, is by means of the **odd-leg** calipers.

Fig. 118

Finding the centre of a round bar with the odd-leg dividers. These are set roughly to half diameter, and lines scribed from opposing sides. The centre of the scribed space is the centre of the bar. In practice the lines would be set closer together.

The drawing (Fig. 118) is practically self-explanatory, but it may be

Fig. 116

An accurate method of centring round stock. Centre-drill in operation on bar held in the fixed steady.

pointed out that the calipers are set to approximately half the bar diameter, and a series of lines scribed from opposite sides of the bar. From these, the centre may easily be found and centre punched.

With Scribing Block

As may be seen in the picture (Fig. 119) this operation is essentially similar to the previous one, except that the bar is mounted on "V" blocks on the surface plate. A scribing block is then set to mark the end of the bar at approximately half its diameter, and several lines scribed at different points by revolving the bar in the "V" blocks.

Fig. 120
(*Right*) Bell punch for centring round bars. (*Left*) Ordinary centre-punch. (*Centre*) Automatic centre-punch which may be used without a hammer.

Copper Sulphate Solution

Light scribe lines on bright steel surfaces are not easily visible, and for this reason the steel surface is

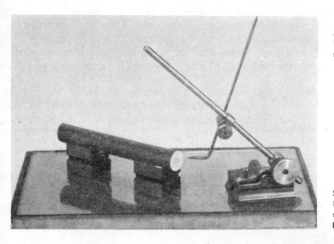

Fig. 119
A method similar to that of Fig. 118. Centring a bar with surface plate, " V " blocks and surface gauge.

Fig. 121
Section of simple bell-punch. It is essential that, in operation, the punch be truly in line with the axis of the work.

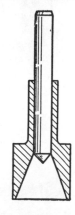

With the Bell Punch

A photograph of this tool is given in Fig. 120, with a sectional drawing in Fig. 121. As will be evident, the "bell" will accommodate all sizes of round bar up to its maximum, and that the punch can always mark the centre of these. Bell punches need careful use, however, as unless the punch is held truly in line with the shaft during punching operations, the punch dot will not lie at the centre of the bar.

generally prepared in some manner. As a temporary measure **engineers' marking blue** may be lightly smeared on, so that scribe lines may be more readily seen. Marking blue is, of course, only useful when the surface is not to be touched in any other way, so that a more permanent method is often advisable. This may be provided by wiping the steel surface with a clean rag which has been dipped in a **copper sulphate solution.** A tablespoonful of the sulphate crystals, which may be obtained from any good chemist's shop, should be dissolved in a medicine bottle full of water, with a few drops of sulphuric acid added.

Provided that the steel is clean and free from grease it will immediately receive a thin, dull, film of copper deposit through which the lightest scribe lines will show brightly.

Marking Out Castings

The methods employed for marking out castings are exactly those as used for forgings, and for work machined out of the solid, so that the main essentials as applied for castings will do equally well for all. Therefore, castings only will be considered here.

Preparing Castings for Marking Out

All casting imperfections such as ridges and "flash" should be first removed with a file, and the casting generally cleaned up so that it will seat firmly on the marking table.

It is almost impossible to mark out a rough casting the surface of which has not been prepared in some way, as the light scribe lines cannot be seen on the rough surface. A paste composed of chalk and water, to which a little glue has been added, should be brushed over the job, and allowed to dry. The glue prevents the white coating from coming off as the job is handled. Scribe lines are clearly visible on this surface.

Preliminaries to Marking Out

Whenever a casting or other workpiece is to be marked out, the seasoned engineer first checks it up to see that it is large enough to finish to the required size, and that such things as lugs, bosses, and the like, are correctly located. These often become seriously misplaced through careless withdrawal of the pattern during sand casting operations. A few rough measurements with the rule are usually enough to

Fig. 122

Simple scribing operation using the surface plate and the scribing block. Note that the casting has been whitened with a chalk paste so that the scribe line will show clearly.

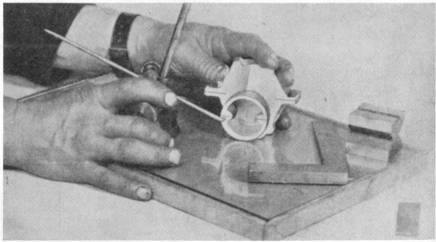

Fig. 123
A firm seating for the workpiece is essential in marking out. Small cylinder-head casting mounted on "V " block.

show that all is right—or wrong, as the case may be. The precaution is a sensible one, as few things are so annoying as to find that a job will not "clean up" after considerable machining has been done upon it.

At the same time a close inspection should be made for visible "blow holes" or other deformities which might prejudice the success of the finished job.

Some Principles of Marking Out

In marking out any kind of work the operation is much facilitated if a **machined face** can be obtained, to which all measurements can be related. This is not always possible, but, when it is, this face should always be machined first before marking out commences. The job will, of course, have been checked for size, so that it will be known how

much preparatory machining can be undertaken. The illustration (Fig. 95) in the previous chapter does, in fact, show the operation of machining the base of a casting prior to marking out.

Where no machined face is possible, the job should be packed up as firmly and truly as possible on the surface plate, and a **centre line** scribed right round the work. This will form a **reference line** from which all other measurements will be taken. This centre line should be marked out with the scribing block, the point of which is set to the correct centre height of the job.

The utility of this centre or reference line will be seen in the following typical illustration. Let us suppose that the job calls for a point to be struck $\frac{3}{8}$ in. above the centre line. The first thing to do is to measure, by rule, the height of the scriber point above the surface plate, as positioned for scribing the reference line. This measurement should be noted. The point of the scribing block may now be reset, by rule, by adding ¾ in. to the centre height measurement, and the new line scribed on the casting. This line will, of course, be parallel to the original reference line.

When thus setting a scribing block to height it is essential that the rule be truly vertical to the surface plate. This is rendered easier by holding the rule against an angle plate, as may be seen in Fig. 124. The operator's hands have been omitted for clarity.

The usefulness of thus referring all measurements to the surface plate is best found when marking out complicated castings, where related points may not all lie on the same plane; or in setting out related points on two sides of a casting, where direct measurement between them is impossible.

Right-angle Lines

Should any point have to be marked out at 90 deg. to the horizontal lines, this may be done by standing a try square on the surface plate, and scribing along the edge of the blade.

Where several sets of parallel lines must be at right angles to the hori-

zontal lines, however, it is a better plan to set the job up on end, so that the original horizontal lines become vertical ones. The original reference line may be set truly vertical by checking off the surface plate, against the try square. One is now in a position to mark out any lines at right angles to the original ones, using, of course, the scribing block. It may be necessary to set out a new reference line at 90 deg. to the first, but always remember that the original reference line is the master one, and all measurements should be related to this if possible.

Duplicating Reference Lines

It sometimes occurs that the original reference lines must be turned away during operations, so that the means of checking up, or re-setting the job, are lost. It is a good plan in such cases to scribe a "dummy" line, parallel to the one to be removed, on a part of the job not so affected.

Centre Punching

When all the centres have been marked out by means of crossed lines they should be centre punched

at the points of intersection, thus indicating where holes or bores are wanted. Use a small punch, and make light and small punch marks. They are more easy to correct than large ones, and are, in any event, more accurate.

Accurate centre punching is by no means so easy as it may appear. The punch should first be held at an acute angle to the work, and the punch point carefully located on the intersecting lines. Then, gently swing the punch into a vertical position, and tap lightly with a small hammer. Now inspect the punch mark through a watchmaker's eyeglass, to ascertain that it is really in the right spot. If inaccurate, the dot may be "drawn" over by inclining the punch and tapping in the right direction. When inspection shows that the correct position has been attained, a light tap may be given, with the punch in a vertical position, to clean up the dot.

Where bores have to be turned in a workpiece it is usual not only to indicate the centre by a dot in this manner, but also to inscribe a circle on the workface with dividers set to the correct radius. If light punch dots are made at intervals around the scribed circle it is then possible, by accurate boring, to cut away half of the dots. This is known as "splitting the dots", and is much used in professional workshops where the marking out is often done by a mechanic other than the turner. Thus, if any error transpires in the finished job, it may be seen at a glance if the marking out or the lathe setting has been at fault. The procedure is useful to the amateur turner, as it forms a ready means of seeing if the set-up has been accurate, or if the job has moved during operations.

Automatic centre punches such as that shown in Fig. 120 do not seem to receive the attention of amateurs which they deserve. With this type the point of the punch is located on the workpiece, and the body pressed downwards, when, by means of a spring arrangement, a ·blow is imparted to the punch. The force of the blow may be varied by adjusting a screwed cap on the punch body. The writer has always found these punches reliable, and much easier to use accurately than the orthodox hammer and punch. They are inexpensive.

The Use of Parallels

Mention has been made of the helpfulness of having a machined face which may be placed firmly on the surface plate, and from which all subsequent marking out may be done. It sometimes transpires, however, that

Fig. 125
The use of parallels, in marking out, to support master surfaces from which marking out must be done.

Fig. 126
The utility of the surface plate and scribing block demonstrated. Related points on various planes may be
correctly marked off. If necessary, related points on the opposite side of the casting could be just as simply located.

the machined face of the workpiece cannot be stood directly on the surface plate, owing to some un-machined surface protruding. In this case the job may be located on parallels, as may be seen in Fig. 125. Here, the undersides of the lugs have been machined, and it is supposed that locations are to be marked out in relation to these machined surfaces.

The Use of Odd-leg Calipers and Dividers

It is a sad thing to have to admit, but it is nevertheless too often true, that many amateur jobs are doomed to failure at the marking-out stage, which is, after all, the basis of many undertakings. Carelessness, and lack of the correct technique, are the chief faults, while inaccurate meas-urement also adds its quota of failures. For instance, it is common practice for the uninitiated to set off vital measurements directly on to the job with rule and scriber.

Accurate measurements cannot be set out in this way, especially if several points must be set off one from another. The correct procedure is to set the dividers accurately to the rule, and transfer to the workpiece. When placed directly on the work, the thickness of the rule itself makes it extremely difficult to locate the scriber at the exact point of measure-ment.

Odd-leg calipers provide a ready means of scribing lines parallel to a machined edge or for setting out the position of holes in relationship to an edge. The drawing (Fig. 127) shows, as an instance, how they may be used to locate holes at the corners of a workpiece. This is a typical example of the many applications of which the odd-leg calipers are capable.

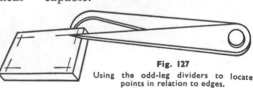

Fig. 127
Using the odd-leg dividers to locate
points in relation to edges.

CHAPTER 10

PLAIN TURNING AND BORING

IN spite of the many varied and complicated jobs of which the amateur's lathe is capable, the greater part of lathe work does, indeed, fall under the above heading, and plain turning and boring must be the first things which the amateur must master. When the handling of the machine during simple operations has become, as it were, second nature, the mastery of the more complicated processes will follow almost as a matter of course.

Outlook

It may serve a good purpose to introduce some observations not usually considered to be within the scope of mechanical textbooks. One of the advantages of being amateurs, however, is that we may often disregard with advantage not only some accepted "rules" of engineering, but of journalism also.

There is little doubt that one's attitude of mind, and outlook, influences profoundly the quality of one's work, and the speed with which proficiency is acquired. Most amateur engineers are capable of doing much better work than they think; which leads us to the golden rule of model engineering— "Have a try!" To be scared of a job is fatal, and leads to more failures than anything else.

The second great enemy to success is **haste.** In no other occupation is it more necessary to "make haste slowly". No better advice can be given to the beginner and expert alike than to be Confident and Careful. Model engineering is, above all, a hobby which does not respond

favourably to uncertainty or to haphazard methods.

A habit which the beginner in model engineering will find of inestimable value is that of mentally running over the various steps in manufacture, determining what first to do, and arranging the further processes in their logical sequence. Failure to do this will often result in undue difficulties in some subsequent operation, or even an inability to do the operation at all.

Some Wise Precautions

When any job has been mounted on the lathe for turning, and the tool correctly set, the next step is **not** to take a cut! Before doing this the wise turner will always move the saddle along the bed of the lathe by hand, so as to make sure that nothing is fouling anywhere. Similarly, the cross-slide should be wound inwards, so as to see that no obstruction exists there also. In particular, it should be checked that the **saddle lock** is not in operation before the self-act feed is engaged. This has been done time and again to the detriment of everything concerned.

It must be emphasised that the lathe should never be left with the self-act or screwcutting lever in the engaged position; nor should any impediment or obstruction be left which might prevent the free operation of the machine. The danger of the lathe being accidentally or unthinkingly switched on while in these conditions is too obvious for further comment.

A similar danger exists in the

foolish and very prevalent habit of leaving the chuck key in the chuck. It is fatally easy to switch the lathe on without this being noticed, whereupon the key is either flung across the workshop, or strikes the bed a resounding blow. And so we get another dent in the precious lathe ways, which dent, short of regrinding the bed, can never be removed.

Speed, Depth of Cut, Feed and Cutting Speed

In discussing lathe work four terms will be constantly met: namely, **speed, depth of cut, feed,** and **cutting speed.** The speed means the rate of revolutions per minute at which the work is turned. Depth of cut designates the amount which the tool is advanced laterally into the work; that is, the cut determines the amount by which the work is reduced in diameter. The feed, on the other hand, refers to the amount that the tool is advanced per revolution longitudinally along the work, or, the rate at which a given cut is applied. Thus the lathe may be set to revolve at 20 r.p.m., to turn off a shaving of metal $\frac{1}{4}$ in. in width (the cut), and of 0·005 in. in thickness (the feed). This combination would be known as slow speed, heavy cut, fine feed. Almost infinite combinations of speed, feed and cut may be arranged, depending upon the lathe used, the size and quality of the material to be turned, and the finish required.

Cutting Speed really indicates the speed at which the material passes the tip of the cutting tool, and is always given in feet per minute. It depends not only upon the speed at which the work is revolving but also upon the diameter of the work itself; in other words, cutting speed is identical with the periphery speed of the work.

It should be remembered that the cut is always half the amount by

Fig. 128
Dividing head body mounted on cross-side of lathe for boring with boring bar.

which the diameter of the job is reduced; that is, a cut of $\frac{1}{4}$ in. will reduce the diameter $\frac{1}{2}$ in.

When roughing out a job it is handy to know that a slow speed, heavy cut and heavy feed remove most metal in a given time.

The Self-act or Automatic Feed

On all screwcutting lathes it is possible to gear the leadscrew to the mandrel in such a manner that the lathe carriage—carrying the tool —may be made to move slowly along the lathe ways. This makes it possible to advance automatically the tool along the work, thus giving automatic feed, the amount of which will depend upon the ratio of gearing between the lathe mandrel and the leadscrew.

The manner in which the gear train is calculated and assembled is explained in Chapter 12, which is devoted to **Screwcutting,** as self-act and screwcutting are allied processes.

Automatic feed is a great convenience for the turner, especially on long work where manual operation becomes tedious. In addition, as automatic feed is constant, a better finish on the work usually results. Finishing cuts of any length should always be made with a self-acting fine feed.

Speeds and Feeds

Once again it is necessary to depart from textbook methods, it being usual to devote much space to lists of cutting speeds and feeds suitable for various metals. To the professional these are important matters, as he is concerned with maximum production, and the removal of the greatest quantity of metal in the shortest time and in the most economical way.

While speed and economy are not usually so important to the amateur, it is not because of this that the accepted tables are useless. Cutting speeds and feeds are always calculated on the assumption that the lathe in question is of the large and heavy professional type. One does not encounter the typical amateur lathe in professional workshops, except it be for some special purpose analogous to amateur practice. In these instances speed and feed calculations are not usually applied, except for very small work. This is not decrying the amateur class of machine, nor suggesting that it has not professional uses. It is simply pointing out that calculations based on large—and expensive—heavy duty machines cannot be expected to hold good for the majority of the cheaper and lighter lathes, except where very small work is involved. Nor does it mean that some sturdy and well-designed exceptions do not exist, but even should the amateur be the lucky possessor of such a machine, even then it may be found impossible to work to the accepted professional standards.

The reason is, of course, that the amateur's lathe is invariably called upon to handle work which is much too big for it. That it does so at all is a great credit to all concerned. The amateur will cheerfully turn up cast iron locomotive wheels of 8 in. diameter; part-off 4 in. diameter steel stock; turn heavy castings, and, in fact, tackle any job which may be crowded into the long-suffering machine. Under these conditions orthodox speeds and feeds will not hold.

Nor is it really necessary to worry about them; the lathe itself will quickly register its protest to abuse, so that the amateur will soon know that he is in error. The rule is: **when in doubt, reduce the speed.** The beginner will be surprised how often he must use backgear.

So that the amateur may try out the experiment for himself a short

Fig. 129
Another method of holding work on the cross-slide. Boring the banjo of the home-made dividing head on a 3½-in. lathe. This picture demonstrates well the usefulness of the angle plate.

list of some of the accepted cutting speeds is given, using high-speed tools. The list is also useful as indicating the ratio between the cutting speed of various metals.

	ft. per min.
Annealed High-Speed, and Stainless Steel	50
Annealed Carbon Steel	60
Cast Iron, Mild Steel, Wrought Iron	80
Brass	200
Aluminium and its Alloys	300

The revolutions per minute necessary to give these cutting speeds may be found by the following simple formula:

$$\frac{\text{Cutting Speed}}{\text{Quarter of Work Diameter}} = \text{r.p.m.}$$

Example:—

To find the cutting speed for a brass bar 8 in. in diameter:—

$$\frac{200}{2} = 100 \text{ r.p.m.}$$

Cutting Lubricants

These important aids to good workmanship are too neglected by the average amateur turner. Quite often the only cutting lubricant used is ordinary lubricating oil, which is not satisfactory for general use.

Brass and **cast iron** are best worked without cutting lubricant, but **steel** and **aluminium** and its **alloys** always require it. Correct lubrication keeps the tool tip cool, and thus gives longer life; the finish on work is also improved, and easier to obtain.

For **steels,** lard oil is an excellent cutting lubricant; it may also be used for copper, although some grades may be found to work best when dry.

Aluminium and **alloys** seem to respond best to paraffin oil as a lubricant. Aluminium has the habit of attaching itself to the tool, so that a little pile builds itself up on the tool tip. This destroys the effective shape and edge of the tool. Paraffin prevents this.

Probably the best and most universal cutting lubricant is that known as soluble cutting oil which is now used professionally to the exclusion of all else for general work. Soluble cutting oil is a brown, oily compound which emulsifies when mixed with water into a white, milky fluid. It is manufactured by several firms in this country, but is usually obtainable from them only in bulk quantity. It may, however, be purchased from many local engineering stockists in one gallon cans.

A suitable concentration is made with one part soluble oil to six parts of water. It is excellent stuff, and provides the answer to the amateur's problem. Failing this, the old-fashioned soap-and-water, or "suds" mixture may be used, but this tends to rust the lathe and other metal parts, whereas the soluble oil will not do so.

Large lathes, especially capstans and automatics, are provided with a pump which forces a jet of lubricant on to the work. This arrangement is not practicable in the home workshop, as a great deal is bound to be splashed about. The amateur had best apply the lubricant with a soft mop brush, from a small can kept near the lathe. This is quite satisfactory.

Roughing-out

A great aid to the logical development of work is the process known as roughing-out. This is simply a preliminary shaping of the job, with all surplus metal cut away to within about ·020 in. of finished size. All shoulders, steps, collars, and suchlike, should be machined in, so that only the finishing cuts are left to be done. It must be remembered that all dimensions must be left oversize to allow for " cleaning-up".

The advantages of roughing-out are that the surplus metal may be removed with a tool capable of heavy cuts, replacing with a re-sharpened tool for the final finishing operations. One also gets a better idea of the job in general, and machining operations are more easily determined. In addition, holding methods for the delicate finishing cuts may be lighter than the heavy grips necessary for roughing cuts, so that a greater variety of chucking methods is sometimes presented.

Fig. 130
The first operation in turning. The lower picture shows a small lathe mandrel in its finished state, while the top picture shows the preliminary roughing-out stage.

Further, should an error be made—such as roughing down undersize—good, finished work is not destroyed.

When turning jobs between centres roughing-out is essential, as the centre adjustment always requires several alterations as the job proceeds. A final adjustment for finishing is necessary, and this setting must never be touched during the final cut.

It is an excellent plan, where possible, to rough-out with one end of the job held in the three-jaw chuck, the other end being supported by the tailstock centre. The success of between-centre turning depends mainly on the correct alignment and adjustment of the centres, as has been pointed out in Chapter 8.

Finishing

The art of obtaining a fine, high finish on work in various metals is mostly a matter of experience, but, nevertheless, some general guidance can be given. Tools must be sharp, and set to correct centre height, and it is advisable to retouch them on the grinder before making the final cut. Blunt tools may either tear the surface, or may not be capable of taking off the small amount sometimes necessary to obtain correct finished size.

Brass

High speed, slow feed and light cut, using either of the tools shown at (D) and (E) in Fig. 64, Chapter 6, will produce a high finish on brass, bronze and allied metals. The tool (D) may have the tip lightly "stoned off" with a slip oilstone. No cutting lubricant is needed. Depth of cut about 0·010 in.

Mild Steel

Tool (A), (B) or (C) in Fig. 64 may be used for finishing; tool (A), especially, giving a high polish finish if set to "rub" as indicated in Fig.

63. The tip may also be lightly "stoned" to a minute radius. Generally speaking, a light cut (0·010 in.), fine feed, and slow speed, with plenty of cutting lubricant, will be found the easiest way to obtain a high degree of finish on mild and other free-cutting steels. Should difficulty be experienced, first check the tool for sharpness and right setting; if correct, **reduce speed**. Use slow back-gear if necessary.

Cast Steel, Nickel Steel, Silver Steel, etc.

–These materials—classed as "high-grade" steels—are often finished best at high speed, with fine feed and cut. Tools must be exceptionally sharp and well lubricated, as much heat is generated at the cutting tip. So many new steels are now upon the market, however, that each may well be a law unto itself, so that the turner is forced to fall back upon experiment. Do not leave the experiment until the finishing cut, but try to obtain a good finish early in operations. You will then know the right procedure when the time comes.

Copper

High speed; fine feed; fine cut; this is the secret here, using any of the steel-turning tools—very sharp. Copper always should be **cut** to a finish and not rubbed, and a lubricant may help. Often, plain lubricating oil may be best, and may be used when drilling copper.

Aluminium, Dural and Alloys

Use the steel-finishing tools and procedure, except that high speed is required. Lubricate plentifully with soluble oil or paraffin.

Cast Iron

This should be worked dry, and steel-cutting tools again used—preferably that shown at (C) in Fig. 64.

Fine feed is necessary, but the cut may be increased to about 0·020 in. as cast iron, especially the inferior grades, tends to push the tool off when very fine cuts are used, thus causing rubbing. Low speed is essential.

The scale on cast iron castings is often hard and troublesome to remove, as it often contains moulding sand which quickly wears away the tool point. A deep cut should, therefore, be always used when removing the "skin". Tools tipped with any of the cemented carbide products are invaluable for this work.

Strictly speaking, cast iron cannot be turned to a high finish such as we understand for steel. If a polish is required emery cloth and oil should be employed, but do not forget to make a small allowance (about 0·001 in.) on turning diameter, if a correct size is essential.

Filing and Polishing in the Lathe

It is generally considered bad practice to file work to size in the lathe, and in professional workshops a howl of derision arises from the turners should one of their fellows be spotted doing so. In spite of this, there are occasions when a file may be legitimately used, as in adding a slight taper to a stub mandrel (Chapter 8). A fine file may also be used for taking off the sharp edges on turned work (no good turner ever leaves dead sharp edges to cut the fingers). The rule is: keep both the work and file moving at all times; if the file is held stationary against the revolving work flats will be in evidence upon it.

Polishing with emery cloth is legitimate turning practice, but always use **oil** and **emery cloth** for polishing steel. A good finish cannot be obtained on brass or aluminium with emery cloth, dry or oiled, and

Fig. 131

How *not* to file in the lathe: using a file without a handle is a most dangerous practice. Should the file strike the revolving chuck jaw the tang will pierce the hand!

its use should be avoided. Above all, never use a file in the lathe without a handle! If the file catches the work or the spinning chuck jaws the tang may be driven deeply into the hand.

Tolerances

In the pursuit of his hobby the model engineer is bound to meet with specifications calling for any of the generally accepted standards of fit. These may be classed as follows:—

(1) **Running Fits.** This embraces all classes of running work such as bearings. There exist lengthy tables of fit tolerances for different classes of work, but for the amateur the requirements may be summed up by saying that the shaft or other component must be free to rotate with no perceptible side shake.

(2) **Push Fits.** This means that the shaft may be pushed into the hole by hand, but is not free to rotate.

(3) **Drive Fits.** Fits wherein a hammer must be used to drive the spindle into the hole.

(4) **Force Fits.** Where a press or screw are required to force parts together.

(5) **Shrink Fits.** This term embraces all those fits which require that the outer component be expanded by heat before the parts can be united. Red heat is indicated. The allowance for shrink fits varies with the size of the job, but a satisfactory working formula is to allow 0·001 in. for every inch in diameter. Thus, if a ring must be shrunk on a shaft of 2 in. diameter, the ring must be bored 1·998 in. This tolerance may be made slightly more for sizes above 3 in. diameter, and slightly less on diameters of less than $\frac{1}{2}$ in.

Parting-off

Most turners, amateur and professional alike, have encountered trouble at some time or another during the process of parting-off work in the lathe. It has already been pointed out that lack of clearance in the parting tool is a prolific source of trouble, but there exist other pitfalls for the unwary. It is a common experience that, while apparently cutting well, the tool suddenly seizes in the job—often with disastrous results.

This may be caused by the parting tool not being square with the longitudinal axis of the work, so that it is forced in "on the slant". This virtually destroys the side clearance, and binding results.

Apart from this fault the most usual cause of calamity is slackness and/or backlash in the cross-slide of the lathe. When the tool is advancing, the backlash is taken up in one direction by the pressure of the feed screw, but there is nothing to prevent the cross-slide itself from being pulled forward, to the extent of the backlash—often quite an appreciable amount. If, therefore, the tool tends to be caught in the work, it is pulled forward still more, so that the tool digs deeply into the work and a jam-up results.

The trouble is most prolific on old lathes where considerable wear may have taken place on the thrust bearing, feed screw, and nut. Much can be done to minimise the trouble by a careful adjustment of the thrust, which is usually possible. Nothing can be done with a worn feed screw and nut, beyond replacing them.

The nuisance can, however, be somewhat mitigated by tightening the adjusting screws on the cross-slide bearing, so that the slide is quite stiff to move. This stiffness may act as a brake on any unwanted forward movement.

Slack head bearings may also lead to parting-off troubles; the work, in this instance, being lifted up or pulled forward on to the tool. Adjustment here is also the only cure.

Provided that the tool is correctly ground and shaped, and that no slackness exists in the lathe, parting-off should not present any terrors. For diameters above 1 in. backgear should be engaged if steel is being operated on. The job should be plentifully flooded with cutting lubricant, and the tool forced into the job with a firm, steady and even pressure. A parting tool should always be "kept at work", and the pressure of the cut not allowed to slacken. Parting-off calls for **slow speed** and **coarse cut.** In this case, of course, the **cut** really becomes the **feed.**

In particular, parting-off calls for a firm set-up, and the parting cut should always be made close up to the chuck jaws. Much overhang will cause "chatter" and jamming. On no account attempt to part-off work between centres!

Parting-off Large Steel or Cast Iron Work

When work of large diameter must be parted-off, it is not advisable to make the part in one cut. First, it is difficult for the chips and swarf to get clear from a deep, narrow channel, and a seize-up may result. It is also difficult to get adequate lubricant down the narrow slot, with a brush, to the tip of the tool. In addition, it is necessary to have the tool "backed-off" for a considerable distance, thus causing it to have a thin, weak neck which may be easily broken.

Deep cuts are best taken in stages, in the manner shown in Fig. 132. With this method the parting tool is first run in to a reasonable depth; it is then withdrawn, and another cut taken directly alongside the first, making a wide aperture. Into this the parting tool is again inserted, and a further cut taken, leaving

clearance for the side of the tool in the original aperture. This system is an almost certain guarantee against parting-off troubles.

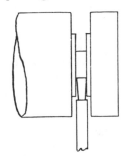

Fig. 132
Parting-off large diameters. Clearance is provided for the tool by taking side-by-side cuts in the initial stages.

When the lathe has much slackness in the head bearings better results may often be had by mounting the parting tool in an inverted position at the rear end of the cross-slide, and cutting by winding the slide forward. This "up-side-down" method may be seen in the photograph (Fig. 220) in Chapter 16. The downward cutting pressure prevents the lathe mandrel from lifting in its bearings.

The turner may follow any of the above procedures when parting-off cast iron. If the iron has an outer scale it is advisable to remove this first with a suitable roughing tool before the parting tool is used. It may be found, otherwise, that the scale has taken the edge from the parting-off blade.

Parting-off Brass

This follows the same general procedure as used for steel, except that the speed may be considerably higher, and the parting tool ground without top rake or lip.

When parting-off brass at high speed the metal chips break into very small pieces, and fly off in a fine, continuous spray with considerable velocity. These chips can be dangerous to the eyes, and are the worst things in the world for working into the flesh in the form of splinters. The amateur is advised to stand well out of the way, or, better still, to rig up a temporary guard of perspex or celluloid, somewhat after the manner shown in Fig. 133. Here, a sheet of perspex has been slotted to fit over the toolpost. Transparent guards are compulsory in some factories where this kind of work is prevalent.

Boring

The boring of holes forms one of the chief functions of the lathe, and, broadly speaking, two methods may be used; namely, that in which the work is revolved against a stationary boring tool held in the toolpost, and that in which the work is clamped to the cross-slide of the lathe, and the tool revolved in the lathe head. Drilling from the tailstock is also possible.

It will thus be seen that for boring purposes the lathe is a very versatile machine, and that almost any kind of job may be undertaken upon it.

Single-Point Boring

In Chapter 6 (Figs. 67 and 68) some recognised types of boring tools are illustrated, and their uses are described. Such tools are known as "single-point tools", the reason for which is obvious. The vast majority of boring work is done with them. The shanks of such tools should be reasonably stiff, but, as has been pointed out, a slight springiness is an advantage.

Single-point boring tools have a tendency to "push-off" from the work as boring proceeds. This effect is cumulative, so that it is quite common to find that a hole, intended to be parallel, is, in fact, tapered—the widest part being at the end from which the tool is entered. This may be avoided by occasionally taking several cuts at the same tool setting. This is known as "working out the spring" and should be done frequently, especially when nearing the final cut.

Another practice is to allow the tool to cut both going in and on the

Fig. 133
A simple precaution when working on brass. Chip-screen of perspex or thick celluloid mounted on toolpost.

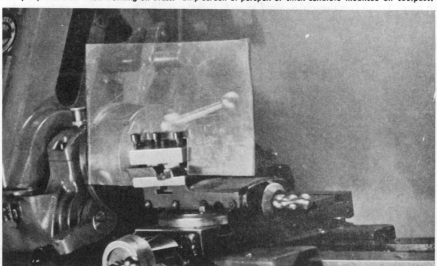

return. For the back cut the tool setting should not be altered. The beginner should be wary here, however, because quite often the tool makes a deeper cut on the return than on the entry, the reason being that on the return journey a different, and possibly sharper, part of the tool is being used. For this reason it is advisable never to make the final cut on the return or it may be found that the hole has been bored oversize. Nevertheless, backcutting is useful during the preliminary boring cuts, as it tends to keep the hole parallel.

When nearing the critical diameter the final cuts should be made on the same tool setting, relying on the spring of the tool to take out just that minute amount so often necessary to a perfect fit.

It should be noted that bearing holes or bushes, except those of very small diameter, should be bored to be a push fit on the shafts concerned, the final fitting being done by scraping when the bush is *in situ*. Small bearing holes and bushes, which are too small to scrape, should, likewise, be finished with a hand reamer when in position.

Tool Clearance

Although the shank of the tool should be as sturdy as will allow for a little springiness, it is highly necessary that plenty of clearance be left between shank and bore, so that the cutting chips may be free to get away. A tool shank which almost fills the hole will, in all likelihood, lead to disaster, as the chips and swarf will become packed between the tool-shank and the wall of the bore, thus forcing the cutting point into the job. Boring to size is, of course, impossible under these conditions. Better too much clearance than too little.

Attention has already been drawn to the necessity of providing clear-ance, behind the job, for the tool point, when boring holes which go right through the work. Such holes are known as **"open bores"**.

Blind Holes

These, on the other hand, are those which do not go right through the job, but have a closed bottom. Such holes have two dimensions—diameter and depth—and the beginner is often perplexed when combining these two measurements accurately at the final cut. The drawing (Fig. 134) shows a simple method of doing so. The hole should be bored to within a few thousandths of an inch of diameter and depth; the operator should then concentrate on the **depth** only, taking light cuts along the bottom of the hole until correct depth has been reached. The tool should then be run into the wall of the bore for a few thousandths of an inch, thus making a slight under-cut in the extreme corner. This is shown, in an exaggerated manner, in the drawing.

Attention may now be given to the diameter, and as the tool nears the bottom of the hole it will be heard to "go off cut" as it meets the groove, thus indicating that the bottom has been reached. In very few cases is it necessary for a blind hole to have an absolutely square corner at the bottom.

Fig. 134
Boring blind holes to correct diameter and depth.
Method is fully explained in the text.

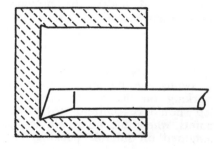

Fig. 135
A model locomotive cylinder packed to height on a wooden block for boring on the cross-slide. Wooden packing, however, is not recommended for accurate working as the packing is seldom truly flat.

All the notes which have been given on external finishing apply with equal force to internal work, except that it is unusual to attain correct size in one finishing cut. This usually has to be carefully worked up to, using the spring of the tool, as indicated.

Work on the Boring Table

It will be remembered that in Chapter 1 it was pointed out that on removing the top-slide of the lathe the cross-slide might be used as a table, upon which work might be clamped; and that it was later emphasised that the top of the cross-slide should always be provided with a number of "T" slots, into which the holding down bolts might be located. The utility of this arrangement is found when it comes to boring large work which cannot be swung over the lathe bed. When working on the boring table, the job should be centre-dotted at the points where the holes are to be, mounted on suitable packing, and

firmly bolted down. The centre dot may be located for height against a lathe centre plugged into the lathe mandrel. A clearance hole may then be drilled with a large drill held in the lathe head.

A typical boring bar—also known as a **"fly-cutter bar"**—is shown in the drawing (Fig. 69); it should be noted that it is made from a suitable length of mild steel bar, centred at each end. Through the bar a hole is drilled to take the cutter bit, which is locked into place with an Allen screw. The cutter bit may be ground up from a broken centre-drill, or the hardened shank of an ordinary drill of appropriate size. This type of bar is particularly suited for roughing-out purposes.

The illustration (B) indicates a variation of this cutter, which is extremely useful for finishing holes parallel and to size. As will be seen, this is a double-edged cutter, which may be ground-up from a piece of broken file. It is secured by Allen screws.

Fig. 136

Setting a boring bar cutter to correct radius of cut. Half the diameter of the boring bar is deducted from the micrometer reading.

Boring bars should be as stiff and large as possible, but the necessity for chip clearance still holds good. The cutter should be situated in the centre of the bar, which must be slightly over twice the length of the job, to allow the cutter to come clear through the bore at each end. Slow speed, and fine cut and feed are necessary for a good finish, with

Fig. 137

Using a boring bar for facing the end of a workpiece. The fly-cutter is, of course, sharpened on the side face.

Fig. 138
The utility of the small lathe is well demonstrated in this picture. Large aluminium casting bolted to cross-slide for boring and facing operations using the boring bar.

plenty of cutting lubricant where called for.

Setting Boring Bar Cutters to Size

For good results the boring bar should be truly centred at each end, otherwise the cutter will swing in an arc larger than the set radius. This also happens when the bar is bent. The advantage of a truly running bar is found in setting the cutter to any given radius. The illustration (Fig. 136) shows how to set the cutter to a definite radius of cut. The measurement is taken with a micrometer from one side of the bar to the tip of the tool; half the diameter of the bar is then deducted from the total measurement; the result indi-

cates the radius which the tip of the tool will describe.

Facing on the Boring Table

In addition, facing of work may be done with the cutter-bar. Fig. 137 shows this operation, and the cutter has its sharpened edges on the side.

The advantage of working with the boring-bar is that large work which could not possibly be swung may be undertaken. It is also an unrivalled method when two or more holes, in the same plane, must be bored parallel to each other. It is advantageous to tighten the slide screws to give a stiff movement, as there is a tendency for the cutter to displace the job if backlash in the slide is apparent.

CHAPTER 11

TAPER TURNING, CRANKSHAFT TURNING, DISC AND BALL TURNING

ONE of the most widely used engineering methods of joining two components together is by means of the male and female tapers, and it is small wonder that this is so when the advantages of this fixing are considered. No other method—short of bolting or welding rigidly together—will provide so firm a grip; yet, in spite of this solidity, the united components may be almost instantly released. The lathe itself offers a good example of the ideal use of tapers; namely, those in the head mandrel and the tailstock, so that the turner may see their efficiency for himself.

It stands to reason, therefore, that the beginner who intends to take all classes of work in his stride, must early master the technique of taper turning—even if only to make accessories for his own lathe. Nor is the process difficult, considering that the efficiency depends entirely upon a perfectly mating fit.

Method of Turning Tapers

At the moment only **external** or **male tapers** will be considered, because, although most of the principles still hold good, **internal** or **female** tapers do not so readily lend themselves to demonstration.

There are four generally accepted methods of forming tapers in the lathe, namely: by swivelling the top slide; by off-setting the tailstock; by means of a **taper turning attachment**, or by interconnecting the lead-screw feed and the cross-slide feed by means of gearing. The two latter systems are chiefly used when large quantities of taper turning have to be dealt with, although for those prepared to spend a few pounds on lathe refinements, the taper-turning attachment forms a simple and easily adjustable means. The amateur is, however, mostly concerned with **top-slide** and **set-over** methods.

Measuring Tapers

The amount by which a taper decreases is always stated in inches per foot of length, and tables are given at the end of this book of the popular standard tapers — Morse, Brown and Sharpe, and Jarno.

Setting tapers to pure measurement involves some calculations—which are given later—and although the necessary formula is of the simplest, calculating for odd lengths of taper can become somewhat involved. Tapers also vary in size, and the matter is complicated because, in some instances, the taper per foot varies with the size also. Thus, the Morse No. 1 tapers 0·600 in. per foot; the No. 2 tapers 0·602 in. per foot, while the Morse No. 4 tapers 0·632 in. per foot. The tapers of Brown and Sharpe also differ with size, although some regularity of grouping is maintained. The Jarno taper—which seems the most logical of them all—does not vary throughout the whole range of nineteen sizes. Why this taper is not more used is a puzzle to most working engineers, but not, apparently, to the designers.

The amateur is greatly aided by the use of **taper test pieces,** to which taper work may be fitted; in the instance of an external taper—a correct female, and for a female taper—a correct male plug-gauge. Fortunately, accurate test gauges exist in the head and tailstock of the lathe and in the external tapers of the lathe centres. The size in question will be that most frequently used, because accessories for the lathe will form the great bulk of amateur taper turning. Should a range of test pieces be required, these may be most cheaply obtained by buying a set of **taper sleeves** which are used for adapting one size of taper to another; for instance, in fitting a No. 1 Morse-shanked tool into a No. 2 socket. In the smaller sizes the sleeves are quite cheap.

Tapers are rather awkward things to measure accurately by micrometer; the difficulty being to determine the exact distance between given diameters. Probably the most successful way is to chalk the surface of the pattern, and to scribe two lines around it at the set distance—revolving the pattern in the lathe against a scriber. Care must then be taken that the measurements are made exactly across these lines.

Tool Height

It is necessary when turning tapers that the tool be placed at exact centre height, and it should be set to the tip of a lathe-centre plugged into the head or tailstock. The reason for this may be seen in Fig. 139, where an exaggerated example is given. We here suppose that the tool has been set well below centre height—say $\frac{1}{2}$ in.—and that the small end of the taper has a radius of only $\frac{3}{8}$ in. It will be seen that while the tool will cut on the larger diameters, when it reaches parts of the work with a radius less than the amount which the tool is below centre height, no cut can take place. What is true for

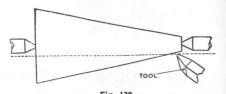

Fig. 139

Diagram illustrating necessity for tool to be set at dead-centre height for taper turning. Note that low-set tool misses the smaller diameter entirely.

this example still holds good no matter what the diameter of the work or low-set of the tool.

A Word of Caution

A common mistake made by the beginner when taper turning, is to take too deep a cut, especially when nearing the finished size. In taper turning a little goes a very long way, in so far as a very small amount taken off the diameter will allow a taper to enter its socket seemingly out of all proportion to the amount of metal removed. Finishing cuts should not be more than about 0·005 in. deep, otherwise it may be found that a " nearly " fitting taper will suddenly become too small for the socket in question.

Taper Turning by Top-Slide

This is the simplest method, entailing nothing more than angling the top-slide to conform with the taper to be cut. The limitation is that the length of the taper is confined to the maximum movement of the top-slide.

Setting the slide to the correct angle is best done from a test piece —such as one of the lathe's own centres. This may be mounted by gripping a piece of metal in the chuck, facing it, and centring it with a centre-drill. Into this hole the point of the lathe centre is located, the other end being supported on the back centre. If you possess a female lathe centre this may be plugged into the headstock, and the centring of the piece of metal obviated. It is essential, of course, that the tailstock be in line with the head, as for straight turning.

Having mounted the pattern the top slide must now be set to it. The best way of doing this is, undoubtedly, by means of the **test dial-indicator** or **" clock "**. This should be held in the toolpost, and the clock plunger located against the test piece to show a zero reading. The top-slide should then be set so that the reading remains at zero when the top-slide is wound back and forth. It is highly necessary that the clock plunger be at dead centre height, otherwise, for reasons which we have seen, the angle of the slide will not conform correctly.

Failing the use of a test indicator the slide may be set to the tip of the turning tool. In this instance, the tool must just touch the pattern all the way along, as the top-slide is traversed. A piece of white paper placed on the lathe bed below the work will help one to see any minute gap between tool-tip and pattern. It may also help if the pattern is lightly chalked so that the tool may scribe a line along it. As a guide, the top-slide may be set to an angle of about $1\frac{1}{4}$ deg. as a starting point for Morse tapers.

Fitting Tapers to the Socket

Before proceeding to details of the between-centres method, a few hints on fitting tapers to their respective sockets may be of assistance. The taper should be roughed-out until it will enter the socket a reasonable amount—say to within $\frac{3}{4}$ in. of the finished distance. If no test socket is available into which the taper may be tried, one must use the mandrel or tailstock of the lathe, so that it will become necessary to remove the work from the headstock. Do not,

however, remove the job from the chuck, but screw off the chuck itself, leaving the work undisturbed. If you un-chuck it it is highly improbable that you will be able to replace it accurately.

Now, draw three chalk lines, equally spaced, along the length of the taper, and lightly locate it in the test piece. It should then be partially rotated, back and forth, and withdrawn. Should the male taper be incorrect it will be seen that the chalk marks have been rubbed off where the tapers have touched, but will be intact on those places where they have not mated. From this it may be gathered that the angle is too great or too small, and the top-slide setting may be corrected accordingly. Extremely small adjustment to the setting should be made, a light cut taken, and the job again tested for fit. If an extremely good fit is wanted **engineers' marking blue** may be used in place of the chalk.

When very small differences of fit exist it is permissible to remove the last minute errors with a fine Swiss file. This is more likely to be successful than trying to adjust the top-slide to minutes of a degree.

It is unnecessary to state that both the socket and the job must be perfectly clean before testing for fit.

Taper Turning between Centres

Long tapers, where the length exceeds the travel of the top-slide, must be turned by methods other than the above, and this generally means for the amateur turning between centres. In this method the job is mounted on the lathe centres in the usual way, but the tailstock is set over, towards the operator, so that the end of the job is displaced from the lathe axis. The drawing (Fig. 140) makes the system clear.

When dealing with long tapers, setting up by direct measurement is

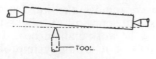

Fig. 140

Diagram illustrating method of forming tapers by off-setting the lathe centres.

usually essential, because unless one has a test piece of a length exactly similar to that of the job, setting by the " clock method ", just described, is not possible. The reason is that the amount by which the tailstock must be off-set varies with the length of the work. Let us imagine, for instance, that we have a job 1 ft. long which requires a taper of $\frac{1}{2}$ in. to the foot. Setting the tailstock over for $\frac{1}{4}$ in. will, of course, give us the correct setting. Now let us imagine that we have a bar **2 ft. long** requiring a similar degree of taper. If the tailstock be simply shifted along the bed for a distance of 2 ft., without altering the cross-setting, and the job is turned, we shall then cut a taper of only $\frac{1}{2}$ in. in 2 ft.—exactly half of the taper required.

From this circumstance we can evolve a simple formula to determine the amount of off-set which must be given to the tailstock for any given length of job or degree of taper, as follows:

$$\frac{\text{Length of Work (in.)} \times \text{Taper per in.}}{2} =$$

Off-set in in.

Example:

Find the amount of tailstock off-set required for a No. 1 Morse taper (0·600 in. per ft., or 0·050 in. per in.) 5 in. long:

$$\frac{5 \times 0·050}{2} = \frac{0·250}{2} = 0·125 \text{ in.}$$

It will be noted that the taper per ft. is the inclusive taper; hence the division by two.

When considering the length of a job it must be remembered that the points of the lathe centres enter the centre holes for a short distance; thus, in effect, making the job shorter. Centre holes should always be as small as is consistent with the size of the work, and where extreme accuracy is required the amount which the two centres enter into the holes must be deducted from the total length for calculation purposes.

Setting-over the Tailstock

The necessary off-set having been determined, it remains to move the tailstock the necessary amount. This is, once again, simplified by our old friend the **test dial-indicator**. It is necessary only to locate the clock plunger against the tailstock barrel—with the tailstock in the central position for straight turning—and to move the tailstock by means of the adjusting screws until the clock registers the correct amount of movement.

Failing a test dial-indicator, the distance can be measured by the index on the cross-slide.

Starting with the tailstock once more in the central position, take a piece of silver steel, round-off the nose, and clamp it in the toolpost. Bring the rounded end of this tool up to the tailstock barrel so that it will just nip a cigarette paper. Then turn the cross-slide feedscrew back to take up the backlash, but still nipping the cigarette paper. Note the reading on the index dial.

Now continue to withdraw the cross-slide from the tailstock barrel until the required amount of off-set is measured on the index. The tailstock may now be adjusted towards the tip of the silver steel, until the cigarette paper is once more just nipped between them.

Internal or Female Tapers

These are much more difficult to determine by direct measurement, so that internal tapers are almost invariably finished with **taper reamers** in the standard sizes. For sizes and tapers where no reamer is available it is necessary to turn first a similar external taper as a test piece. When, however, the angle of the taper is not of great importance—so long as the parts mate correctly—the internal taper should always be bored first, and the male taper fitted to it.

The model engineer often encounters taper fits, such as the fitting of a flywheel to a taper shaft, and the home-made reamer, shown in Fig. 83, in Chapter 7, is invaluable here. The taper on the shaft should be turned first; then, without disturbing the tool setting, the taper should be duplicated on a suitable piece of silver steel or cast steel. This may then be filed and ground to half its diameter and hardened and tempered as stated. The resultant taper hole should be a good fit on the shaft.

When boring internal tapers all the rules for external turning should be observed, especially the necessity for setting the tool at the correct height, and the taking of light cuts.

Crankshaft Turning

All model engineers will, at some time or another, inevitably encounter the turning of a crankshaft, for there is hardly an engine of any sort, steam, petrol or compressed air, that does not require one.

The **overhung crankshaft** such as may be seen Fig. 101, in Chapter 8 presents only a problem of simple off-setting on faceplate or chuck, and comment is not necessary.

The making of a **double-webbed crankshaft,** as pictured in Fig. 141, is rather more complicated. Several methods of actual technique may be

Fig. 141
A finished crankshaft for a model steam engine.

used, but in all of them the principle remains the same; namely, turning the shaft between the lathe centres from two sets of centre holes spaced the amount of the crank-throw apart.

The following paragraphs describe what is, probably, the simplest and most accepted method.

A piece of steel should be selected of sufficient diameter to accommodate the crank webs, and should be faced to length. Mount it on " V " blocks on the surface plate, somewhat in the manner shown in Fig. 119, in Chapter 9, and with the scribing block strike off a horizontal line across each end of the bar, at centre height. Now revolve the bar on the " V " blocks so that these lines become vertical. With the scribing block at the same setting, strike off another line at each end of the bar, crossing the original line at right angles. Next, set the scribing block, by rule, the exact amount of the crank-throw, above the centre line, and without disturbing the bar, strike off another line on each end.

Fig. 142
Method of setting out ends of material for twin-centre system of crankshaft turning.

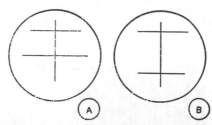

Fig. 143
First stage in turning the crankshaft shown in Fig. 141.

These should now look something like the drawing at (A) in Fig. 142. At the points where the lines intersect, centre holes should be accurately drilled with a centre drill. Although the drawing (A) shows one pair of intersecting lines located exactly on the centre of the bar, it is, of course, possible to arrange that both pairs of centres are off-set, as at (B). This should be done when the throw of the crank is large, as by this method the shaft may be turned from a bar of minimum diameter.

Some of the surplus metal may now be removed. The bar should be mounted on its **true** centres in the lathe, and the ends of the shafts roughened down, leaving the centre intact for the width of the journal and webs. It is important, however, not to cut into the off-set centre holes. The job at this stage may be seen in Fig. 143. In this picture the centre holes have been shown much larger than is really necessary, for the sake of clarity.

The job may now be re-mounted in the lathe, but this time on the **off-set** centres, and the webs roughly turned over their outside diameters. The journal may now be turned. For roughing this out a sturdy parting tool is the thing to use, and one may be seen in operation in the picture in Fig. 144. Having removed the surplus, the journal should now be finish turned, using a tool of parting-tool shape but with a rounded nose. This will give a radiused corner where the journal and shafts join the webs; this is correct crankshaft procedure. The job at this stage is seen in Fig. 145.

As the job will be revolving

Fig. 144
Turning the crankpin of the model shaft. A stout parting tool with rounded nose is ideal for this work. Note the job set on the eccentric centres.

Fig. 145
The crankshaft with the crankpin finished. It is now mounted on the true centre and the bearing shafts finish turned.

eccentrically low backgear speed is essential.

The shafts may now be finish turned; this, of course, by mounting the job on its true centres. During this process the off-set centres will be turned away, so it is necessary that all operations on the journal be complete. Finishing the web diameters now completes the job.

Supporting the Webs

It will be readily understood that when the journal has been turned, and the work remounted for finishing the shafts, there exists a weak portion at the centre of the crankshaft. It is necessary to support this in some manner, otherwise the working pressures when turning the shafts may tend to close the webs together. For large shafts screw-jacks are usually employed, and these are fitted between the webs and carefully adjusted to withstand the strains. Small crankshafts, such as the amateur is most likely to encounter, are best

supported by a piece of metal turned to be a tight push fit between the webs. It may be secured from flying out, as the job revolves, with a strip of insulating tape, binding the block to the journal. Fig. 146 presents a sketch of the arrangement.

Alternative Techniques

The crankshaft illustrated has **disc webs**, but quite often a shaft is wanted in which the webs are rectangular in shape. Turning from a solid round bar is, in this instance, wasteful of both time and material, so that the shaft is best made from a flat piece of steel, which is roughly shaped with a hacksaw. The drawing (Fig. 147) shows how the crankshaft blank may be roughed out.

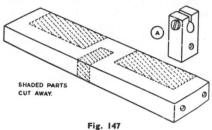

SHADED PARTS CUT AWAY.

Fig. 147
Forming a crankshaft blank from flat material. The small drawing at (a) illustrates a removable cheek for use when the integral cheeks are not provided.

The inexperienced may find difficulty in making the inside cuts with the saw, so a practical method is illustrated in Fig. 148. The order in which the cuts are made is shown by numbers. A rough file may be used to clean up any irregularities.

Fig. 146
Method of supporting the webs with a well-fitting wedge piece. This may be bound to the crankpin with nsulating tape.

Fig. 148
Diagram showing method of sawing material for crankshaft blank. The sequence of cuts is numbered.

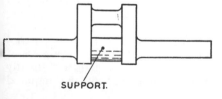

SUPPORT.

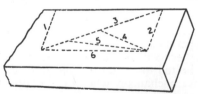

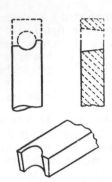

Fig. 149
Form tool for smal ball-turning. The upper drawings show how such a tool may be formed with drill and taper reamer. (See text.)

It will be noted that blanks of metal have been left at the ends of the shafts so that the two pairs of centre holes may be accommodated. These end blanks are, of course, turned off when the shafts are being finished. It is sometimes recommended that the shafts be finish turned completely circular as a first step, and that removable end blocks —such as is shown at (A) in Fig. 147 —be fitted for turning the journal. These blocks carry the off-set centre holes, and are secured to the shafts by a nipping screw. While these may be of use for large crankshafts, they form an awkward and uncertain method for small work, because it is difficult to get the blocks to grip tightly enough to withstand the turning strains. Any movement during the turning of the journal, is, of course, fatal.

Many of the crankshaft forgings sold with " kits of parts " are made without integral end-blocks, and this method must, perforce, be resorted to.

Ball Turning

Turning large metal balls to be truly spherical is a most difficult operation with amateur equipment. It calls for the use of a **ball-turning apparatus,** a thing which few model makers will possess. The apparatus is bolted to the lathe cross-slide, and has mechanism whereby the tip of

the turning tool is made to describe a radius by the operation of a feedscrew.

Fortunately, large balls are mostly required by the amateur for such purposes as capping levers, and as extreme accuracy is not wanted, roughing out on the lathe, and finishing with file and emery cloth, will usually suffice.

Small balls may be accurately turned by means of a form tool, such as is shown in Fig. 149. These tools may be made from cast steel bar, or from old files. The simplest method of shaping the tool is to drill a hole of the correct diameter through the steel bar, and to taper it with a home-made reamer, having a taper of about 6 deg. inclusive. This provides the " backing-off " on the cutting edge. The bar may then be sawn in two, so that the hole is unequally divided, and the end trimmed to shape with a file, giving cutting clearance by backing-off on the filed parts. The tool is then hardened and tempered.

If old files are used they will, of course, have to be softened for drilling and filing. Softening is best done by placing the file in a kitchen fire, and leaving it all night. Cooling will thus be gradual as the fire dies down, and this is the correct softening technique.

Turning Ebonite Balls

Ebonite balls have become increasingly popular for capping the levers on modern machinery, and it may well be that the amateur's own lathe may be improved in appearance and convenience by fitting them.

Balls of soft materials—such as ebonite or wood—should be roughed out with a broad tool, by eye, using the cross-slide and the lathe-carriage, and then finished with the simple tool shown in Fig. 150. This is a piece of steel tubing, of a diameter slightly smaller than that of the required

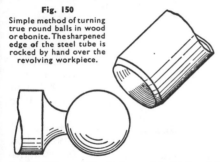

Fig. 150
Simple method of turning true round balls in wood or ebonite. The sharpened edge of the steel tube is rocked by hand over the revolving workpiece.

ball. The wall of the tubing should be faced-off square at one end, and given an external chamfer, to make a cutting edge.

The work should be revolved at high speed, and the tubing cupped over the partly finished ball, and rocked around the job in all directions, by hand, using a firm pressure. This will cut off all the rough and irregular places, so that a perfect ball will be obtained. Polishing should be done with fine emery-cloth and oil, which gives a high finish. Wooden balls, are of course, finished with fine glasspaper and then oiled.

Turning Blank Discs

One of the most puzzling jobs which the model engineer is likely to encounter is the turning of thin, blank discs from sheet metal. Sheet metal is always difficult to machine, solely because its lack of bulk makes it a most awkward material to hold during the machining operations. Blank discs are quite often required

Fig. 151
Components necessary for turning blank discs such as that shown at (D). (A) mandrel, (B) pressure pad, (C) folded emery cloth.

for such things as cover-plates, and frequently no holes by which they may be secured while machining are permissible. Of course, in those cases where a central hole may be allowed, the common method of turning the outer diameter is to secure a nut and bolt through the centre hole, and to hold the shank of the bolt in the three-jaw chuck, and this system presents few difficulties. It is when the disc must be completely plain, such as the one shown at (D) in Fig. 151, that the beginner —and very often the " old hand "— becomes puzzled.

A popular method which will serve for brass, steel, or any " solderable " metal is to turn and face a piece of brass rod, and to solder the piece of sheet metal to it. The disc is then turned, and, when finished, the disc is unsweated from the rod. This is a somewhat roundabout and messy system, and cannot, of course, be used for aluminium or its alloys. An old dodge, which is quite efficient is to face a large piece of wood in the lathe, and to stick the sheet metal to it with melted shellac.

The approved system of turning blank discs, however, is by means of a

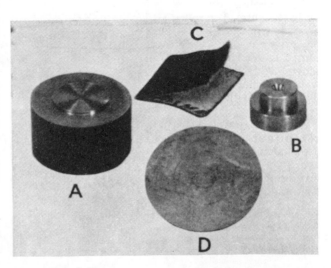

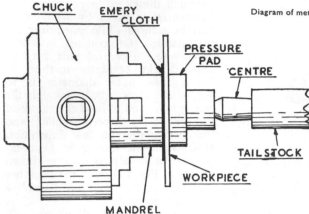

Fig. 152
Diagram of method of turning blank discs.

CHUCK
EMERY CLOTH
PRESSURE PAD
CENTRE
TAILSTOCK
WORKPIECE
MANDREL

object of the emery-cloth is, of course, to provide a friction grip between the revolving face and the job.

The piece of metal to be turned should be roughly clipped to shape. Having clamped the job securely in the lathe, it should be revolved at high speed, and the tool withdrawn from the work to its fullest extent. The tool should be brought up very carefully to the job. If too heavy a cut is attempted at first the tool will jam in the job, and you will have to start all over again.

Take very light cuts with slow hand feed—not more than 0·005 in. deep —until the outstanding irregularities have been removed.

Do not stand in line with the job when working upon it, as a sudden jam-up may cause the disc to spin out of the lathe.

" pressure-pad ". Briefly, the system consists of holding the discs by compression between the head and the tailstock, using a revolving tailstock-centre for preference.

In Fig. 152 the pressure-pad system is explained. Here it will be seen that a piece of brass of fairly large diameter is held in the three-jaw chuck, and faced true. Against this we place a piece of emery-cloth, folded so that the abrasive sides are outwards, and against this emery-cloth the piece of metal to be turned is clamped by the pressure pad, which revolves on the back-centre. The pressure pad is simply a piece of brass, turned to the shape shown, with a fairly deep centre hole drilled in with a centre-drill.

All these simple components are depicted in Fig. 151, and the whole lot may be made up in ten minutes. The

Fig. 153
Turning a blank disc with the components shown in Figs. 151 and 152.

CHAPTER 12

SCREWCUTTING

ALTHOUGH it is true to say that all engineering practice has been based on the use of the lathe, nothing has become so deeply embedded in the very roots of mechanics as has the screw thread. There is hardly any piece of mechanism to-day that does not embody somewhere an example of the screw principle—a principle which owes its very existence to the lathe. The importance of screwcutting is, therefore, as vital to the amateur as to the professional engineer, and neither the one nor the other will progress very far in his art without it. Fortunately, screwcutting in the lathe is a simple practice, the results of which are out of all proportion to the difficulties encountered.

Pitch and Lead

A screw thread has five characteristics: length, diameter, thread form, pitch and lead; but only the last two are likely to puzzle the beginner. On a single-start thread—with which we are at the moment concerned—pitch and lead are, however, identical, and may be expressed in two ways: (a) in threads per inch of length, and (b) in so many inches pitch or lead. This means, in other words, the amount in inches which a screw will advance per single revolution. Thus, a screw of 8 t.p.i. (threads per inch) will advance $\frac{1}{8}$ in. per single turn; its pitch or lead may be designated as being of eight threads per inch or of one-eighth inch pitch. With multiple threads—of which more later—pitch and lead do not mean the same thing. Metric threads are, of course, ex-

pressed as being of " x mm. pitch ".

The Principles of Screwcutting

If we glance at the illustration (Fig. 1) at the beginning of this book, we shall see that at the point marked (17) has been shown the lead-screw. It has been explained that this is a long screw—usually 8 or 10 t.p.i. in amateur machines—which may be coupled to the headstock by means of gearing. It will be remembered that the lathe carriage, bearing the lathe tool, can be engaged at will with the leadscrew, so that, as the leadscrew is turned, the carriage will be moved along the lathe bed, in exactly the same manner as a nut may be moved along a threaded bolt.

For the sake of simplicity let us confine ourselves to a lathe having a leadscrew of 8 t.p.i.—although the same principles hold good for a leadscrew of any pitch. If the leadscrew is coupled to the head mandrel in an even ratio of gearing, that is, if one revolution of the leadscrew equals one revolution of the mandrel, it is obvious that if a suitable tool is applied to a piece of work in the chuck a thread corresponding in pitch to that of the leadscrew will be reproduced on the workpiece. In early screwcutting lathes this was, indeed, the practice; the machine being provided with numerous, easily changed leadscrews of various thread pitches.

The inconvenience and expense of this arrangement was soon apparent, so that a system was evolved whereby the ratio of revolution between the work and the leadscrew might be varied by means of gearing between the two. Thus, in the instance of our 8 t.p.i. leadscrew, if the mandrel is geared to revolve twice as fast as the leadscrew, a screw of double the number of threads per inch will be cut; that is, 16 t.p.i. Should the ratio be yet further increased to 3 to 1 a thread of 24 t.p.i. will be obtained, and so on throughout the whole practical range. Conversely, should the leadscrew be geared to revolve at twice mandrel speed—that is, if the leadscrew revolves twice during one revolution of the workpiece — a thread of half the leadscrew pitch will be cut—4 t.p.i.

Gearing

The foregoing is the simple theory of screwcutting in the lathe, and it is evident that some slight knowledge of the principles of gearing is necessary before suitable gear trains can be set up, even when working from the usual gear-change charts. The novice is often puzzled as to what, in fact, does constitute a gear train, so, for his benefit, Fig. 154 shows the simplest possible form.

Here we see a gearwheel having 70 teeth meshed with one having 35 teeth; that is, one is twice the size of the other. If the large wheel is revolved once the smaller will, of course, turn twice, and is therefore said to be **geared up** in the ratio of 2 to 1. If, on the other hand, the power is applied from the small wheel, two turns will be necessary before the large wheel will complete one revolution. The large wheel is now said to be **geared down** in a 2 to 1 ratio. The wheel which applies the power is called the **driver,** while the other is known as the **driven.**

Intermediate Gears

The photograph (Fig. 155) shows these same two gearwheels meshed together through an intermediate gear. **No matter what size of inter-**mediate gear wheel is used the ratio of gearing between the two outer wheels always remains the same, in this case 2 to 1. The middle gearwheel serves only to transmit the drive from one wheel to another, and to reverse the direction of motion of one of the outer wheels. For this reason it is known as the **idler wheel,** and any number of idler wheels may be employed in series to link the driver and driven gears, but the ratio of gearing between these two always remains the same. The system is called a **simple gear train.**

Compound Gear Trains

It will thus be seen that a simple gear train can be used only to yield the ratio of gearing consistent with the difference between the diameters

Fig. 154
Simple gear giving a 2-1 step-up-or-down, according to which wheel supplies the drive.

35

70

Fig. 155
Simple gear train with intermediate " idler " wheel.
The idler wheel does not affect the ratios between the
outer gears.

of two given gearwheels. The disadvantage is that when large differences of gear ratio are required, one of the gearwheels must be impossibly large. For instance, should we require a six-to-one step-down from a gearwheel of 2 in. diameter the driven wheel would have to be 12 in. across. The complications which would arise with larger ratios, such as 30 to 1, can easily be imagined!

Fortunately, these limitations of space can be overcome by other methods of gearing, which brings us to a consideration of the **compound gear train,** pictured in Fig. 156. Here we see that our driver wheel is once more of 35 teeth, and that the driven is again of 70 teeth. Instead, however, of being coupled by a single gearwheel, two intermediate gearwheels are employed—**placed side by side and coupled together on a common mounting.**

Now, the smaller intermediate gearwheel has 20 teeth, and the larger has 60 teeth, so that their ratio is 3 to 1, and it will be noted that the driver wheel (35) is engaged with the 60-tooth intermediate. The driven wheel (70) engages with the 20-tooth intermediate gear. We have thus interposed a step-down of 3 to 1 between our original wheels, which already possess in themselves a 2 to 1 step-down ratio. The effect of this is to give a step-down ratio of 6 to 1 $(2 \times 3 = 6)$. Any gear ratio may be thus obtained, as it is quite possible to use two or more compound intermediates. Thus, if another similar compound intermediate were inserted the reduction in gearing would be 18 to 1 $(2 \times 3 \times 3 = 18)$. It is necessary to remember only that the ratios of step-up or step-down given by each stage of gearing must be multiplied together. The order in which the gears are arranged is not important provided that the correct step-up-or-down sequence is preserved.

Calculating Gear Trains for Screwcutting

Again we depart from the usual textbook procedure, where many good pages are employed to demonstrate the manner of calculating screwcutting gear trains. This, I feel, for the amateur turner, is a complete waste of time, which can be much better employed in actually using the lathe. In the first place, it is seldom or never that the amateur mechanic must calculate a gear train for himself, because every lathe is supplied with a chart—usually an engraved plate screwed to the lathe—whereon all the threads possible with the change wheels supplied are worked out, and the sizes and positions of the gearwheels stated.

Secondly, even if no chart exists, published lists of the gear trains necessary for almost any possible thread and leadscrew are easily obtainable. Such lists covering amateur requirements are given at the end of this book. I am personally acquainted with model engineers of wide repute who have never worked out a gear train in their lives.

The matter which has already been given here on gear trains is necessary to an understanding of many gear charts. As for calculation methods, the formulae will be given, together with the briefest instructions. Look at them; forget them; but remember where they may be found.

(*a*) Calculate ratio between lead of leadscrew and lead of thread to be cut; thus:

Lead of Leadscrew
Lead of Thread to be Cut

Example:
Lead of Leadscrew = 8
Lead of Thread to be Cut = 32
$$\tfrac{8}{32} = \tfrac{1}{4}$$

(*b*) Work must, therefore, revolve four times while the leadscrew revolves once; that is the leadscrew must be geared down in a ratio of 4 to 1.

Example:
Mandrel gear   ..   20 teeth
Leadscrew gear   ..   80 teeth

(*c*) If no 80-tooth wheel is available a compound gear train must be used. In the example this may be found by inspection; thus:
$$\tfrac{1}{2} \times \tfrac{1}{2} = \tfrac{1}{4}$$
Two step-down ratios of 2 to 1 may be used; thus:
Mandrel Gear   ..   20 teeth

Intermediate Compound   ..   40—30 teeth
Leadscrew Gear   ..   60 teeth

(*d*) Where gears cannot be found by inspection the rule is: divide each number into separate numbers, which, when multiplied together give the original numbers; thus:
$$\tfrac{1}{4} = \tfrac{1}{2} \times \tfrac{1}{2}$$

(*e*) As gears of 1 and 2 teeth are obviously impossible, multiply the numbers by any convenient number which will give suitable gear wheels. Changewheel sets usually progress in steps of 5 teeth so that the number is usually any convenient multiple of 5. That is, 10, 20, 30, etc.

Fig. 156
A compound gear train with a 3-1 gear ratio mounted between the outer wheels, thus multiplying the original 2-1 ratio by 3; i.e., 6-1.

(*f*) In the example, 20 is the convenient number; thus:

$$\frac{20}{40} \times \frac{20}{40}$$

or:

Mandrel Gear   .. 20 teeth
Intermediate Gear 40—20 teeth
Leadscrew Gear   .. 40 teeth

(*g*) It is probable that the change-wheel set will not contain two 20-tooth gears and two 40-tooth gears. Therefore, one of the pairs of numbers may be multiplied by some other convenient number, say, 30; thus:

$$\frac{20}{40} \times \frac{30}{60}$$

or:

Mandrel Gear   .. 20 teeth
Intermediate Com-
    pound   40—30 teeth
Leadscrew Gear   .. 60 teeth

Thus, by calculation, we have arrived at the gear train obtained by inspection, as in paragraph (*c*).

Thread Forms

Although in modern industry there are a great number of thread forms for special purposes, those which the amateur is likely to encounter are but four in number, viz.: **the " V " thread, the square thread, the acme thread,** and **the buttress thread.**

The " V " Thread

This is the most common type such as is found on the British Standard Whitworth, British Standard Fine (B.S.F.), and British Association (B.A.), and in the American A.S.M.E. and U.S. Standard Form. French and International Metric threads also employ the " V " form. Strictly speaking, none of these is of the pure " V " form, the tops and roots of the

threads being rounded in the British, and flatted in the American and Metric types. The home mechanic will probably be most concerned with the Whitworth and B.S.F. forms, a drawing of which is given in Fig. 157, both forms being identical.

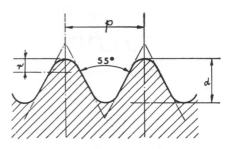

WHITWORTH STD. & B.S.F.

Fig. 157

Formula $\begin{cases} p = \text{pitch} = \dfrac{1}{\text{no. thrds. per in.}} \\ d = \text{depth} = p \times \cdot64033 \\ r = \text{radius} = p \times \cdot1373 \end{cases}$

Although for amateur and most professional work the theoretically correct radius can be ignored, the angle and depth are important. The very simple formula will enable these to be found, as it will be seen that the depth is always ·64 of the pitch.

The included angle of Whitworth and B.S.F. threads is 55 deg.; that of the American and Metric threads is 60 deg., while that of the B.A. thread is $47\frac{1}{2}$ deg. The amateur will not often screwcut the B.A. sizes, as these are invariably formed with taps and dies.

The Square Thread

In the drawing (Fig. 158) is shown the **square thread** which is mainly used to transmit motion, such as that of the lathe cross-slide. The depth is equal to half the lead; that is, a thread of $\frac{1}{8}$ in. lead will have a single depth of $\frac{1}{16}$ in. The width of each thread and each groove will, of course, be $\frac{1}{16}$ in.

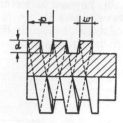

SQUARE FORM.

Fig. 158

$$\text{Formula} \begin{cases} p = \text{pitch} = \dfrac{1}{\text{no. thrds. per in.}} \\ d = \text{depth} = \dfrac{p}{2} \\ w = \text{width} = \dfrac{p}{2} \end{cases}$$

The Acme Thread

This thread is a variation of the square form, and is largely supplanting it in general use for feedscrews on the lathe and other tools. It has some advantages of strength, but is especially adapted to the use of split or half-nuts as commonly used for

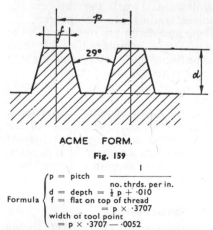

ACME   FORM.

Fig. 159

$$\text{Formula} \begin{cases} p = \text{pitch} = \dfrac{1}{\text{no. thrds. per in.}} \\ d = \text{depth} = \frac{1}{2}\,p + \cdot 010 \\ f = \text{flat on top of thread} \\ \quad = p \times \cdot 3707 \\ \text{width of tool point} \\ \quad = p \times \cdot 3707 - \cdot 0052 \end{cases}$$

quick engagement of the screw. A typical example is met on the lathe carriage of screwcutting lathes.

It will be noted from the diagram (Fig. 159) that the inclusive angle is

29 deg., and that, unlike the square thread, a clearance of ·010 in. is allowed at the top and bottom.

The Buttress Thread

In such things as vices, car jacks and the like, where the thread has always to resist a powerful force applied in one direction only, the buttress thread (Fig. 160) is often employed. As in the square thread, one face is at a right angle to the axis of the screw, but is supported by

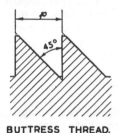

BUTTRESS   THREAD.

Fig. 160

$$p = \text{pitch} = \dfrac{1}{\text{no. thrds. per in.}}$$

a sloping back face. Resistance to shearing is over twice that of the square form, and the buttress should always be employed for conditions of great one-way stress.

Screwcutting Procedure (External " V " Thread)

While screwcutting technique is essentially the same for all types of threads, the external " V " form is the simplest and most often encountered, so that it may serve as the example.

Having turned the workpiece to size, the threading tool is set in the post at exact centre height, and " square " with the work. Fig. 161 shows how this may be facilitated by using the threading-tool gauge to obtain alignment. The correct gear train is mounted up, and the lathe put into slowest backgear. If the workpiece is of small diameter or of any considerable length it should be supported by the tailstock centre.

Now move the lathe carriage, by hand, back and forth to make sure that it has unrestricted movement for the whole length of the cut.

The clasp nut may now be engaged with the leadscrew, the lathe started, and a light trial cut taken. At the end of the cut the tool must be smartly withdrawn by a backward

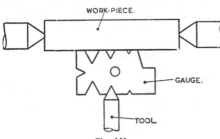

Fig. 161
Method of using screw gauge for setting tool at right-angle to screw axis.

movement of the cross-slide, and the clasp nut may be disengaged. The saddle is now wound back to the starting point, by hand, and the tool reset for the next cut, this time a little deeper. · This procedure is followed until the thread is completed.

The depth of cut should be small, not more than about ·005 in. at a time, while for screws of fine pitch or small diameter even less than this amount should be taken. Setting to the exact depth each time is important, as any excessive depth will tear up the work badly and perhaps break the tool tip. It is here that the **cross-slide index dial** becomes invaluable, as by its aid the cut can be reset to within a thousandth of an inch. And thousandths are important! The correct depth of thread can also be measured by the index reading.

If no index is fitted a chalk mark can be made on the feed screw handle, to correspond with a similar

mark on the cross-slide itself. By making the marks to coincide, the tool setting may be duplicated. It is necessary, of course, to re-chalk the cross-slide handle after each advance in setting. While the method is more or less satisfactory it cannot compare with the index dial for speed and accuracy.

Picking-up the Cut

The system of disengaging the clasp nut at the end of each cut, running back the carriage, by hand, to the start and re-engaging the clasp nut, is only possible when the number of threads to be cut is **an exact multiple of the number of threads on the leadscrew.** Thus, with a leadscrew of 8 t.p.i. direct engagement at any point may be made for 8, 16, 24, 32 threads per inch; and so on for any threads which are an exact multiple of eight.

The complications arise when threads which are not an exact multiple of the leadscrew have to be cut, such as—following our above example—10, 18, 20, 22 and so on. Here, the tool must have a definite point of engagement with the work; that is, the clasp nut must always be engaged at a certain point or points on the leadscrew. If the nut is engaged haphazardly in any position it is highly unlikely that it will be the correct one, so that the tool may not follow the original cut but may enter the work between the correct thread grooves. This, of course, destroys the thread.

Picking-up by Thread Dial Indicator

The **thread dial indicator**—one of which is shown attached to the lathe carriage in our photograph (Fig. 162), forms an easy and certain method of ensuring the correct pick-up point for threads of most pitches.

The device consists of a vertical spindle, having at its lower end a gearwheel, which, by swinging the housing, may be meshed at will with the leadscrew. To the top of the spindle a graduated and numbered disc is attached, which revolves with the lower gear. As the disc is turned the graduations upon it alternately coincide with a fixed mark on the body of the indicator.

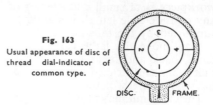

Fig. 163
Usual appearance of disc of thread dial-indicator of common type.

Fig. 162
Thread dial-indicator shown attached to lathe carriage and engaged with the leadscrew.

If the lathe carriage is **not engaged** by the clasp nut, but the **indicator gear wheel is meshed with the revolving leadscrew,** the disc will, of course, also revolve, as we have, in effect, a worm gear arrangement. On the other hand as soon as the clasp nut is engaged, and the lathe carriage starts to move along the bed, **the disc no longer revolves,** because the two movements cancel out; that is, the gearwheel is moving forward along the leadscrew at exactly the same speed as it is being turned backwards, so that no relative rotary movement takes place between the gear wheel and the leadscrew. Advantage is taken of this fact to provide an infallible selection of the " pick-up " position.

The factors governing the " pick-up " of thread dial indicators are (a) the ratio of indicator spindle revolutions to the thread being cut, and (b) the number of markings on the dial. Some variations in the quantities of these factors are occasionally found

on different makes of lathes, but, again confining ourselves to the 8 t.p.i. leadscrew, the following description of the method of operation will serve as a typical example. Suitable indicators for this leadscrew usually have a gearwheel of 16 teeth, and four markings on the dial. Where the leadscrew pitch and other factors are not as in the example, instructions for operation are usually provided by the makers.

(a) Operation is by engaging the clasp nut at the moment when any certain marking on the dial coincides with the fixed mark, as follows:

(b) Threads which are an exact multiple of the leadscrew pitch do not require the use of the indicator.

(c) For even-numbered threads which are not an exact multiple of the leadscrew pitch the clasp nut may be engaged when any mark on the dial coincides with the fixed mark.

(d) Odd-numbered threads should always be engaged at the same number on the dial or on any alternate number.

(e) For half-threads per inch, always engage on the same number on the dial.

(f) For other threads, mm. sizes, etc., the clasp nut should not be disengaged (see following paragraphs).

The Reversing Method

A system which is becoming much used in professional practice is the certain one of leaving the clasp nut permanently engaged with the lead-screw, and, instead of returning to the start by hand, to reverse the direction of the lathe drive. This, of course, runs the carriage backwards to the start by means of the lead-screw.

The modern professional lathe now usually incorporates a reversing clutch mechanism in the headstock gearbox, giving a fast return, but few amateurs' machines will have this expensive refinement. Happily, the position may be quite satisfactorily overcome by simply reversing the direction of rotation of the lathe motor by means of a suitable switch. This does indeed form one of the easiest methods of all for the amateur turner, and is highly suitable for another screwcutting technique to be described later.

The Chalking Process

Those folk whose lathes possess neither a thread dial indicator nor means for reversing the direction of drive must fall back upon a very old system of positioning the cut; namely, that of chalking the change wheels. Here it is necessary to stop the lathe during its first cut, keeping the clasp nut engaged, and to chalk a tooth on the mandrel gear, making a coinciding chalk mark on the headstock. Similarly, a tooth is chalked on the leadscrew gearwheel, and a similar mark made on the lathe bed to coincide with it. The clasp nut may now be disengaged, and the lathe carriage returned to the start as before, but the clasp nut must not be engaged for the following cut until all the chalk marks again coincide. The system is rather awkward, and is not to be compared with the two previous methods.

For short screwcutting jobs the amateur is much better served by stopping the lathe, leaving the clasp nut engaged, and reversing the lathe direction by hand.

Cutting the Thread

It has already been observed that only light cuts should be taken, and that disaster is the sure reward for the heavy handed. In addition, it is advisable to take two or three successive cuts at the same tool setting— say, after every ·025 in. advance. In this way any spring in the tool or job may be " worked out ", and a truer and better-finished screw thread will result.

When roughing out " large " threads—below about 16 t.p.i.—it is an advantage to advance the tool sideways a few thousandths of an inch, by means of the topslide, on occasional cuts. It should also likewise be retarded occasionally. The exact method is to advance the tool about ·003 in. on one cut, and to retard it a like amount on the succeeding cut, and so on. This side-to-side cutting serves to widen the opening of the thread, thus relieving the strain on the tool as it advances

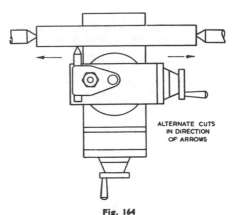

ALTERNATE CUTS
IN DIRECTION
OF ARROWS

Fig. 164
Diagram showing process of roughing threads by alternate movements of the tool.

deeper into the work. Also, as the tool takes most of the roughing cuts on one or other of its edges only, a deeper cut may be obtained without risk of "chatter" or breakage (Fig. 164).

The process should be used with caution, and stopped well before reaching the correct depth of thread. With the bulk of the metal removed, the tool is again set to a central position, and the thread finished with the usual light, undisturbed cuts.

Setting Over the Topslide

An excellent method of screwcutting, especially for " V " threads of any great pitch or depth, is provided by setting over the topslide to conform to the angle of the thread to be cut.

The drawing (Fig. 165) should convey the essentials, and it will be seen that the topslide is set at an angle of 27½ deg. to the lateral axis of the thread. For the sake of demonstration it will be assumed that a Whitworth form is to be cut. As this thread has an inclusive angle of 55 deg. it will be noted that the topslide is set to exactly half this angle.

The lathe and workpiece are set up

Fig. 165
Method of screwcutting by off-setting the topslide. The process is fully explained in the text.

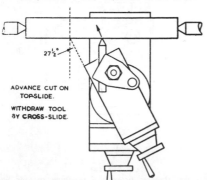

for screwcutting in the usual way, but instead of advancing the tool into the work by means of the **cross-slide,** the topslide is used for this purpose. It will thus be understood that the tool will be entered at an angle of 27½ deg. to the lateral axis of the thread, and will only cut on the forward edge. Thus one side only of the thread is formed by the profile of the tool; the other side of the thread takes its angle from the advance of the topslide itself.

Quite large cuts can be taken in this way, so that it is probably the quickest method of screwcutting. The reason is, of course, that the tool is cutting only on one edge—in the same manner as an ordinary turning tool—therefore the wedging action which takes place in the orthodox method is obviated.

The system has other advantages, but it will be necessary to give a fuller explanation of the procedure before they can be appreciated. Screwcutting is started in the usual way; that is, by advancing the tool by the **cross-slide** and taking a preliminary cut. The reading on the cross-slide index dial should be noted, and, if the dial is an adjustable one, it should be set at zero, or, failing this, a chalk mark made upon it for easy identification of the setting.

At the end of the cut the tool is withdrawn by the cross-slide in the usual way, and the direction of lathe rotation reversed for the return of the carriage to the start. While the carriage is returning, however, the tool may be advanced for the next cut, but this time by means of the topslide. This can be done because the cross-slide has withdrawn the tool from contact with the work.

On again reaching the starting point the cross-slide is once more wound forward to its original setting as indicated by the chalk mark. The lathe is then reversed and another cut taken. The depth of this cut will, of course, depend upon the amount which the **topslide** has been advanced. Briefly, the tool is advanced by the topslide, and withdrawn by the cross-slide, but this must always be returned to its original setting before the cut is taken.

Quite amazing speed of operation may be attained, as the movements become continuous, and no pause is necessary at the start of each cut to reset the tool. It will be appreciated, of course, that should one be cutting an American or Metric thread, which have inclusive angles of 60 deg., the topslide must then be set at an angle of 30 deg. to the lateral axis of the thread. The novice should be careful that the slide is actually set from the axis of the cross-slide, and not from the longitudinal axis of the screw, as this would give an angle of $62\frac{1}{2}$ deg.!

Internal threads can also be cut in this way, but do not lend themselves so readily as the external ones. Exactly the same procedure is followed, except that the topslide must angle from a different direction, so that the tool is moved towards the operator instead of away from him.

Thread Gauges

The amateur will often be required to measure the pitch of screws, as it is frequently required to make threaded parts to fit existing threads. Measuring " V " threads by rule is awkward, especially in the finer pitches, so that a **thread gauge** similar to that shown in Fig. 166 is employed. This tool has a number of blades, each of which is shaped to the pitch and outline of a commonly used size, and successive blades are offered up to the thread until one is found which fits perfectly. The number of threads per inch will be found stamped on the blade.

Acme and square threads, being usually of large pitch are, however, more easily measured with the steel rule, which is placed along the screw and the number of threads within the inch read off. There is a trap for the unwary here, as it must be remembered that the inch measurement

Fig. 166
Thread gauge for measuring pitches of screws.

must encompass **an equal number of threads** and **an equal number of spaces.** Thus, a thread of 8 t.p.i. must have 8 threads and 8 grooves within the inch. The diagram (Fig. 167) conveys the idea. If there appears to be an unequal number then it is quite likely that you have picked upon a thread of metric or diametral pitch, which will, quite often, seem to conform to an inch measurement. In

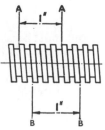

Fig. 167
When measuring threads by rule the measurement should embrace equal threads and equal spaces as at (A) (A). (B) (B) is incorrect.

the diagram the inch measurement encompasses threads and spaces as shown by (A) (A). If (B) (B) is indicated you may be sure that there is something wrong, and it is probable that the screw may not be pitched in English measurement.

At the same time, the thread

should be measured over a distance of several inches, as it is possible that the number of threads to the inch may be fractional. For instance, $3\frac{1}{2}$ threads per inch. Such a thread measured over two inches of its length should, of course, show 7 threads and 7 spaces.

Screwcutting Procedure (Square and Acme Forms)

For obvious reasons the set-over topslide method of screwcutting cannot be used for square or acme form threads, as the form is actually taken from that of the tool itself, which is ground to the correct size and profile. Such tools are, indeed, really form-tools.

In all other particulars screwcutting procedure remains the same, and it is, in fact, quite common practice to rough out both the square and acme threads with an ordinary " V " threading tool, finishing with a cor-

threads are usually of coarse pitch, which means that the helix angle of the thread is fairly large. Unless the angle of the tool conforms with the helix the skirt will rub on the walls of the thread, forcing the tool out of line and widening the groove.

The trouble can be eliminated by the use of the tool holder shown in Fig. 168. It may be made from a short length of square or hexagon steel rod, with a hole drilled in one end for the round tool bit. An Allen screw holds the bit in position. Suitable tools can be made from broken centre-drills or the hardened shanks of high-speed drills. Being circular in section the bit can be partially revolved to conform with the helix angle of the thread to be cut. It is as well to chuck an odd piece of metal, take a trial cut along it, so that the angle can be observed, and set the bit to give the clearance for the skirt.

It will be appreciated that the helix

Fig. 168

Threading tool holder which allows cutter to be turned to conform with helix angle of screw.

rectly ground form-tool. Such roughing out must be used with discretion, however, as it is fatal for the width of the " V " groove to exceed that of the finished screw thread.

It is essential with the square and acme forms that the tool be at a true right-angle to the axis of the work. Should it be tilted so that the side angles are displaced, it will be difficult to make a nut to fit it correctly.

Clearance Angles

The most prolific source of trouble is lack of side clearance in the threading tool. Being used almost exclusively as feed screws, these

angle for any given lead will alter with the diameter of the screw. The smaller this becomes the more acute is the helix angle in relationship to the screw's axis. The drawing (Fig. 169) shows, diagrammatically, two screws of equal lead but of different diameter, and it will be noted that there is a considerable difference in the helix angle.

Tool Width

The width of the tool for a single-start, square form thread must always be exactly half the pitch of the desired thread. For instance, a thread of $\frac{1}{8}$ in. pitch would need a tool of $\frac{1}{16}$ in.

width at the tip; a thread of 10 per in. (i.e. ·100 in. lead) must be ·050 in.

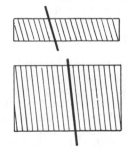

Fig. 169

Diagram showing how helix angle alters according to screw diameter. The pitch in both drawings is identical.

wide, and so on. Inspection of the drawing in Fig. 158 will show why this is so.

The correct width of the tip of the acme form tools can be found from the simple formula accompanying Fig. 159.

Multiple-start Threads

When threads of large pitch must be cut on comparatively slender shafts a difficulty arises owing to the excessive depth of the thread in relationship to the shaft diameter. It may, for instance, be desired to cut a square thread of 4 t.p.i. on a shaft of only $\frac{1}{2}$ in. in diameter. It will be remembered that the tool width is always half the pitch—in this instance, $\frac{1}{8}$ in. The depth of thread is also equal to the width, so that the combined depth would be $\frac{1}{4}$ in., leaving only $\frac{1}{4}$ in. as the core diameter. This would weaken the screw excessively, and would not, in fact, be a mechanical proposition.

The difficulty may be overcome by the use of a multiple-start thread, which may be of two, three or more starts. For the sake of illustration we will confine ourselves to the two-start screw.

A two-start screw is really two screws combined in one; that is, one thread is cut within the helix of the other. Our photograph in Fig. 170 shows that in appearance the two-start 4 t.p.i. screw is similar to a single-start thread of 8 t.p.i. This is due to the fact that each thread and each space is only $\frac{1}{16}$ in. wide;

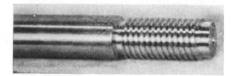

Fig. 170

Two-start thread, showing similarity of appearance to a single-start thread of half the pitch.

in fact, the two 4 t.p.i. threads have been cut with a tool ground to the correct width for a thread of 8 t.p.i.

This should be made clear by our picture of a two-start thread in its initial stage, with only one thread

Fig. 171

Initial stage in cutting a two-start thread. Note wide space between first thread, ready to receive the second.

cut. The wide space between the grooves, ready to receive the second thread, will be noted. Fig. 172 shows that the second thread has been started but not yet finished to depth, and the short register which indicates

Fig. 172

Two-start thread with first thread finished and second thread just started.

the correct thread depth will be seen. It is also advantageous to have the turned recess at the finish of the thread, into which the tool may run after the finish of the cut.

Spacing Multiple Threads

The above paragraphs and pictures should enable the beginner to understand what a multiple-start thread is. As may be imagined, an even spacing of the threads is of vital importance, as it must be remembered that a **two-start nut** has to be cut later to fit the thread. An error in spacing of a couple of thousandths of an inch will make it impossible for the nut to screw on—unless it is cut with a similar error.

Fortunately, quite simple and accurate spacing methods exist. In practice, two are in general use, namely, that of marking the gear wheels, and that using the test dial-indicator.

The first is the older system, and is still probably one of the best. In setting up the gear train it should be arranged that a gearwheel having an even number of teeth should occupy the position on the lathe mandrel. On this wheel two teeth, directly opposite each other, should be marked with chalk. A similar mark should now be made at the space in which one of these teeth engages with the next gearwheel.

Having cut the first thread, the banjo of the lathe carrying the gear train should be lowered, thus disengaging the mandrel wheel, and the mandrel revolved half a turn so that the other chalked tooth will engage in the chalked space. The gears may now be re-meshed, and the second thread cut. Three-start threads will require that the gearwheel on the mandrel be marked in three equally divided spaces, while four marks will be made for a 4-start screw.

Spacing by Test Dial-indicator

Once more our very useful friend the test dial-indicator may be employed. By this method the tool is moved forward to occupy a position exactly between the first threads by measurement.

Assuming that the first thread has been cut, the clasp nut should be left in engagement. The dial-indicator, mounted on a stand or the scribing block base, is placed on the lathe bench, with the plunger depressed against the top-slide. This is then screwed forward for the amount necessary to locate the tool in the centre of the first threads. It should be noted that the amount of movement required is always **half the pitch of the thread;** thus, for a thread of $\frac{1}{4}$ in. pitch (·250 in.) the movement must be ·125 in.

Whereas in a single thread the pitch and lead are the same thing, this is not so with the multiple thread. Here the pitch is taken to indicate the actual distance between each thread, while the lead is the distance which the nut will move for one turn of the screw. A two-start thread may, for instance, be said to have a pitch of $\frac{1}{8}$ in. and a lead of $\frac{1}{4}$ in.

It is as well to remember that when cutting any type of thread the main precautions are **slow speed** and **light cuts.**

Left-hand Threads

It is often desirable that a screw, especially a machine feed-or-lead-screw should have a **left-hand thread** in order that the slide or lathe carriage may be moved forward when the feed-handle is turned in a clockwise direction. The opposite arrangement is extremely awkward, and is not, fortunately, found on modern machines.

When cutting ordinary right-hand threads the tool traverses the work from right to left, and the tumbler gear on the head should be so set. With left-hand threads, however, the cut must be taken from left to right, with the tumbler gear reversed appropriately. If the job is held in chuck or collet it is necessary that a recess should be turned in the work, to core depth, in which the threading tool may be started on its cut. The helix angle of a left-hand thread does, of course, slope in the opposite direction from that of a right-handed screw, and the clearance angle of the tool must be adjusted accordingly.

Internal Threads

All the principles governing the screwcutting of external threads operate equally for internal threads. Light cuts and slow speed are particularly necessary, and slowest backgear should always be used. For " V " form threads the tool illustrated in Fig. 67, Chapter 6, is employed, or a boring tool holder, wherein a loose cutter is held by a nipping screw, may be employed with advantage. Such a bar enables the cutter to be removed for sharpening without disturbing the set-up of the lathe. This tool is also shown in the photograph.

Core Size

The first step in cutting internal " V " screw threads is, of course, to bore the hole. The diameter of this is always equal to the diameter of the mating screw **less the double depth of thread.**

A useful table of thread depths is given at the end of this book, so the amateur will have no difficulty in determining the size of hole necessary for any screw. It will be seen, for instance, that the double depth of thread for a screw of 16 t.p.i. is ·080 in.; thus, the bore necessary for a nut to fit a screw of ¾ in. diameter by 16 t.p.i. will be: ·750 in. — ·080 in. = ·670 in.

L

Core diameter for square threads should be **screw diameter less pitch,** but Acme threads have a clearance of ·010 in. at both top and bottom of the thread. In practice, the **Acme screw** is made to nominal dimensions, but the **bore of the nut** is made .020 in. larger, and the thread cut .020 in. deeper.

Where the nature of the work will permit it is extremely convenient to recess the nut blank for a short distance to indicate the depth of thread. This is shown in Fig. 173, and it will be understood that screwcutting is continued until the tip of the tool just touches the register.

It is particularly necessary when cutting internal threads that successive cuts be frequently taken at the

Fig. 173
Method of registering screw diameter when cutting threaded nuts.

same tool setting—especially the finishing cuts. Internal screwcutting tools tend to " push off " from the bore owing to their spring, and this spring must be " worked out ". It should be unnecessary to emphasise the importance of setting the tool " square " with the job, nor the necessity for perfect form in the tool itself.

Fitting Nuts

Screwcutting threads by pure measurement is a difficult process if accuracy is to be maintained, so that it is usual to have a test piece to which the thread may be mated. In most instances it is possible to use for this purpose the screw which the nut must fit.

It is useful to know that a nut which is tight on its screw may be loosened by hammering it with a hide mallet while it is on the screw. Hammering off the screw tends to tighten it, but the practice is to be avoided as the nut is distorted.

Fitting Nuts of Square and Acme Form

This is probably the most difficult of all screwcutting jobs, as quite often the nut will, for no apparent reason, refuse to go on to the screw.

In this situation, first check that the pitch of nut and screw are identical. Silly as this may seem, mistakes of this sort have often been made—and not only by amateurs either! Next check that the nut thread has been cut deeply enough, and that the core diameter is not too small. Assuming these are correct, there only remains thread width to consider. Without touching any of the lathe settings, draw the tool backwards, towards the tailstock, about ·001 in., by means of the topslide, and take another cut through the nut. Moving the tool in this way causes it to cut on the back edge, thus widening the groove. If the tool is advanced, towards the headstock, it will cut on the front edge, and will probably "chatter". Continue the widening operation until the screw will enter.

Cutting Left-hand Nuts

Remembering that left-hand external screws are cut from the headstock towards the tailstock it seems reasonable that left-hand nuts should be cut in the same way; that is, by starting the cut from within the chuck and working outwards. This is, however, awkward, and the amateur will find the system outlined in Fig. 174 much better. It will be apparent that the tip of the threading tool points towards the back of the lathe, in the opposite way from that of the tool used for right-handed threads. The cut is taken with the lathe turning in reverse, and the gear train arranged so that the tool will feed-in from the

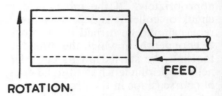

ROTATION.

FEED

Fig. 174
Diagram showing method of cutting left-hand nuts allowing tool to be fed in from the front.

outside when thus revolving. The tumbler reverse gear is invaluable here for determining the direction in which the leadscrew shall revolve.

Fitting Multiple-start Nuts

Nuts for multiple-thread screws are extremely tricky things to fit, because although only one thread may be at fault it is impossible to tell which one it is! If the pitch, core and depth are correct all that can be done is to widen each groove in turn not more than ·001 in. at a time—and to try the fit after each cut. Very great care is necessary as the nut may easily become too loose on the screw.

Helix Angle Clearance

It is again highly important that the skirt of the internal threading tool has plenty of clearance within the helix of the groove. For this purpose the tool holder indicated in Fig. 175 is recommended. In prin-

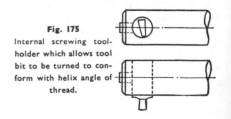

Fig. 175
Internal screwing toolholder which allows tool bit to be turned to conform with helix angle of thread.

ciple it is the same as the external tool of Fig. 168; that is, a round cutting bit which may be turned to give clearance is used. The bar is particularly adaptable, as it may be employed for both left- and right-handed threads.

Taps and Dies

Most screws of small diameter and standard pitches can be cut with **taps** and **dies** operated from the tailstock. Taps may be gripped in a drill chuck, or held in a tap wrench, the cut being started by pressure from the back centre. Low back-gear speed is necessary, and the tap should be well lubricated; **lard oil** is particularly good for operation on steel or aluminium alloys. A taper tap should be run through first, followed by a plug tap.

It may be found that there is less danger of tap breakage if the tap is simply started on its cut under power, and the thread completed by hand. With deep holes it is highly necessary that the tap be frequently withdrawn to clear away the metal chips. Neglect of this usually means a broken tap and a spoiled job.

The **tailstock die-holder** shown in Fig. 40, Chapter 4, is the ideal tool for using dies in the lathe. Such dies are usually adjustable, and the first cut should be made with the die opened up a small amount. Then readjust for the finishing cut. Lubricate well and see that the die does not become clogged with chips

Taps and dies used in the manner outlined above make a useful adjunct to screwcutting, and it may often be found advantageous to rough out a thread by screwcutting, and to finish it with a tap or die. The screwcutting ensures that the thread will be " square " with the axis of the job, as otherwise there is a danger that taps and dies, used alone, may produce a " drunken " thread.

Thread Chasers

On plain lathes threads must be cut with taps, dies, or **thread chasers.** In appearance, chasers resemble thickened wood-chisels, the ends of which are profiled to the various forms and pitches. They are used by hand, and supported at the end on a toolrest. When brought into contact with the revolving work the chaser is drawn along at approximate "thread speed ", and the thread begins to appear. When the thread is partially formed the chaser will carry along it, until correct depth is attained. The chaser is withdrawn at the end of each cut, and re-entered at the start.

Cutting threads in this manner is an art not quickly acquired, and, except for certain purposes—notably those of the instrument trade—is falling into disuse. Nevertheless, chasers are valuable for " dressing " worn or damaged threads, or they may be used as screwcutting tools in the normal way, and will give extremely good thread form. Chasers for internal threads are also available.

CHAPTER 13

MILLING, SHAPING AND GRINDING IN THE LATHE

THE use of the lathe for any but legitimate turning purposes is a practice confined almost exclusively to the amateur mechanic. Reasons are not far to seek, for it is obvious that the lathe cannot compete in speed of production or in scope with machines designed and extensively developed for special purposes. To the professional time is money, so that it pays him to spend some hundreds of pounds on, for instance, a milling machine, rather than devote the time necessary for converting the lathe into another machine altogether.

Happily, the model mechanic is not so greatly hampered by these considerations, so that he is usually prepared to spend some time and trouble, if, in the end, his single machine tool will do the work he requires. As for the usefulness of the lathe in this role it may be said at once that, except for limitations in size, most work which may be done on a milling machine may be successfully undertaken.

Limitations

The most serious limitation which the lathe has for milling purposes is the lack of a rise-and-fall movement. A secondary weakness is that the travel of the cross-slide is comparatively short, so that the length of the work which may be undertaken is somewhat curtailed. Lastly, the slides of the amateur lathe are of light construction, so that heavy milling and shaping cuts cannot be made.

Methods

Two systems of milling may be employed. In the one, the work is secured to the cross-slide, and the tool rotated in the headstock. In the second, the work is held at the headstock and the cutting tool revolved in a suitable spindle attached to the cross-slide. Both methods have their peculiar uses as will be seen.

The Vertical Slide

If advantage is to be taken of the full possibilities, the **vertical slide,** shown in Fig. 176, is an indispensable accessory. It is designed to overcome the lathe's greatest milling disability —lack of rise-and-fall movement. The accessory takes the form of a movable slide, which may be bolted in a vertical position by its right-angled baseplate to the top surface of the cross-slide. The face of the vertical slide is provided with a number of " T " slots by means of which the workpiece may be bolted to it.

The slide illustrated is known as the **universal swivelling type,** by reason of the fact that not only may it be swung from the vertical in one direction, but also at angles to the axis of the lathe bed. Some vertical slides do not embody these movements, but are fixed rigidly to the right-angled baseplate, so that the face of the slide is always presented vertically at 90 deg. to the lathe axis. This limits its usefulness to a great extent. Other types of slide are encountered where only one of the swivelling movements is incorporated.

Fig. 176

The accessory which converts the lathe into a milling machine—the vertical slide. That shown is known as " the universal swivelling type ".

General Observations

Not being specially designed to withstand the type of cut which milling imposes, certain precautions are necessary for lathe milling operations.

Most lathe cross-slides and feedscrews are rather lightly constructed, although quite adequate for the turning stresses which they are designed to withstand. For this reason " chatter " is likely to be encountered when milling, and it is advisable to tighten the cross-slide adjustment by means of the side screws, making the slide to move rather stiffly.

The same consideration calls for considerable care in the selection of feeds and speeds, and, except in the case of certain forms of cutter, a low speed and feed are desirable.

When using the circular type of cutter, or the fly cutter—both of which are dealt with in the following paragraphs—it is advisable to feed the work into the cutter against its direction of rotation. If the work is fed in **with** the direction of rotation, so that the cutter tends to draw the work towards itself, it may be found that the cutter will snatch, and pull the work forward, due to the backlash in the lathe slide.

Types of Cutters

Whereas in turning operations the work revolves against a stationary tool, in milling the tool revolves against the work.

The picture (Fig. 177) shows a selection of milling cutters, such as are generally useful to the amateur. At (A) may be seen a small circular saw, which, though not generally classed as a milling cutter, is one in effect. At (B) may be seen a similar cutter of greater thickness, used for milling narrow grooves, while at (C) is another of even greater thickness. Such cutters are obtainable in a variety of diameters and thicknesses, in keeping with the work to be undertaken.

The tool shown at (D) may be classed as a true milling cutter. It is used for various purposes, such as the milling of wide grooves, or the cutting of semi-circular depressions. Although obtainable in a great variety of sizes and widths only the smaller sizes are of real use to the amateur. A heavy and stiff machine is necessary for use with large or wide cutters such as this, and considerable power is required to operate them at the full width of cut.

The small cutter indicated at (E) is one used for cutting the flutes in thread taps. The cutting teeth are

Fig. 177
Milling Cutters (A) small
slitting saw, (B) and (C)
similar cutters of greater
thickness, (D) small slab
cutter, (E) tap or reamer
fluting cutter.

Fig. 177
Milling Cutters (A) small
slitting saw, (B) and (C)
similar cutters of greater
thickness, (D) small slab
cutter, (E) tap or reamer
fluting cutter.

ground to a convex radius, which does, of course, reproduce as a concave groove in the work. Useful as this cutter is in itself, it serves to illustrate a whole range of types. These are the **profile cutters.** The drawing (Fig. 178) illustrates some sections of these, and it will be seen that they have a profiled tooth form, which will reproduce the reverse on the workpiece. Thus, the convex radius-cutter at (A) will mill a radiused groove, while the cutter at (B) will produce a rib of semicircular section. Above each cutter-section is shown the work which it will reproduce.

At (E) in the drawing is illustrated a **gear-tooth cutter**—probably the most useful and widely used of all profile tools. The small drawing shows the shape of the cut which is made, and the sketch has been continued in dotted line to show how the gear formation is obtained by spacing the cuts around a circumference.

The Side and Face Cutter

Probably the most useful of all plain cutters, it is similar in appearance to (D) in Fig. 177, except that teeth are continued up the cutter sides. The tool cuts on both sides and the face, and is capable, therefore, of forming deep, shouldered work. Wide grooves may also be cut, as the tool may be fed into the work sideways, thus widening the channel to any extent.

If circular cutters are used to mill a groove of specified width, it is necessary that they be truly mounted on the arbor. Two such arbors are sketched in Fig. 179. Should the cutters wobble on the shaft

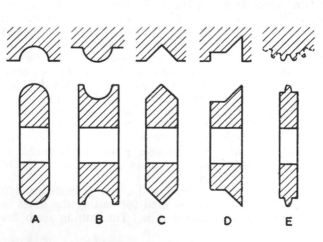

A   B   C   D   E

Fig. 178
A few typical types of form milling cutters. That shown at (E) is a gear cutter.

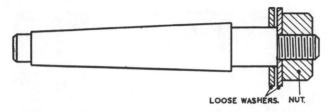

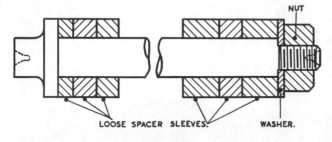

Fig. 179
Useful types of arbors for
use with circular cutters.

MORSE TAPER ARBOR.

CENTRES ARBOR.

tremely well to milling in the lathe, because the usual vertical slide set-up presents the work in an ideal manner for end mill operations. Such tools can, indeed, replace the orthodox circular cutter to a great extent, and may be found more convenient to use.

As a case in point, the pictures (Figs. 180 and 181) show similar jobs being undertaken by the two types of cutters. In Fig. 180 a step is being milled in a 'rectangular piece of metal, using a circular cutter, with the job mounted on the cross-slide of the lathe. It has been necessary to pack the work

they will, of course, cut a groove wider than the actual width of the tool.

End Mills

This form of tool lends itself ex-

Fig. 180
Milling a step in a workpiece packed and bolted to the lathe cross-slide.

Fig. 181
Milling a similar job to that shown in Fig. 180, using an end mill.

up with parallels to obtain the correct depth of cut. Fig. 181 shows the same job mounted on the vertical slide, with an end mill in operation. The absence of the somewhat awkward packing pieces will be noted, as the depth of cut can be regulated by adjustment of the slides. In this photograph it will be observed that the end mill has been plugged directly into the lathe mandrel, being provided with a taper shank for this purpose. The tool is also shown in Fig. 182 (A). The overhang of the tool is

thus much lessened, and the risk of "chatter" reduced to a minimum. When the tool is gripped in the chuck it is a surprisingly long way from the lathe mandrel! A parallel shank end mill is depicted at (B).

The tool (C) is known as a **counterbore,** which is an end mill with a short pilot shank attached. Its

Fig. 182
Typical end mills the uses of which are explained in the text.

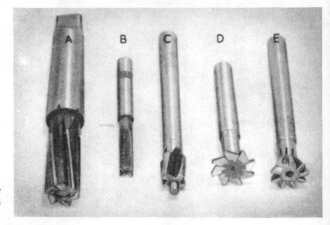

function is to cut a seating around a previously drilled hole. The pilot shank may be bushed to fit various sizes of holes, and the counterbore may, of course, be obtained in various diameters. The tool is also of use for counterboring in the drilling machine, as it is held steady by the pilot. The drawing (Fig. 183) shows a home-made counterbore which is simple to manufacture. A piece of silver steel of the required diameter is drilled to take the pilot spigot; the two cutting edges are then filed up by hand, and the tool hardened and tempered to medium straw colour.

At (D) in the photograph is pictured a **woodruff cutter** which gets its name from the fact that it is often

Fig. 184
Milling a " T " slot in the lathe. Note that a plain slot has first been milled.

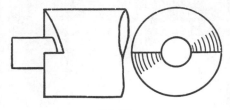

Fig. 183
Drawing of easily made counterbore end mill.

used to cut seatings for the semi-circular woodruff keys. One of its main uses, however, is for milling the undercuts in such things as " T " slots as used on machine tables. The procedure is shown in the picture (Fig. 184), where it will be seen that a plain slot is first milled across the job with an end mill. The cutter is seen entered for the undercut.

The final tool illustrated at (E) in Fig. 182, is a **60-deg. angle cutter,** such as would be used for milling the " V " slides of machine tools and instruments. The bulk of the metal is first removed with an end mill or side-and-face cutter, and the " V " grooves milled in afterwards. One

advantage of roughing out by end mill on the vertical slide is that both the roughing out and the finishing of the " Vs " can be done at the one setting.

It will be appreciated that the above selection of cutters is but a small proportion of those available; they have been presented rather as representative of their classes, and as indicating general methods rather than particular cases.

End mills may be run at higher speeds than is possible with other types of cutters. The actual speed depends upon the rigidity of the lathe and set-up, and upon the material being cut. Brass, aluminium and the like permit of higher speed than do steel and cast iron. The novice must, therefore, experiment to some extent until the best permissible speed is found.

Short drills, ground as shown at (E) in Fig. 77, Chapter 7, make excellent end mills, so that the amateur need never be at a loss for any special sizes.

Fly Cutters

Milling cutters are expensive items, and quite a small number may cost several pounds. Fortunately, this ever-present obstacle of £ s. d. can be partially overcome by the use of **fly cutters**, which are really single-toothed milling cutters. They are held in a boring bar such as is illustrated in Fig. 69 in Chapter 6.

In this drawing the cutter, as depicted, is suitable for the boring of plain holes, but it will be evident that if the tip of the cutter is shaped to a given profile any of the cutters shown in Fig. 178 may be simulated.

The fly cutter is suitable for almost any amateur work, its accuracy depending upon the skill of the amateur in shaping the profile. It lends itself particularly to the cutting of gears, as a finished gear of similar pitch may usually be found to act as a template to which the tool may be shaped.

Grinding accurate profiles by hand is a difficult job, and the amateur is well advised to make the cutter bits from soft cast or silver steel. They may be carefully filed to shape, backed-off and hardened.

Slotting with the Fly Cutter

In Fig. 129, Chapter 10, will be seen a set-up for boring a banjo plate. While the picture shows a round hole being bored with a boring bar and a fly cutter, it is obvious that were the job moved forward on successive cuts, by means of the cross-slide, an elongated hole or slot would be obtained.

The set-up is useful for milling large and deep slots through metal of

Fig. 185
Gang milling in the lathe Two identical cutters are mounted on a common arbor with spacing collar between.

any great thickness where an end mill of the required size would not be practicable.

Gang Milling

The operation of two or more circular cutters mounted upon a common arbor is known as **gang milling,** and an example is seen in Fig. 185. Here, two parallel flats are being milled on the end of a short stud-bolt, the cutters being spaced by a distance-piece of the appropriate length. The system is particularly applicable when a number of identical pieces are required, and it will be appreciated that form cutters and saws can be similarly used.

Sawing in the Lathe

With the exercise of a little ingenuity on the part of the amateur, the lathe can be converted into a most excellent circular-saw bench, capable of handling quite a large variety of work.

It is necessary that the saw be mounted upon an arbor running between centres, and that some form of slotted table be fixed to the cross-slide at a suitable height. Such an arrangement will be within the scope of the home mechanic.

A typical circular-saw bench is shown in Fig. 186, as supplied by one well-known lathe manufacturer. It has all the desirable features of design, including rise-and-fall, tilting table, and adjustable fence.

When sawing metal a medium or low speed of revolution is desirable, as considerable wear takes place on the saw if it is overrun. A cutting lubricant should be plentifully flooded over the work to keep the saw as cool as is possible.

Fig. 186

A most useful accessory, the saw table. This mounts on the lathe cross-slide, while the saw is spun on an arbor between centres.

(Courtesy Myford Eng. Co., Ltd.)

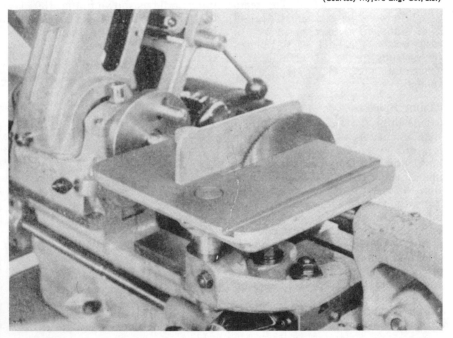

Fig. 187

The simple milling spindle (*left*) may be swivelled and adjusted for height. That shown on the right has direct or geared drive, and is most efficient for drilling from the cross-slide. Note the lever feed.

On the other hand, wood sawing requires that the saw be revolved at high speed. Small, metal cutting saws are not generally satisfactory for operation on wood, as the teeth have little or no " set ". The teeth of wood saws have a great deal of " set " in order to give plenty of clearance to the back of the blade. If this rubs in the cut great heat is generated and the saw rapidly spoiled.

Milling Spindles

Operating the tool from the cross-slide by means of a **milling spindle** is useful when the workpiece must have radial milling work carried out upon it, such as the milling of circular slots or the cutting of gearwheels. Thus, the milling cutter may be set in motion, and the work, on faceplate or chuck, revolved to give a circular groove, or if only partially revolved, a semi-circular groove. A groove is given only as an illustration as, of course, semi-circular profiles and the like may be worked.

Many types of milling spindles exist, some having rise-and-fall move-ments, and provision for belt tensioning by means of jockey pulleys. Useful as these somewhat elaborate arrangements are, it must not be overlooked that such a simple milling spindle as shown in Fig. 189 may be given a rise-and-fall movement by bolting it to the vertical slide. Various types of milling spindles are illustrated.

Fig. 188

An unusual type of milling attachment driven by worm and pinion gearing. A small cutter will be seen mounted on the shaft.

Fig. 189

Probably the simplest type of milling or drilling spindle, shown mounted for cutting a slot in a drive dog. The belt to the overhead drive is plainly seen.

The Overhead Drive

In Chapter 3 mention was made of the **overhead drive,** and we now come to its practical application. If the work is held in the headstock on the face-plate or in the chuck, and the cutter mounted in a spindle on the cross-slide, some means of revolving the cutter is necessary.

Fitting a separate motor to the milling spindle is not a proposition on small lathes, as the weight is apt to be excessive. The overhead drive provides a means of revolving the cutter by a belt—usually a round belt as used on sewing machines— and Fig. 189 shows such a drive applied to a simple milling and drilling spindle. A groove is being milled in a clutch dog.

It will be appreciated that some form of belt tensioning is necessary, so that the belt may keep tight when the milling spindle is raised or lowered. A spring-loaded arm, bearing a jockey pulley, is probably the most satisfactory method, but it is necessary that any such tensioning device must move with the milling spindle along the lathe bed if much movement is required. Fortunately, very little longitudinal movement is usually wanted, so that the stretch of the belt may often serve.

Dividing or Indexing

Radial work, such as the cutting of gearwheels, or the drilling of a series of holes on a set radius, obviously calls for some method of spacing the cuts. This leads to the important matter of **dividing,** or **indexing.**

There are manufactured, commercially, numerous appliances for this purpose; they are known as **dividing heads,** and while being ideal for the job, they are, unfortunately, expensive. Essentially, they consist of a worm-driven reduction gear arrangement, the movement of which is regulated by templates—called dividing plates—drilled with a number of series of spaced holes. No more than this may be said here, as the actual instructions for operation are somewhat complicated, and are usually provided by the manufacturer.

Most amateurs can, however, get along with simpler and cheaper methods, as the lathe offers a good selection of " dividing plates " in the shape of the lathe gear wheels.

The simplest method of using these is shown in Fig. 194, where the bull wheel on the lathe spindle is thus employed. A spring-loaded plunger is fixed by a bracket to the headstock, so that the plunger may be located between any of the gear teeth. These may be sub-divided into multiples of the whole, and quite a useful range of divisions is often provided. Probably the most useful wheel is one having 60 teeth.

Fig. 191

A commercial dividing head for attachment to a 3½-in. lathe. Indexing is obtained through a worm gear off a dividing plate. The attachment is shown mounted on a universal swivelling vertical slide.
(Courtesy Myford Eng. Co., Ltd.)

A Home-made Dividing Head

A very much greater range of divisions may, however, be obtained with the **lathe change wheels,** as these

Fig. 190

Practical application of milling in the lathe. Machining the hornblocks for a model locomotive.

Fig. 192

Another type of commercial dividing attachment shown in operation on a gearcutting job. Note the dividing plate on the left of the picture.

may be geared together in a train, in exactly the same manner as for screwcutting.

The illustration (Fig. 195) and the greatly reduced drawing (Fig. 196) show a simple divided head which is not beyond the powers of any model engineer to make, as it entails nothing more than plain turning operations. It consists of a casting, through which runs a spindle, screwed at the nose to take the lathe chucks, and bored to fit collets if these are available. One end of the spindle is keyed, so that any of the lathe change wheels may be attached to it, and will turn with it. A banjo is also provided, which may be swivelled and locked upon

the body, and which carries a number of adjustable studs, and collars similarly keyed so that any two change wheels may be mounted together. A spring-loaded plunger is also provided, and this may be located anywhere upon the slots in the banjo, and locked into position.

Method of Using

If Fig. 195 is studied, it will be seen that if a single gear wheel be mounted upon the spindle, and the plunger placed so that it will locate into the spaces between the gear teeth, a number of divisions equalling those of the gear wheel may be obtained by indexing in each space. Alternatively, the spaces on the gear wheel itself may be sub-divided, thus giving divisions in multiples of the gear teeth. For instance, a 40-tooth wheel might be indexed at every fourth tooth, thus giving 10 divisions. As explained earlier, lathe change wheels usually range upwards in steps of 5 teeth, starting at 20 teeth.

Similarly, any of the actual wheel divisions, or multiples thereof, may be doubled by gearing up the wheel in a 2 to 1 ratio. Gear trains of any magnitude may be used, governed only by the range of change wheels available. Thus, for instance, to index 250 divisions it is necessary only to gear up a 50-tooth wheel in a 5 to 1 ratio, locating the plunger in every space of the driver wheel.

This method alone will provide the amateur with a wide range of divisions, but there are still further possi-bilities. A concrete example will be demonstrated from the photograph in Fig. 195.

It has been assumed that it is desired to divide a workpiece into 18 equally spaced divisions. If we were to mount a 45-tooth wheel on the spindle, and index every fifth division, we should, of course, get 9 divisions; by gearing up the 45-tooth wheel in a ratio of 2 to 1, and indexing every fifth tooth on the driver wheel, the number of divisions would become 18 $\frac{(45 \times 2)}{5} = 18$). A 3 to 1 step-up would yield 27 divi-sions; a 4 to 1 would give 36 divi-sions, and so on. It will be seen that the dividing head in the picture is set up with a 45-tooth wheel on the spindle, a compound intermediate of 20-40, coupled with an idler wheel

Fig. 193
The well-equipped amateur may handle almost any job. Here we see an escapement wheel for a clock being cut on a small lathe, indexing being carried out from the lathe head.   (*Photo by K. N. Harris.*)

it has, of course, its limitations. The rule is: **the number of teeth on the spindle wheel must contain a multiple of the desired number.**

As a measure of the utility of this dividing head the photograph (Fig. 197) shows it mounted in the lathe for cutting a gearwheel of 72 teeth. It has been bolted to the vertical slide, thus giving universal movement. The cutter will be seen mounted on a taper-shank mandrel plugged into the head, while the gear blank is held in a collet in the dividing spindle. The method of obtaining the 72 divisions is interesting, and serves well to illustrate our point. The

for convenience in mounting the gears.

In this way the range is enormously increased. Let us take another example, and imagine that we require 21 divisions. We select for our spindle wheel a 35-tooth gear; if we index every fifth space we will obtain 7 divisions $\frac{(35}{5} = 7)$. By gearing up 3 to 1, and taking every fifth tooth on the driver wheel we do, of course, obtain our 21 divisions $\frac{(35 \times 3}{5} = 21)$. The wide scope of this method will be appreciated, yet

multiple of 72 which was chosen was 8. A 40-tooth wheel on the spindle, indexed every fifth tooth will yield this number. Thus, if it is geared 9 to 1 the 72 divisions are obtained. $(8 \times 9 = 72)$.

Wheels with a single ratio of 9 to 1 were not available, so two compound intermediates of 3 to 1 were selected. The first compound intermediate is 75—25, and the second is 60—20, indexing being carried out on every fifth tooth of the 60 wheel $\frac{(40 \times 3 \times 3}{5}$ $= 72)$. It will be seen that an idler wheel has been employed to link

M

the 40- and the 25-tooth wheels, but it does not, as was pointed out in Chapter 12, affect the gear ratios. As the 25-tooth wheel does, in fact, lie behind the 75-wheel it is not seen in the photograph. It is interesting to note that had the 60-tooth wheel been indexed every two teeth, 180 divisions would have been obtained, while indexing every tenth tooth would, of course, yield 36 divisions.

Sufficient has been said to show the method of using, and the utility of this device. The application of the set-up shown to the milling of flutes in home-made taps and reamers is a case in point.

Shaping in the Lathe

Shaping is a method of removing metal by a planing action, neither the work nor the tool being revolved.

Its application in the lathe is limited, as considerable strain is imposed on the machine, and planing or shaping operations should be carried out with discretion. Its use is, in fact, confined almost solely to the cutting of long keyways in shafts, and as such keyways are required from time to time the lathe is often called upon once more to prove its versatility.

The shaft should be firmly

Fig. 195
Home-made dividing head using the lathe change wheels. A vast number of division ranges may be obtained by gearing and compounding as in screwcutting. This novel device was made in the author's workshop.

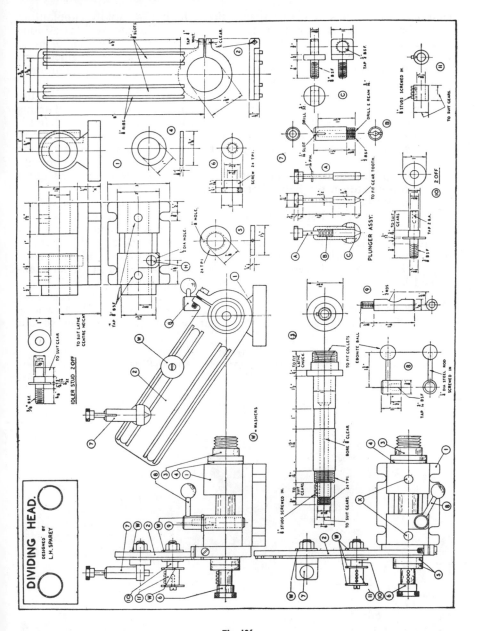

Fig. 196
Greatly reduced drawing of the home-made dividing head. The simple design puts it within the powers of even the beginner.

mounted in the chuck and supported by the back centre, and the mandrel locked by engaging the backgear wheels but leaving the bull wheel locked to the pulleys. Long work should also be supported by the travelling steady.

A parting tool is mounted in the toolpost, on its side, with the cutting edge facing the chuck. The lathe carriage is run along the bed by hand.

Small depth of cut is essential, and excessive pressure on the handwheel should never be exerted. It is also necessary that the tool should finish its cut off the job, or, if this is not possible, a hole should be drilled into which the tool may run. In Fig. 199 we see a keyway being shaped in this way.

Grinding in the Lathe

In professional engineering practice grinding is rapidly supplanting the old " finish turning " for all jobs where precision is required. A high, accurate finish can be obtained, and hardened parts used for jobs hitherto left soft.

Laudable as this practice is, the amateur cannot hope to emulate his professional brother, and " finish turning " must still be relied upon for most jobs. In spite of this, some work may, at times, call for grinding, a case in point being the truing-up of hardened lathe centres.

Grinding can, in fact, be carried out very well in the lathe, as it is necessary only to clamp some form of grinding spindle, with overhead drive, in the toolpost. My advice is, however, **never grind in the lathe unless it is absolutely necessary!** If you do, take the uttermost precautions against grit. All grinding wheels wear away a little in use, and should

Fig. 197
In action! Cutting a 72-tooth gearwheel with the home-made dividing head. Full operational instructions are given in the text.

to guard against this destructive demon, but there is no certain way to prevent grit from entering the bearings of a lathe!

The lathe bed may be somewhat protected by covering it up as much as possible with a large, damp cloth, and a similar cloth may be draped around the headstock. This is a difficult job, however, as there is danger of the cloth being caught up and whirled around the belt or spindle, when the grit will be most effectively deposited just where you do not want it.

any of this dust enter the bearings, or get beneath the slides, the days of the lathe are numbered.

Machines made for grinding purposes have special precautions, such as felt-packed bearing glands, telescopic covers, and overhung slides,

The foregoing may seem to present a somewhat gloomy outlook, but it is necessary as a warning to the

Fig. 200
Toolpost grinder constructed by the author. Plain, external-cone bearings, and ballraces, are combined in this design.

Fig. 199
Although the lathe has limited application for shaping purposes, quite useful jobs may be undertaken, such as the cutting of long keyways as shown here.

uninitiated. Grind if you must, but do as little of it as is possible.

The picture (Fig. 200) shows a home-made grinding spindle of the author's for attachment to the cross-slide of the lathe. No method of fixing is shown, as this may be left to the ingenuity of the amateur. One suggestion is that it be bolted to a sturdy, flat plate, with long " U " bolts, the plate having holes for the holding-down bolts. The spindle may be mounted at the centre height of the lathe, as it is never necessary to depart from this position. A drawing is also given in Fig. 202

Fig. 201
The parts of the toolpost grinder are well displayed in this picture. While essentially simple, accurate workmanship is necessary.

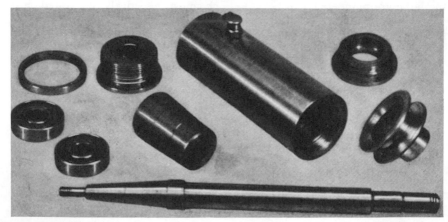

where it will be seen that the attachment is suitable for both internal and external grinding.

Small grinding wheels must be run at high speed to be efficient, about 5,000 r.p.m. is about the minimum, while 20,000 r.p.m., or more, is the ideal. A word of warning! Always clamp up the grinding wheel between two stout paper washers, placed between the wheel and the metal clamping washers, and do not tighten the clamping nut excessively. Neglect of these precautions may result in a burst wheel, and at 5,000 r.p.m. this is, to say the least, best avoided.

Before using the grinding wheel at any time true it up on its spindle with a diamond wheel-truer, to ensure balance and concentric running. If you have no diamond a piece of broken emery wheel, held against the revolving stone, will do almost as well.

Grinding calls for extremely light cuts—certainly not more than ·001 in. at a time. Best results are obtained when the wheel is only just touching the job. Grinding is for finishing work; not for roughing out.

The work to be ground should be revolved against the direction of the stone, at a speed of about 300 r.p.m. or thereabouts, depending on the diameter of the job. Always arrange the direction of rotation so that the grinding wheel is turning in such a manner that the sparks fly away from the operator. If you do not, and are not wearing goggles, you will get a great deal of grit in the eyes.

Making Small Grinding Wheels

Small grinding wheels may be made from the broken pieces of a larger wheel. After selecting a suitable piece of stone, a hole must first be made through it. This can be done quite simply, using the drilling machine and a suitable size of drill.

Fig. 203

One of the most useful accessories which the amateur can possess is a lathe filing jig, as shown here. By its aid accurate hexagon, square, triangular and other sections may be filed by hand.

The secret is to revolve the drill slowly, and to drill the stone by means of a series of smart blows applied by the drilling machine handle. This method of drilling, by means of tapping the work with the revolving drill, will yield clean, round holes through any grinding wheel.

The drilled fragment is now mounted on a suitable spindle, set up in the lathe and revolved at fast speed, when it may be trued by holding another piece of grindstone against the revolving stone.

Filing Jigs

While not, strictly speaking, connected with milling, shaping or grinding, the **filing jig,** as shown in Fig. 203, may aptly conclude this chapter.

The device is clamped to the cross-slide of the lathe, and is provided with two hardened rollers which serve as a guide for the file. Height adjustment is provided. It is invaluable for filing flats, hexagons, etc., on bar held in the lathe chuck. In operation the jig is brought up close to the work, adjusted for height to allow just the right depth of cut, and filing continued until the file rides squarely on the rollers. Some form of indexing of the lathe head—such as that shown in Fig. 194—is required for positioning the flats of triangular, square, hexagon or like sections.

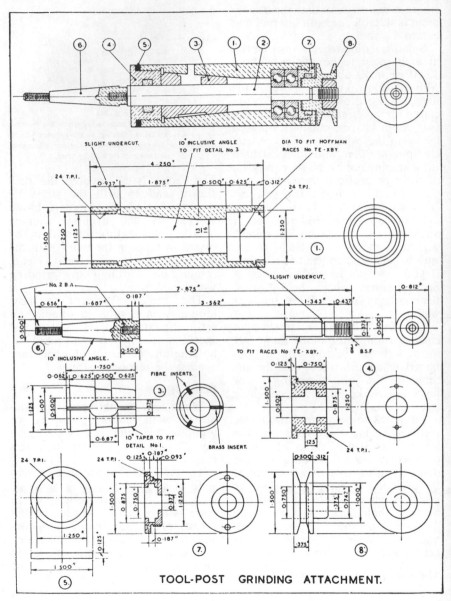

Fig. 202

Greatly reduced drawing of the toolpost grinding attachment. Methods of fixing to the lathe are suggested in the text.

CHAPTER 14

LAPPING

OF all the operations which a model engineer is called upon to perform from time to time, **lapping** is probably the one about which he knows least, and, in consequence, fears most. Being intimately connected with "fine limit" work, its difficulties have become in some measure exaggerated, principally because failure is the rule rather than the exception unless the correct methods are employed. The purposes of lapping are two-fold: first to obtain a good finish and, secondly, a good fit between two components—usually, in model engineering work, the cylinder and piston of steam or petrol engines, or piston-valves, and such like. Flat surfaces, such as steam-slide-valves and rotary-disc-valves for internal combustion engines, may also be lapped to a fit, but conical or spherical surfaces do not lend themselves to the process, for reasons which will be apparent later. Now, the terms good finish and good fit, in the sense in which we are employing them, are really the same thing. A good fit only means a perfect contact between two surfaces, so it is obvious that if the surfaces are not perfectly even, and free from valleys and high-spots—in other words, if the finish is not good—intimate contact cannot be achieved. Taking as an example one of the most common model-engineering "fits", that between the piston and cylinder of an internal combustion engine, it is often found that while the fit of the piston within the cylinder appears perfect, or even tight, there is a leakage of compression between the two. This inconsistency is known as a "false fit", and is due to one or both of two things. These are a bad finish on the mating surfaces or lack of circularity of the bore or piston. At the moment we are concerned only with the first, although it is true that correct lapping will have a great influence upon the second.

What is Lapping?

Confining our remarks, for the sake of simplicity, to the case of the cylinder and piston cited above, lapping may be described as the finishing of the bore upon a prepared mandrel or "lap", which is revolved at high speed, using an abrasive as a cutting agent. Similarly, the piston is finished in an "external-lap" (sometimes called a "female-lap"), which is also revolved and used with an abrasive in the same manner. It may be pointed out that many model engineers believe that lapping means the actual mating together with a fine abrasive of the piston and cylinder; that is, the lapping of the piston itself within the cylinder. Although, strictly speaking, the term does cover this condition, results are seldom or never satisfactory, because if the fit between the two components is to be of a high degree of accuracy, there is not room for the usual types of abrasive used. In practice, however, by taking the right precautions, a very limited amount of intimate lapping can be done satisfactorily, as will be explained later.

Laps

Although there are many kinds of

Fig. 204
Common types of laps:
(*top*) plain laps, (*centre*)
truing laps, (*lower*) expanding laps, showing
wedge.

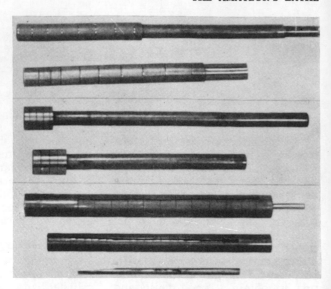

laps, we will, for the sake of simplicity, confine ourselves at the moment to only two—the **plain-lap** and an efficient **expanding-lap**, which, used intelligently, will cover all our needs. These are for cylindrical lapping, and are of both internal and external types. Taking first the plain internal laps (two of which are shown in Fig. 204), it will be seen that these are just plain, cylindrical pieces of metal, into which a series of rings have been turned. These rings are to hold the lapping compound, and do, to a limited degree, prevent the lapping compound from accumulating at the ends of the lap, due to the reciprocating movement of lapping. It will be appreciated that these plain laps must be absolutely parallel and circular in the first place.

Truing-Laps

Two of these are illustrated in our picture (Fig. 204), and it will be noted that they are identical with the plain laps just described, except that they are shorter in length. Their purpose is to true up bores which have become constricted in places during the lapping process.

Expanding Laps

In our third picture (Fig. 204) will

Fig. 205
Drawing of simple expanding
lap.

be seen a highly successful type of expanding lap—probably the most useful of all. Those shown in the picture are of copper rod. Reference to the drawing (Fig. 205) will indicate that these copper rods are capable of expansion by forcing the internal wedge into the longitudinal slot. The method of making is as follows:

The piece of copper rod selected should be at least four times the length of the component which it is intended to lap, and of such a diameter that it is an easy slide fit within the prepared bore. Chuck the rod in the lathe, and, with a sharp-pointed tool, turn a series of shallow rings at about half-inch distances along the rod. Selecting a drill about one-third the diameter of the rod, drill the rod from one end as deeply as possible, preferably about half its length. Now remove

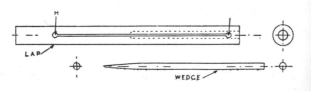

from the lathe and drill the two holes (H) (H) right through the diameter of the rod. At one end, in fact, a series of holes may be drilled close together, so as to provide a "start" for a hacksaw blade. The longitudinal slot may now be made, cutting right through the rod from one hole to another. It will be noted that there is a short plain portion left at one end; this is to grip in the chuck when lapping.

Fig. 206
External split laps with wedges.

The wedge consists of a piece of silver-steel, which is a slide fit in the longitudinal hole. One end of the silver-steel is filed into a wedge shape, so that when inserted into the rod the wedge will register into the slot. Thus, by tapping the wedge farther into the lap, expansion of the lap will take place.

It will be recognised, of course, that, as this expansion occurs, the lap will bulge slightly in the middle, and will, in effect, be barrel shaped. Provided that the lap is not expanded beyond legitimate limits—that is, that the whole lap is not too small for the intended bore—this barreling will be found to be an advantage, as, by careful use, a bore which is tending to become out of parallel may be corrected by applying the "tight" portion of the lap to the constricted place in the bore.

External or Female Laps

To ensure that a piston, for instance, is truly circular, parallel, and of high finish, lapping is almost essential in the home workshop, where expensive grinding or honing machines are rare. For this purpose the external laps shown in Figs. 206 and 207 will be required. Those in the photograph are of cast iron. The bore should be made a slide fit on the component to be lapped, and sufficient thickness should be left in the lap walls. This is necessary because three slots have to be milled or sawn

down the length of the lap, as shown in the illustrations. One of these slots cuts right through into the bore of the lap, as indicated at (A) in Fig. 207. The other two, however, only penetrate to half the thickness of the wall (B) and (C). Their object is to provide some degree of flexibility, so that the lap may be expanded by the small, steel wedge illustrated. On cutting the lap through at (A) it will always be found that the lap closes up sometimes to quite a considerable degree, so that the wedge is necessary to enable the lap to embrace the workpiece easily.

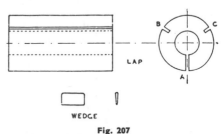

Fig. 207
Drawing of external laps shown in Fig. 206

It will be as well here to issue a word of warning about the small wedge. This should be made so that it is **below the outside of the lap** when in position, and the corners should be well rounded off with a file. Laps may sometimes jam on the work, especially if one attempts to enter or remove the lap while the work is in motion. Should this happen while the lap is gripped in the hand, a serious wound may result if the above precautions are neglected.

Materials from which laps should be made will, of course, vary with the material of the job. Broadly speaking, the lap material should be softer than that of the workpiece; for instance, steel should be lapped with a copper or cast-iron lap, and even brass or aluminium may be used. For cast-iron bores use copper or brass, and for brass or gunmetal bores use either copper or aluminium. It is sometimes recommended that a **lead** lap should be used, but the writer has always found these most unsatisfactory. There is an extreme tendency for lead laps to tear up and seize in the bore, resulting in deep scores in the work, and a ruined job.

Abrasives

The question of abrasives has been so thoroughly gone into by commercial firms that there is, to-day, a correct cutting compound for every type of material. Most of these firms are usually only too willing to assist the model engineer with advice. There is no doubt that the use of the correct lapping compound makes smooth the path.

Two easily obtained materials which have given satisfaction in the home workshop are fine valve grinding paste, and metal polish. These, with the addition of jeweller's rouge and white lead, will tackle almost any model engineering job.

When using "loose" abrasives such as these, it is highly important that the abrasive be all removed from the job after lapping, or when changing from one abrasive to a finer one. Any trace left in the finished job will continue to cut when the job is assembled, and the running

life will be about nil! Scrub the work out with paraffin oil, then again in **clean** paraffin oil. Finally, the work should be again scrubbed out with hot water and soap. Finishing with white lead and oil, before the cleaning processes, helps to "pick up" any loose abrasive.

Because of this cleaning difficulty many experienced engineers do not use a "loose" abrasive, but employ what is called a "charged lap". Here, the lap is rolled in dry abrasive powder such as diamond dust or flour emery, between two steel plates, so that the powder becomes embedded in the lap. It is then carefully wiped down, and all surplus powder removed. Although entailing a little more work, this is probably the safest method, as the danger of the cutting compound entering the pores of the lapped metal is much reduced. A roughing lap charged with Oakey's knife powder and lubricated with paraffin oil is very successful. Similarly, a lap charged with the finest grade of **crocus powder** lubricated with paraffin oil, or even used dry, gives a high, "safe" finish. Diamond dust, which may be obtained from any large engineers' warehouse, is the best of all, but is, of course, expensive. Very little is required, however, and a couple of "pinches", if carefully preserved, will last a lifetime. A lap charged with diamond dust, and used dry, gives the finest finish of all; furthermore, the lap does not tend to be worn away.

Operation

It must be understood that lapping is a finishing process, and that it is not intended as a means of removing large amounts of metal, nor for truing up bores which are badly tapered or out of round. The bore to be lapped, therefore, should be as good as it is possible to produce.

The bore should be carefully finished on the lathe to a plug-gauge about 0·004 in. smaller than a finishing reamer. Model engineers usually find no difficulty in accommodating the size of their bores to reamer size, and designs for petrol engines and the like should be made with this in view. When putting through the reamer, support it with a centre in the tailstock, and allow the reamer' to "float"—that is, to take its own course—as this will tend to keep the reamer from cutting taper. Do not stop the lathe until the reamer is withdrawn again.

Now make an accurate plug-gauge, 0·002 in. larger than the reamered hole. This gauge need be only about ⅜ in. long, with rounded edges. This should be the size of our finished bore. We may now proceed to lap, using, at first, a **plain** lap charged with fine valve-grinding paste and oil. Revolve the lap at the fastest lathe speed, and, grasping the job in the hand, run it up and down the lap, twisting the wrist with a "half-turn" motion as the work is run up and down. Continue this in moderation until all reamer marks are removed. Now wash the job thoroughly in paraffin oil.

We may now take the expanding lap, and adjusting it for size, proceed to lap the job with metal polish until a high-class finish has been produced. Continue this fine lapping until the plug-gauge will just enter one or both ends. Owing to the imperceptible rocking movement which always takes place when lapping, and to the building-up of the lapping compound at each end of the stroke, bores invariably become slightly **bell-mouthed.** For this reason it is often desirable to make the job half an inch or so longer than required, and to turn off the ends afterwards. Presuming that the plug-gauge now just

enters, replace the expanding lap by a short, **truing-lap,** and, using metal polish, lap out the tight parts of the bore until the plug-gauge will just push tightly through. We are now somewhere near parallel. We must now replace the expanding lap in the chuck, and adjusting for size, carefully lap for a few moments with **metal polish and oil.** Keep the lap rather on the tight side, and try to lap evenly over the tightest portion. You will feel the job slightly gripping as you pass over the highest point of the lap. Continue in this manner until the plug-gauge enters and slides smoothly through the bore. Remember, however, that the job must be thoroughly washed in paraffin, and then soap and water, before trying the gauge at any time. Finally, remove all traces of the metal polish from the lap, and charge it with white-lead and oil. This will produce a very high finish indeed.

Lapping the piston proceeds in the same manner; the piston having been turned to within 0·002 in. of finished size. In this case, however, the job is revolved in the lathe, and the lap held in the hand. Reduce the size of the piston with fine grinding paste until it is just too tight to enter the bore, then lap with metal polish until a good, slide-fit is obtained. Please observe the thorough washing process before every trial for fit. When the job is considered satisfactory, place a tiny smear of jeweller's rouge on the piston, flood copiously with oil, and lap the piston up and down within the bore a few times by hand. Finally, scrub all parts well in hot water and soap, and assemble with plenty of oil.

For successful results the job and the lap must be kept in relative movement to each other apart from the ordinary rotation; hence the reciprocating and twisting-hand movements used. With taper forms, however, this movement cannot be imparted, resulting in the building up of lapping compound at certain spots. This causes grooves to appear in the job, besides causing the male and female tapers to assume different angles. Very slight hand-lapping with fine abrasive material can, however, be indulged in on conical surfaces, provided that care is taken not to overdo it.

Parallel Laps

It will be appreciated that the expanding lap of Fig. 205 does not remain parallel when the wedge is driven in, but assumes a barrel shape. It may seem to be somewhat of an anomaly that a barrel-shaped lap should be used to produce a parallel hole, but from a good experience of this type of lap I can assure readers that it is not. The lap has been used principally for the finishing of cylinder bores for model petrol and diesel engines, which, with the latter species at any rate, is an exacting type of work.

Under certain conditions it is probable that a consistently parallel expanding lap may be a better proposition, provided that one has the skill necessary to produce a tool which will really remain parallel in all conditions. This is not so easy as it may seem, as some

Fig. 208
Alternative types of expanding laps, designed to remain parallel on expansion. See text for full particulars.

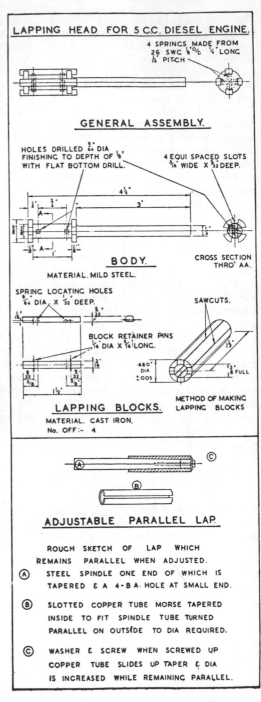

very precise machining of the internal parts of the lap is required.

The matter will be amplified by a glance at the lap shown at the bottom of the drawing in Fig. 208. It will be seen that expansion is attained by means of a male taper sliding within a female taper. Accuracy of parallelism depends entirely upon a perfect mating of the two tapers, as the slightest disparity will cause one end of the lap to expand more than the other. Making two such perfect tapers is not a simple job, yet, if the difficulties can be overcome, the arrangement forms a very efficient lap.

Fig. 209

Flat lapping-plate of cast iron. The diagonal grooving retains the lapping compound.

The lapping head shown at the top of the drawing (Fig. 208), though dimensioned for a specific size of bore, may, of course, be proportioned for any other sizes. Its novelty lies in the fact that it is self-expanding, the grinding surfaces of the lap being pressed against the work by internal springs. Although more complicated than the previous lapping head, this self-expanding tool is probably more easy to make accurately, but careful turning and milling are required.

The greatest snag, however, with parallel laps is that they pre-suppose a perfectly parallel bore in the first place; a thing very difficult to achieve with the limited and often inaccurate tools at the disposal of the amateur. Even a reamered hole is, more often than not, out of parallel, it being quite usual to find that the end of the bore from which the reamer was entered is slightly larger than the other end.

Flat Lapping

Flat, lapped surfaces are often wanted for slide-valve seatings, rotary disc valves and the like.

The illustration in Fig. 209 shows a **lapping plate,** consisting of a stout piece of cast iron, one surface of which is machined flat. Across the surface is cut a number of diagonal, parallel lines; these retain the lapping compound.

In operation, the plate is smeared with a suitable abrasive and the job rubbed over the plate, using a firm, even pressure. The rubbing motion should be in the form of a large figure "8", and the direction of rotation changed from time to time. This particular form of movement helps to ensure that each part of the lapped surface has an even pressure applied to it. If a straight up-and-down, or across movement, or a circular movement is used, it is probable that certain parts of the job will be cut down more than others.

CHAPTER 15

METAL SPINNING, SPRING WINDING, TURNING RUBBER, ETC.

THIS chapter will be devoted to some unusual jobs which the amateur may from time to time encounter. It is, in fact, just such "odd" knowledge as this which adds so enormously to the scope and versatility of the amateur's lathe.

Metal Spinning

Many forms of work which might in the usual run be turned from the solid are often easier to make, and more economical of material, if made from sheet metal. Typical examples are tubular petrol tanks for model petrol engines, metal lids, and flanged cover plates. Such simple forms, provided that they have not too deep a "draw", may be made by the amateur turner by the process of **spinning.** Essentially,

Fig. 210

The simple components required for spinning in the lathe. (A) formed chuck; (B) pressure pad; (C) material to be spun; (D) metal lid spun by the methods outlined in this chapter.

this process consists of shaping a disc of sheet metal over a prepared **former,** by means of pressure applied while the job is revolving in the lathe.

Metal spinning is a highly skilled art, and it is not pretended that the raw amateur may even approach the wonderful and beautiful work turned out by the professional spinner; nevertheless, simple forms are quite within the average capacity, if a few rules are observed.

At (D) in Fig. 210 may be seen a flanged metal lid, such as presents a typical example of simple metal spinning in aluminium, brass or copper. At (C) may be noted the disc from which such a lid would be formed. (A) indicates the metal "chuck", which is simply a piece of brass or steel, faced-off, and turned to the internal diameter of the lid. The component at (B) is a **pressure-pad,** such as we have already encountered for the turning of blank discs.

The photograph in Fig. 211 shows the assembly mounted up for spinning operations, and it will be observed that the metal disc (C) is clamped tightly between the formed chuck (A) and the pressure-pad (B). Pressure is applied from the tailstock through a revolving-centre (D). A plain centre may be used, in which case it must be well lubricated.

Clamped in the toolpost will be seen a **spinning-rest.** This comprises a stiff, steel bar into which two $\frac{1}{4}$-in. steel pegs have been driven, spaced about $\frac{5}{8}$ in. apart. The pegs provide

Fig. 211

Set-up for metal spinning. (A) formed chuck; (B) pressure pad; (C) metal disc; (D) running centre, highly suitable for spinning purposes. Note the spinning rest clamped in toolpost.

a fulcrum against which the **spinning-tool** may be levered on to the work.

The drawing (Fig. 212) depicts the spinning-tool. This should be made from cast or silver steel, hardened and tempered, and the rounded end given an extremely high polish. The better the polish the better and easier the work.

From the picture (Fig. 211) the modus operandi becomes obvious. The lathe is set to spin at high speed, and the overlapping portion of the aluminium disc is spun over the formed chuck. One or two technicalities must, however, be observed.

First, the metal disc must be soft; that is, it must be annealed. To anneal brass and copper it is necessary to make the metal red hot and to plunge it immediately into cold water, but aluminium should not be heated quite red. The action of coercing the metal to shape tends to harden it again, so that it may be necessary to remove it from the chuck at certain stages and re-anneal. This is most

important, as metal which is toughening up cannot be spun satisfactorily.

During the process of spinning, **soap** must be used as a lubricant between the work and the tool. If the job is allowed to become "dry" tear-ups and scratches may result.

Spinning technique is more a matter of experience than of instruction, but one important point should be noted. Always start to exert the tool pressure **from the outer edge of the disc.** If pressure is

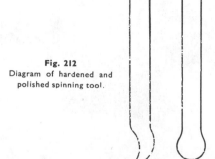

Fig. 212

Diagram of hardened and polished spinning tool.

N

first applied from the "corner" of the job it will be found that the metal will spread, and that folds will form which are often impossible to remove. It must be remembered that, in addition to shaping the metal, spinning also thins and spreads it, and this must be allowed for when selecting the gauge of sheet. With deep "draws" the metal thins out perceptibly.

This consideration is apt to cause miscalculation of the size of the disc necessary for any given job, the amateur invariably making the disc too large. No specific formula can be given for the calculation of exact size as this depends on the shape of the work, the depth of the draw, and the gauge and type of metal. Nevertheless, the amateur will be on guard against over estimation, as too much metal allowance causes folds to develop, and makes the job unworkable. On the other hand, metal which is a little tight on allowance can usually be spread to the required size, at the sacrifice of a little thickness.

When the job has been satisfactorily spun to shape, it will be found that the edge is ragged and irregular. This edge may be trued-up with a parting tool while the work is still held on the chuck. Similarly, any polishing may also be done while thus mounted.

Winding Springs

Most of us have, at various times, wound small springs upon the lathe, and the job has appeared so simple that it would seem that little could be said upon the subject. However, most things have the knack of being not so simple as they would appear and there is a right and a wrong way of doing almost everything. Winding springs is no exception. Of course, simple helical springs of no definite diameter or pitch (yes! springs have a pitch, just like a screw thread) may be run off on the lathe by running the spring wire along a piece of rod by hand, but if springs of a certain diameter and pitch are required—such as compression springs which must fit within a tube— something better than this haphazard method is required.

As will be seen in the illustration (Fig. 213) the tools are of the simplest kind, namely, a piece of stout steel bar, which may be gripped in the

Fig. 213

Set-up for winding springs. The lathe is put into the screwcutting gear nearest to pitch of spring.

toolpost, and a length of suitable mild-steel rod. Through the bar a hole must be drilled through which the wire may run, and a similar hole must be drilled through the round rod, to serve as an anchorage for the end of the wire. In the picture, the wire will be seen protruding through this hole. The loose end of the wire is held in the hand, and the coil allowed to lie upon the floor. Everything must be done to see that nothing will impede the steady movement of the wire, as a sudden catch up will not only spoil the spring, but may be dangerous if the wire suddenly breaks.

The first thing to determine when winding springs is the ·diameter that we require the finished product to be, and to attain this with any certainty when released from the mandrel is not an easy matter. All springs will expand to a greater or lesser degree, the amount depending upon the gauge of wire used, its quality, and the tightness with which it has been wound. Fortunately, by holding the wire in the hand while winding, an average tightness is soon acquired. As a guide, for 20 s.w.g. or under, the finished spring will expand in diameter approximately twice that of the mandrel upon which it is wound. Thus, if a half-inch diameter spring is required, the mandrel used should be of one-quarter inch diameter.

When using wire of greater gauge than this, it may be anticipated that the expansion will not be so great, and mandrels of slightly larger diameters in proportion to the finished size may be used, until, when working with gauges of around No. 12 or No. 14, the expansion will be judged to be an amount equal to about twice the diameter of the wire used. Thus, a mandrel will be chosen of a diameter twice the gauge of the wire smaller than the desired spring.

In any case, a little experiment will soon determine the exact size of mandrel to be used, and it is very rarely that the spring diameter is of importance to a few thousandths of an inch.

Having threaded the end of the wire through the hole in the rectangular bar, it should be pushed through the hole in the mandrel, and bent so as to provide an anchorage. Now, set the lathe up in screw-cutting gear corresponding as near as possible to the gauge of the wire used. For instance, should No. 16 gauge wire be used, set the screw-cutting gears to sixteen to the inch; for No. 20 gauge wire set to twenty to the inch, and so on. Then wind on the first few turns by revolving the chuck by hand, so as to take up the slack and, grasping the loose wire firmly, switch on the power. Of course you will have seen that the lathe is put into its slowest back-gear. In this manner a perfect tension spring will be produced.

For compression springs: that is, for those having the coils spaced widely apart, the same procedure is adopted, except that the screw-cutting gear is set up to the desired pitch of the spring, irrespective of the gauge of wire being used. Often it is important that the pitch be exact, especially when making a spring to replace one already broken, as the pitch of the spring greatly determines the power which it exerts.

Another thing to watch, in special cases, is the direction in which the spring is wound, that is, whether the spring is wound **clockwise** or **anti-clockwise**. This is often of great importance, as in those cases where a spring encircles a revolving shaft, the tension holding a clutch into position. Many such instances are to be met with in engineering practice, and should the spring be wound in the wrong direction for the rotation

Fig. 214

An awkward job made easy. Turning rubber components in the small lathe. (A) rubber typewriter feet; (B) rubber motor mountings; (C) rubber collars for feed shaft; (D) two rubber-turning tools of different diameters.

of the shaft, it will tend to unwind as it revolves. The direction of winding is determined by that in which the lathe is revolved: a left-hand spring requiring that the lathe be spun in reverse. In the illustration the spring shown is a right-hand helical tension spring.

It must be clearly understood that home-made springs cannot equal those made by specialists with the correct equipment. Making springs from spring steel wire which has already been hardened and tempered cannot give the same results, because if the wire can be wound easily into a spiral, it can just as easily be straightened again. Commercial springs are wound while the wire is soft, and then hardened and tempered in the final form, which is such a tricky business that the home mechanic is not advised to try to make springs in this way. Nevertheless, those which he may wind from spring wire will be quite suitable for most purposes. Spring steel wire of good quality should be always used, as the soft stuff is useless. Useful springs may also be wound from

bronze wire, and these are suitable for such purposes as the pressure springs used on some types of commutator brushes.

In conclusion, always take care especially in the matter of ensuring that the wire cannot catch up during operations. A flying end of a piece of spring wire can be dangerous!

Turning Rubber and Leather

Rubber is such untractable material that it is not generally appreciated that it can be turned to a definite shape and size on the ordinary lathe. The desirability of turning rubber is often felt for such things as bottle stoppers, sealing rings, and rubber feet for clocks and instruments, yet most of us have been unsuccessful in our attempts! This is because rubber cannot be turned by orthodox methods, but requires special tools and technique of its own.

The illustration (Fig. 214) shows several rubber articles turned by the writer. Those at (A) are a pair of rubber feet for the typewriter upon which this chapter was typed! (B) shows two motor mountings made for a friend, while (C) shows three rubber collars made for the paper-rollers of a recording machine.

Unfortunately, rubber cannot be turned in the same manner as metal, that is, by means of a tool held in the toolpost of the lathe. The special tools indicated at (D) in the photograph must be used. These consist of pieces of steel, bored to an internal diameter equal to the outer diameter of the desired job. The walls of these tubes are as thin as possible, and the edges are sharpened. For casual work it is not necessary that these tools be hardened.

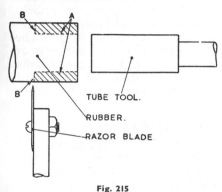

Fig. 215
Method of turning rubber with the tools shown in Fig. 214.

The method of operation may best be conveyed by citing an actual job, so we will instance the rubber feet (A) in Fig. 214. From the drawing (Fig. 215) let us follow the sequence of operations. In this instance the piece of rubber was gripped lightly in the three-jaw chuck, and this method of holding is satisfactory for the majority of work. Thin sheet rubber, from which sealing rings may be made, should be stuck to a smooth piece of wood with rubber solution, and the wood then mounted on the face-

plate. The lathe is revolved at the highest speed, and the larger tool fed in from the tailstock to the appropriate depth (Cut A). Without withdrawing the tube-tool from the work, a knife-blade tool is fed in from the toolpost, until it just contacts the tube-tool. On withdrawing the tube-tool the whole of the portion shown shaded in the drawing is drawn off also, in the form of a tube. The larger diameter is thus obtained.

The large tool is now replaced by the smaller one. This is also fed into the job in exactly the same manner as before, the knife tool inserted, and a smaller rubber tube cut off. Thus, the two diameters and the step are formed, and it remains only to part off the larger diameter to length.

Considerable heat is generated during the process, as the friction on the tube-tool is considerable. The tool and job must be plentifully flooded with **plain, cold water** as a lubricant.

An excellent knife tool can be formed by bolting a broken safety-razor blade to a steel shank. The object of leaving the tube-tool entered in the job during the parting-off process is to prevent the parting cut from being made too deeply. Leather and similar materials may all be turned successfully by the above methods.

It is interesting to note that tube-tools, provided with a saw edge, can be used for cutting discs from wooden boards, and similar materials. For casual use great precision of tooth form is not required, and the saw teeth can be filed by hand with a triangular file such as is used for sharpening saws. The teeth can then be "set" with a pair of pliers; each alternate tooth in opposite direction.

CHAPTER 16

PRODUCTION METHODS IN SMALL LATHES

THE speedy production of large numbers of identical parts in engineering practice has become so associated with the capstan and automatic lathe that it is not generally appreciated that the ordinary centre-lathe is, even now, used extensively in industry for this purpose.

" Production Turners "

So much is this so that there exist a large number of lathe operators, known in the trade as "production turners", who earn quite a good living by mass-producing small details on the ordinary lathe.

The reason why such work is always in demand, even by manufacturers who own large numbers of capstan and automatic lathes, is that these machines are not an economic proposition unless the "run", as it is called, numbers many thousands of identical parts. Unless the production quantity is to be high, the time and trouble spent in setting up a capstan or automatic machine is too great, especially if special cams are required for the automatics. Thus, any parts numbering less than about two or three thousand are usually made by production turners, whose specialised knowledge of this type of work enables them to produce the parts at a speed and cheapness which are truly amazing. Instances of this chiefly occur in the manufacture of specialised machines, with a limited market.

It sometimes occurs in the home workshop that the model engineer is called upon to make a number of identical parts—sometimes, as is the case with scale nuts and bolts, running into many hundred—and the amateur may quite often be puzzled as to the quickest and most precise method of making them. Many of the tricks used by the professional production-turner may here be used to good account, especially as many of them require only the very simplest of accessories. Most of the methods embody the use of improvised "stops", so that once the correct distances and measurements have been found, the lathe may be operated against these stops, in exactly the same manner as a capstan lathe.

A Practical Example

For the sake of illustration it may be simpler to take as an instance a specific job, so let us refer to Fig. 216, which is a photograph of some details made by the writer by the methods to be described. We will, therefore, fix upon that detail marked (A) in the illustration. This component is of brass, and was made for a friend who wanted 120 of them for a special purpose; a plus-minus limit of $\cdot001$ was allowed. The whole lot was made in less than a day. As may be seen, the detail consists of a turned body, a turned step, and a screwed shank; while at the other end are milled two opposing flats with a hole drilled through.

The first step was to obtain brass rod of the required diameter—$\frac{5}{8}$ in. in this instance. This was the finished outside size, so that an operation was saved here. Next step was to part off 120 pieces dead to length, with a few extra lengths as spares. Parting off

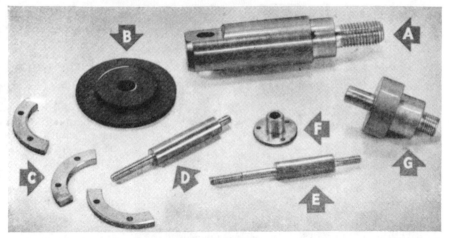

Fig. 216

Some production parts made by the methods outlined in this chapter. (A) Special fitment (120 off). (B) Commutator bush in fibre for small electric motor (50 off). (C) Commutator segments (150 off). (D) Spacing posts. (E) Spacing posts (200 off). (F) Bearing bush (100 off). (G) Armature bush (50 off).

brings us to a consideration of the gadget shown in Fig. 217. This is simply a taper sleeve with a piece of turned steel inserted rigidly into it. This forms a stop, which is inserted into the tailstock barrel. We may now turn to Fig. 218, which shows the parting off process. The tailstock and barrel are clamped up hard at a convenient distance from the chuck, the brass stock is pulled forward until it bears hard against the end of the stop. The parting tool is now moved into position so that it will part off to exact length, trial-and-error methods being used. As will be readily understood, as one piece is parted off, it is necessary only to

release the chuck, pull forward the brass rod until it touches the stop, and insert the parting tool; and so on, until all the pieces are obtained. It will be obvious, of course, that the position of the parting tool is not altered along the bed of the lathe during the whole of these operations; in fact, if some means of locking the carriage to the bed is provided on the lathe it should be used. We now have our 120 lengths of brass rod, which should be checked occasionally as parting off proceeds, to see that correct length is being maintained. A remarkable degree of accuracy can be attained.

Referring again to the detail in Fig.

Fig. 217
Stop for mandrel or tailstock.

Fig. 218
Parting-off to identical length
against stop held in tailstock
barrel.

pieces are gripped in the chuck, they will, being all of the same length, protrude an equal amount in every case.

We may now take a trial workpiece, insert it into the chuck, and tighten up, making sure that it is

216, the next process is to turn the two smaller diameters—one of which is threaded. For this purpose we require two "stops", which are simply made from two lengths of the brass rod. Part off two pieces about 5 in. long, and square off the ends. Now measure the length of the largest diameter step; actually it is $\frac{5}{16}$ in. long, so now proceed to reduce the length of one of the brass stops until it is exactly $\frac{5}{16}$ in. shorter than the other.

pressed hard up against the internal stop meanwhile. Then take the shortest stop-rod, rest it on the lathe bed, and move the lathe carriage until the stop is clamped tightly between the carriage and the head casting of the lathe. This operation may be seen in Fig. 219. We may now proceed to turn the brass down to the diameter of the step, keeping the lathe carriage pressed firmly against the stop, and **moving the tool only by**

Now remove the stop, shown in Fig. 217, from the tailstock, and plug it into the lathe mandrel, leaving the chuck in position. This forms a stop behind the chuck jaws, so that when the work-

Fig. 219
Distance stop placed between
headstock and lathe carriage
to determine length of cut.

means of the topslide. When the correct diameter has been reached, the reading on the cross-slide dial should be noted, and marked with chalk, so that the position may be again duplicated. Then, by means of the topslide only, continue to turn back until the correct length of the larger step has been reached.

It will now be obvious that, provided we do **not now touch the topslide,** we may, by registering on our cross-slide dial, always attain a duplicate diameter, and that, by moving the whole lathe carriage by

the first diameter, the other will locate for the second diameter. All that is now necessary is to insert the longer stop-bar between the carriage and the head, and turn the hand-wheel until the carriage is hard up against it. This will, of course, only allow the tool to cut to a distance of $\frac{5}{16}$ in. shorter than the first stop-bar, that being, you remember, the difference in their lengths. The top-slide is not moved during this second operation.

The above description may seem a little complicated, but it is not really

Fig. 220
Set-up for making small screws, using inverted parting-off tool on rear of cross-slide.

means of the handwheel until it presses firmly up against the stop-bar, also attain a duplicate length of cut; so that we are now set up for doing the first diameter step. However, we also require another diameter, upon which to die the $\frac{5}{16}$ in. B.S.F. thread.

Removing the first stop-bar, proceed to turn down the job to $\frac{5}{16}$ in. diameter for a short distance, making a second chalk mark on the cross-slide dial to indicate this diameter also. We have now two marks on the dial; one will advance the tool to cut

so. A great many words are required to describe simple operations, which, in practice, are automatic. Essentially, the operations are simply those of setting the cross-slide to two correct diameters, and inserting stop-rods between the carriage and the headstock casting, so that predetermined lengths of cut may always be attained. The topslide is merely used for positioning the tool in relationship to the stop-bar in the first place. The cutting of the thread by means of a tailstock die holder need not be described.

Milling and Sawing Processes

The milling of the detail (A) in Fig. 216, followed the **gang-milling** process already described in Chapter 13. The illustration (Fig. 185) is, in fact, a picture of this very component being milled. True parallelism of the milled faces is thus ensured, and the depth of cut is regulated by duplicating the setting of the cross-slide index scale. By working on these and similar lines, a variety of repetition milling and sawing jobs may be accomplished. A case in point is shown by the commutator segments marked (C) in Fig. 216. These segments were first parted off as a ring, the holes jig-drilled, and then sawn into three parts in the lathe. As a sawing jig, a flat piece of metal was used, having two pins driven into it to locate in the drilled holes. This jig was clamped to the cross-slide of the lathe, and a small circular saw mounted on a mandrel in the chuck. Sawing was done by advancing the cross-slide, and positioning the pins upon different holes for each of the three cuts. The model engineer will readily see various applications of these systems.

Making Small Screws

Of all the tedious jobs which the model maker is called upon to perform, probably the making of a large quantity of small screws (or nuts) is the worst. By using simple production methods, however, even this undertaking may be relieved and even made interesting, as there is something very satisfactory about a machining set-up which is working well.

The photograph (Fig. 220) shows an improvised set-up for this job, which calls for no special equipment other than that found in the usual amateur kit. Simply, the set-up consists of a tool set in the toolpost for turning the screw diameter; a stop set behind the tool for determining the length of the cut, a tailstock die-holder for the thread, and a parting-tool, inverted, and set at the opposite end of the cross-slide. In the picture, the parting tool is shown clamped to a small angle plate, which is, in turn, clamped to the cross-slide, and this arrangement is quite rigid enough for use on small brass or steel screws. However, this arrangement is so useful that it is well worth while to make a special

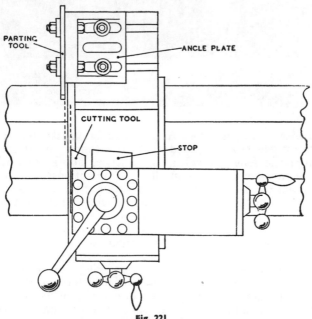

Fig. 221
Diagram explaining the set-up shown in Fig. 220.

Fig. 222

The tailstock turret tool-holder mounted in tailstock, with lever feed attachment in position. This combination gives the home mechanic facilities found only on capstan lathes.

back tool-holder, as its uses are by no means confined to the making of nuts and bolts. It forms a very well established method among production turners, and is worthy of a sketch (Fig. 221). This depicts a plan view. The chief feature to note is that the distance between the tip of the turning tool and that of the parting tool (shown in dotted line in the drawing) determines the length of the head of the screw, and this distance may be adjusted by moving the top-slide of the lathe. The length of the screw itself is determined by the position of the flat piece of metal which is clamped to the toolpost just behind the tool. The diameter of the screw is set on the cross-slide index dial, and the cut is taken by means of the handwheel on the lathe carriage, until the tip of the screw blank just touches the stop. The cutting tool is then withdrawn and the movement continued so that the parting tool cuts off the screw—the thread, of course, having been formed by means of the tailstock die-holder. In setting up it is necessary, therefore, to ensure that there is sufficient room between the two tools to allow the die-holder to function.

Making Nuts

Small nuts may be made by essentially the same methods, except that the turning tool should be a form-tool shaped to part off and chamfer. This form-tool serves to face-off the nuts and to impart the chamfer, while the rear tool parts off as before. By this method no stops are required, as the lengths of the nuts are determined by the longitudinal distance between the tools.

If this system is used in conjunction with a turret tailstock-tool-holder, literally hundreds of nuts may be made in a few hours from suitable hexagon rod, quite equal in all respects to the purchased article. Such a turret tool-holder has been already shown in Fig. 42, together with a working drawing from which the amateur may construct one for himself. The illustration shows the tool-holder set up with a variety of tools, but for small nuts the majority of them can be dispensed with and a short, stub drill and a second-tap are all that is required. Short, broken drills, reground, should always be used if possible, as there is less likelihood of these "wandering".

It will be seen that very few special accessories are required for quite a variety of repetition work in small lathes. The few special pieces of equipment which may be of advantage are, in any case, useful for other turning purposes other than reproduction work. Notably, we may draw attention to the lever tailstock feed, pictured in Fig. 222. With this equipment very fast operation of tailstock tools may be obtained; in fact, the amateur is almost provided with the facilities of a small capstan, especially if the turret tool-holder is also embodied. In amateur practice, as in professional, special equipment is the secret of fast and easy work.

Cross-slide Stops

A feature not often encountered on small "amateur" lathes is the provision of cross-slide stops. These usually take the form of adjustable screw stops, attached to the cross-slide so as to allow them to be set to give a predetermined amount of movement. The screw is usually housed in a bracket attached to the lathe carriage, with a fixed block mounted on the side of the cross-slide. On moving the slide inwards the block comes in contact with the stopscrew, which has been set to allow the required movement.

The arrangement permits an instantaneous duplication of tool setting, and can be invaluable for some classes of repetition work. The provision of such a stop is possible on most small lathes without undue difficulty, and is well worth the fitting as it has uses in the screwcutting method, using the angled top-slide described in Chapter 12.

Diameter Gauges

A very useful gadget, which facilitates the quick setting of tools to cut given diameters, is a **diameter gauge.** This can be easily made by the home mechanic, as it consists only of a taper shank—made to plug into the tailstock barrel—bearing a piece of metal about 2 in. in diameter, turned in a series of steps, each of a definite size, say, $1\frac{3}{4}$ in., $1\frac{1}{2}$ in., $1\frac{1}{4}$ in., and so on. Each step should be marked with its diameter with number punches.

In use, the gauge is located in the tailstock so that the tip of the tool may be registered against the desired diameter. While not accurate enough for precision work, the gauge is invaluable for roughing-out purposes, as the tool can be instantly set to cut just a little larger than is desired, so that roughing cuts of maximum depth can be taken without the constant need for measurement, or the danger of roughing-out too deeply.

Lathe-carriage Stop

In the previous pages the use of metal rods as lathe-carriage stops has been mentioned, and these, while being quite effective, are rather a temporary expedient. A more permanent type of carriage stop is to be preferred, especially as this may be used for purposes other than that of quantity production.

From Figs. 223A and 223B it will be seen that the arrangement is quite a simple affair, as it consists only of a fabricated block, which may be clamped into any position along the front lathe-way. Through this block runs a threaded rod, bearing adjusting nuts, and this rod is secured to the lathe carriage by screwing into the threaded hole provided for the threading indicator. The stop described is designed to fit to the Myford range of $3\frac{1}{2}$-in. lathes, but slight modification will make it suitable for almost any machine. It is to be particularly noted that the block is clamped to the lathe-way by means of a $\frac{1}{4}$-in. B.S.F. Allen screw, and it is most important to remember that a loose gib strip, shown at E in Fig. 223B, is interposed between the point of the clamping screw and the lathe bed. Failure to use this strip may result in damage to the machine.

Using the Stop for Determining Length of Cut

While the diameter of work is easily measured by micrometer or vernier, the length of shoulders, or the depth of holes, are not easily measured with any accuracy, except,

Fig. 223A
Carriage stop attached to a $3\frac{1}{2}$-in. lathe, showing the screwed rod located in the hole provided for the threading indicator illustrated in Fig. 162.

perhaps, with a depth micrometer, which few amateurs will possess.

The lathe stop described does, however, form a ready means of turning shoulders, or boring holes, to an accurate pre-determined measurement. Following our usual procedure, we will illustrate the

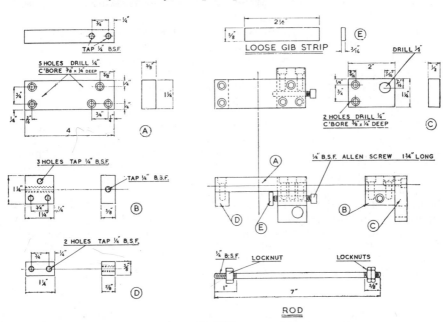

Fig. 223B
Constructional drawing for the mild-steel lathe-carriage stop shown in Fig. 223A.

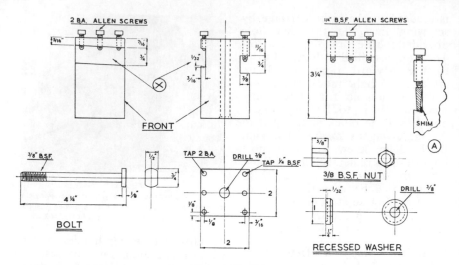

Fig. 224

Back toolpost (mild steel) to hold both turning and parting tools. Note that the slot for the parting tool (marked X) slopes downwards, towards the front of the toolpost. By sliding the tool back or forth a certain adjustment of tool height is attained. The toolpost is designed to take the "Eclipse" $\frac{11}{16}$ in. parting blade, which has a wedge-shaped section. Ideally, the back face of the slot should be sloped to conform with this tool angle, but as this may be a somewhat difficult operation with amateur equipment an alternative method is shown in the small sketch, marked A. Here, a small packing-strip is laid along the bottom edge of the blade, thus packing it to a vertical position. In the drawing, the strip is shown in full black, and need be only a strip of shim steel about ·010 in thick.

method by assuming a hypothetical instance, say, the boring of a hole in a workpiece, exactly 1 in. deep.

Assuming that the workpiece is in the chuck, and the boring tool in the toolpost, the first step is to clamp up the stop on the lathe bed to an approximate position suitable for the job. The lathe carriage is now wound forward, so that it bears hard upon the stop, and cannot move forward. While held in this position, the boring tool is moved, **by the top slide** of the lathe, until its tip just touches the face of the work to be bored. The forward pressure on the lathe carriage may now be relaxed, and, without altering any other setting, the tool is wound

forward **by the top-slide,** exactly 1 in., using the indicator dial to measure the movement.

It will now be understood that the boring tool protrudes exactly 1 in. past the original stop position, so that if turning proceeds, and the carriage is brought hard up to the stop on each cut, the hole will be bored to a depth corresponding to the amount that the top-slide was wound forward, i.e. 1 in.

Back Toolpost for Holding both Turning and Parting Tools

A constructional drawing of a back toolpost for holding both turning and parting tools is described and illustrated in Fig, 224.

CHAPTER 17

CARE OF THE LATHE AND ITS ACCESSORIES

CONSIDERING that the lathe is often the most valuable single possession which the amateur may own, it is surprising how little care is often taken of it. The reason is, perhaps, that the lathe is such a hardy, unfailing servant that the results of neglect appear but gradually, until that unhappy time when the cumulative effects of misuse become only too apparent.

An enquiry conducted by a well-known engineering concern into the causes of machine wear disclosed that the prime factor was **faulty lubrication.** Swarf and metal dust came second, while high on the list of evils were the damage done by work coming adrift through faulty chucking, jamming of machines by unintentional engagement of the self-acts, and the dropping of tools and work upon the lathe ways.

Lubrication

Of whichever of the above faults the amateur may or may not be guilty the most inexcusable is under-lubrication. Nor would the average amateur plead guilty to this charge, as none but the true vandal would neglect the oilcan. Nevertheless, many good machines have been spoiled, by even the best intentioned owners, through neglect of the less obvious points of wear. Perhaps the most neglected part is the belt pulley on the mandrel. The intelligent turner will find that he must use backgear much more frequently than might be supposed, so that the belt pulley will quite often be running free, with the lathe mandrel as a

bearing. Yet countless numbers of amateurs fail to oil these components. Repeated neglect causes wear on both the pulley and mandrel, and gives rise to an annoying rattle when the lathe is used in open speed.

The best advice which can be given on the lubrication of any mechanism is that **noise means wear.** Secondary advice is a caution against using too thick an oil, especially on the head bearings. Use good quality thin oil—little and often.

Swarf and Dust

These enemies are so connected with the cleaning of the lathe that they cannot be separated from it. Swarf and metal dust constitute a serious problem; they get between the slides and scratch the lathe ways. Some lathes, designed by folk who know their job, are fitted with oil-soaked wiper pads attached to the lathe carriage, and these are a great protection. The pads must, however, be removed from time to time, cleaned, re-soaked in oil, and replaced. Most model engineers, are, in any case, ingenious enough to contrive wiper pads for their own machines. The trouble involved is well repaid.

Cleanliness is always essential, but some swarf and metal dust are more destructive than others. Immediately you have finished turning **cast iron** wipe away all the dust at once. Cast iron dust—especially when it contains sand from castings —mixed with oil forms a most efficient lapping compound. The best precaution of all is to cover over as much of the lathe bed as is possible

Fig. 225

A 5-c.c. compression ignition engine designed and constructed by the author. Drawings of this little engine have been published and some thousand amateurs have built examples, and developed a pleasant correspondence with the author from all over the world.

with a damped cloth prior to turning cast iron.

Brass chips may also be destructive, and will lap themselves into cast iron! After brass turning never "blow" the fine chips away when cleaning down. You will force them between the slides and beneath the saddle. Cleaning down with the compressed-air gun is prohibited in all the best regulated engineering works, and blowing with the mouth can be almost as bad.

After turning wood—probably for pattern making—do not leave the chips and sawdust on the lathe for long periods. Sawdust soaks up the oil and collects the damp and forms a lovely "rusting poultice" on the machine.

The Sacred Lathe Bed

Were I asked to form a judgment on the character and ability of any turner I should first take a glance at the bed of his lathe. Dents and scrapes are always a sign of carelessness. They are indelible by usual methods, and can be effaced only by re-grinding the lathe bed. The chief causes are: (*a*) dropping the chuck when unscrewing, (*b*) work coming adrift owing to bad chucking, (*c*) carelessly knocking out lathe centres so that they drop on the bed, (*e*) leaving the chuck key in the chuck and accidentally switching on the lathe (this makes a lovely dent!), and (*f*) sawing off material in the chuck and allowing the saw to strike the lathe ways, by the impetus of the cut as the saw breaks through. The placing of tools and spanners on the lathe bed is also a prolific cause of small dents.

Attention has already been called to the **lathe board,** featured in Chapter 8. With this in position on the lathe bed you may drop your chucks, knock out the centres with a hammer and drift, and saw off with your eyes closed if you wish! And, when not in active use, it may be placed on the lathe bed, beyond the tailstock, and used as a tray for spanners and tools.

Preserving the Taper Sockets in Head and Tailstock

If good work is to be done under all conditions it is essential that the taper sockets of the head and tailstock be undamaged and true, particularly the head socket. Careful turners have a wooden taper plug which "lives" in the head taper, and is only removed when occasion demands.

Much damage can be done to the internal tapers by scarred and ill-fitting taper-shanks, such as may frequently be found on drills and old chucks. Such shanks cannot fit correctly, and, in consequence, are liable to turn in the sockets under strain. Should a drill, for instance, turn in the head socket when being used it is highly probable that the internal taper will be scored and made useless for any further accurate work! Doubtful shanks should be lightly emery-papered, and the burrs removed with a fine file. As an added precaution, a single sheet of writing paper may be interposed between the shank and the socket, so that, should the shank turn, no damage will be done. In passing, it may be remarked that the use of paper slips in this manner provides a very firm grip on the shank.

Fig. 226
An advanced 10-cc. O.H.V. internal combustion engine which should make an appeal to every craftsman requiring a job where skill in overcoming snags is half the joy of battle!

O

Starting up the Lathe

In cold weather the congealing of the oil in the head bearings will cause considerable drag on the mandrel, so that it is advisable to warm up the lathe by letting it run light for a few minutes before starting to work. This lessens the strain on countershaft, motor and the lathe itself. If the lathe is particularly stiff the lowest open speed should be used.

The importance of checking that free movement of the carriage along the bed is possible before engaging the self-act or screwcutting gears has already been mentioned, but may well do with emphasis here. Particularly, it should be ascertained that there is clearance between the work and the lathe carriage, that the carriage locking bolt is not tight, and that the carriage will not foul the fixed steady if this is being used. Care is particularly necessary when using **collets**, as this brings the carriage nearer to the head than is customary with chucked work. For similar reasons, it is necessary to be sure that the lathe is not left in gear for long periods of disuse, so that a

Fig. 227

Sooner or later every amateur falls for the lure of the marine engine. This delightful picture from the album of K. N. Harris gives an excellent impression of the amount of detail that can be achieved in such a miniature.

Fig. 228

A model steam lorry that is worthy of special inspection as the whole of the turning was carried out on a 37s. 6d. lathe, and the bu:: 'ar's workshop really was the kitchen table. Such an effort should inspire those fortunate enough to possess more elaborate equipment to produce veritable masterpieces.

sudden, forgetful switching-on may cause the lathe carriage to travel. If a screwcutting job must be held over for further operations, and it is not desirable to disengage the clasp nut, place a slip of paper on the toolpost marked: **In Gear.** Even if **you** remember the circumstances, the lathe may be unwittingly switched on by a visiting friend.

Bad Chucking

Chapter 8 gives full emphasis to the dangers ensuing on this practice, but it may be again mentioned here if only in the hope that repetition may serve to impress the importance of the matter upon the unwary. As a rough guess, it is probable that about thirty per cent. of all lathe damage is done through this cause! The best safeguard is to support by the tailstock centre wherever possible.

Bearing Adjustments

A correctly fitted lathe mandrel should be entirely without shake of any sort, while at the same time it should revolve quite freely. Undue tightness of the bearings usually becomes apparent when the lathe is run at high speed for any considerable length of time, the consequent heating up and expansion causing the lathe to slow up. If this trouble becomes apparent only on exceptionally long runs it may be ignored, provided that the lathe shows no signs of distress on normal working.

Usually, the offending bearing can be detected by feeling each in turn for undue heating, and the adjusting screws slightly relaxed. Allow the bearing to cool down before commencing operations again, and flood it with thin oil.

When adjusting bearings, tighten each one in succession; that is, first tighten the rear bearing until no shake is perceptible but the shaft is free to rotate. Then transfer attentions to the other bearing. Now see if the lathe tightens up at high speeds, and adjust accordingly.

Adjusting Slides

Most lathe slides are provided with adjusting screws which exert pressure upon movable, metal strips or "gibs", as they are called, which press upon the sides of the internal slides. These screws should be tightened one at a time, tightening each as much as permissible, yet moving the slide the whole length of its travel after adjusting each screw, to ascertain that the slide is not binding. It is then often necessary to slacken off the screws slightly when all have been tightened, as, though the slide may move freely under the pressure of one or two screws, the collective pressure of all of them may be too great for easy movement. Tight slides put great strain on the feedscrews and nuts.

Meshing Gears

Damage may be done to gear teeth, and the studs on the banjo strained, by meshing gearwheels together too tightly. Conversely, too loose a mesh will cause excessive and uneven wear of the teeth. An old trick which ensures a correct adjustment for the wheels is to mesh them together with a slip of thin paper between the engaging teeth. The paper slip is then run out before commencing work, thus ensuring that there is a small clearance between the gear teeth.

Gears are particularly liable to collect metal dust and chips in the bottoms of the teeth, so that the gear train will run with tight and loose spots. Besides causing strain, the smoothness and quiet running of the lathe is destroyed. A stiff wire brush should be applied to the gearwheels before meshing, and chips which have become bedded into the teeth-bases should be picked out with an old scriber. A light application of grease is the correct lubrication for gear trains.

Overhang

At all times the amateur should endeavour to so adjust and set his lathe that it will cut easily and without "chatter", and with the least strain to the machine. Excessive, unsupported, overhang on work or tools will produce vibration, which, besides ruining the finish of the job, may be injurious to the lathe itself if continually persisted in.

A common cause of vibration is that of having the topslide screwed too far forward, so that a considerable unsupported portion overhangs the lathe carriage. Much leverage is thus exerted. It is necessary, therefore, to see that, when possible, the topslide is positioned in such a manner that it is supported under the toolpost. Similarly, do not allow excessive overhang of the tailstock barrel when turning between centres.

Fig. 229

Still the most popular branch of model engineering—building and running live steam model locomotives.
The illustration shows the well-known technical writer Mr. H. E. White at the controls of his 3½-in. gauge
Pacific " Facilitas " under steam.   A locomotive such as this is capable of pulling a passenger load of some tons
and is perennially popular with enthusiasts of all ages!

HANDY TABLES FOR HOME MECHANICS

SCREWCUTTING CHANGEWHEELS FOR LEADSCREW OF 4 THREADS PER INCH

T.P.I.	Mandrel	1st Stud		2nd Stud		Leadscrew
		Driven	Driver	Driven	Driver	
2	60	Idle		Idle		30
3	80	,,		,,		60
4	30	40	60	,,		45
5	30	45	60	,,		50
6	40	Idle		,,		60
7	30	45	60	,,		70
8	35	Idle		,,		70
9	20	30	40	,,		60
10	20	Idle		,,		50
11	20	,,		,,		55
12	20	,,		,,		60
13	20	,,		,,		65
14	20	,,		,,		70
15	20	,,		,,		75
16	20	,,		,,		80
17	20	,,		,,		85
18	20	,,		,,		90
19	20	,,		,,		95
20	20	,,		,,		100
21	40	60	20	,,		70
22	20	55	30	,,		60
24	20	60	40	,,		80
25	20	50	40	,,		100
26	20	65	30	,,		60
27	20	60	40	,,		90
28	20	70	40	,,		80
30	20	60	40	,,		100
32	20	60	30	,,		80
33	20	55	40	60	35	70
34	25	85	40	Idle		100
35	20	70	40	,,		100
36	20	60	30	,,		90
38	25	95	40	,,		100
39	20	60	40	65	50	100
40	20	80	40	Idle		100
44	20	55	30	60	40	80
48	20	60	25	Idle		100
50	30	75	20	,,		100
56	20	70	25	,,		100
60	20	60	30	75	40	80

SCREWCUTTING CHANGEWHEELS FOR LEADSCREW OF 6 THREADS PER INCH

T.P.I.	Mandrel	1st Stud		2nd Stud		Leadscrew
		Driven	Driver	Driven	Driver	
2	60	Idle		Idle		20
3	60	,,		,,		30
4	60	,,		,,		40
5	60	,,		,,		50
6	20	30	60	,,		40
7	30	,,		,,		35
8	30	,,		,,		40
9	30	,,		,,		45
10	30	,,		,,		50
11	30	,,		,,		55
12	30	,,		,,		60
13	30	,,		,,		65
14	30	,,		,,		70
15	30	50	40	,,		60
16	30	40	35	,,		70
17	30	Idle		,,		85
18	30	60	50	,,		75
19	20	38	30	,,		50
20	20	40	30	,,		50
21	40	60	30	,,		70
22	20	40	30	,,		55
24	20	40	30	,,		60
25	20	50	45	,,		75
26	20	40	30	,,		65
27	20	45	30	40	50	75
28	20	40	30	Idle		70
30	20	50	30	,,		60
32	20	40	30	,,		80
34	20	40	30	,,		85
35	20	50	30	,,		70
36	20	60	25	,,		50
40	20	50	30	40	35	70
42	20	60	30	Idle		70
44	20	40	25	50	30	55
45	20	50	30	45	35	70
48	20	60	30	Idle		80
56	20	70	30	,,		80
60	20	50	30	60	35	70

SCREWCUTTING CHANGEWHEELS FOR LEADSCREW OF 8 THREADS PER INCH

T.P.I.	Mandrel	1st Stud		2nd Stud		Leadscrew
		Driven	Driver	Driven	Driver	
2	50	25	60	Idle		30
3	50	25	60	,,		45
4	60	Idle		,,		30
5	60	30	40	,,		50
6	60	Idle		,,		45
7	40	,,		,,		35
8	60	40	50	,,		75
9	40	Idle		,,		45
10	40	,,		,,		50
11	40	,,		,,		55
12	40	,,		,,		60
13	40	,,		,,		65
14	20	,,		,,		35
15	40	45	30	,,		50
16	20	Idle		,,		40
17	40	,,		,,		85
18	20	,,		,,		45
19	20	38	40	,,		50
20	20	Idle		,,		50
21	20	30	40	,,		70
22	20	Idle		,,		55
24	20	,,		,,		60
25	20	25	20	,,		50
26	20	Idle		,,		65
27	20	30	20	,,		45
28	30	35	20	,,		60
30	20	50	40	,,		60
32	30	40	20	,,		60
33	20	45	30	,,		55
34	20	Idle		,,		85
35	20	50	40	,,		70
36	30	45	20	,,		60
38	20	38	40	50	30	60
39	20	30	25	50	40	65
40	30	50	20	Idle		60
42	20	60	40	,,		70
44	20	55	30	,,		60
45	20	45	40	50	30	60
48	25	50	40	60	35	70
50	20	50	30	Idle		75
56	25	50	30	60	40	70
60	20	50	40	60	35	70

SCREWCUTTING GEARWHEELS FOR LEADSCREW OF 10 THREADS PER INCH

T.P.I.	Mandrel	1st Stud		2nd Stud		Leadscrew
		Driven	Driver	Driven	Driver	
2	50	20	60	Idle		30
3	50	20	40	,,		30
4	50	Idle		,,		20
5	50	,,		,,		25
6	50	,,		,,		30
7	50	,,		,,		35
8	50	,,		,,		40
9	50	,,		,,		45
10	50	20	30	,,		75
11	50	Idle		,,		55
12	25	,,		,,		30
13	20	65	50	,,		20
14	25	Idle		,,		35
15	20	,,		,,		30
16	25	,,		,,		40
17	50	,,		,,		85
18	25	,:		,,		45
19	20	,,		,,		38
20	25	,,		,,		50
21	20	30	50	,,		70
22	25	Idle		,,		55
24	20	40	50	,,		60
25	20	Idle		,,		50
26	25	,,		,,		65
27	20	30	25	,,		45
28	20	40	50	,,		70
30	20	30	25	,,		50
32	25	40	30	,,		60
33	20	30	25	,,		55
34	25	Idle		,,		85
35	20	35	25	,,		50
36	20	30	25	,,		60
38	20	38	30	,,		60
39	20	30	25	,,		65
40	20	40	25	,,		50
42	25	35	20	,,		60
44	20	40	25	,,		55
45	25	45	20	,,		50
48	20	40	25	,,		60
50	20	50	30	,,		60
56	25	40	20	,,		70
60	25	60	20	,		50

Constants for finding Root Diameter of Screw Threads

To find the root diameter of any screw thread, subtract the constant for the number of threads per inch from the outside diameter.

WHITWORTH FORM

T.P.I.	Constants
3	0·426 in.
4	·320
5	·256
6	·213
7	·182
8	·160
9	·142
10	·128
11	·116
12	·106
13	·098
14	·091
16	·080
18	·071
20	·064
22	·058
24	·053
26	·049
27	·047
28	·045
30	·042
32	·040
36	·035
40	·032
44	·029
48	·026
50	·025
56	·022
60	·021

DECIMAL EQUIVALENTS OF DRILL SIZES

NUMBER DRILLS

Drill	Equivalent In.
80	0·013
79½	·0135
79	·014

NUMBER DRILLS (cont.)

Drill	Equivalent In.
78½	0·0145
78	·015
77	·016
76	·018
75	·020
74½	·021
74	·022
73½	·0225
73	·023
72	·024
71½	·025
71	·026
70	·027
69½	·028
69	·029
68½	·02925
68	·030
67	·031
66	·032
65	·033
64	·035
63	·036
62	·037
61	·038
60½	·039
60	·040
59	·041
58	·042
57	·043
56	·0465
55	·052
54	·055
53	·0595
52	·0635
51	·067
50	·070
49	·073
48	·076
47	·0785
46	·081
45	·082
44	·086
43	·089
42	·0935
41	·096
40	·098
39	·0995
38	·101ɔ
37	·104
36	·1065
35	·110
34	·111
33	·113
32	·116
31	·120
30	·1285

NUMBER DRILLS (cont.)

Drill	Equivalent In.
29	0·136
28	·1405
27	·144
26	·147
25	·1495
24	·152
23	·154
22	·157
21	·159
20	·161
19	·166
18	·1695
17	·173
16	·177
15	·180
14	·182
13	·185
12	·189
11	·191
10	·1935
9	·196
8	·199
7	·201
6	·204
5	·2055
4	·209
3	·213
2	·221
1	·228

LETTER DRILLS

Letter	Equivalent
A	0·234
B	·238
C	·242
D	·246
E	·250
F	·257
G	·261
H	·266
I	·272
J	·277
K	·281
L	·290
M	·295
N	·302
O	·316
P	·323
Q	·332
R	·339
S	·348
T	·358
U	·368
V	·377
W	·386
X	·397
Y	·404
Z	·413

BRITISH ASSOCIATION STANDARD THREADS

Number	Pitch mm.	Outside Diameter Inches	Tap Drill Size	Clearance Drill Size
0	1·000	·236	12	B
1	·900	·208	19	3
2	·810	·185	26	$\frac{3}{16}$
3	·730	·161	29	19
4	·660	·142	33	27
5	·590	·126	39	30
6	·530	·110	43	34
7	·480	·098	47	39
8	·430	·087	50	43
9	·390	·075	$\frac{1}{16}$	48
10	·350	·067	54	50
11	·310	·059	56	53
12	·280	·051	61	55

WHITWORTH STANDARD THREADS AND BRITISH STANDARD FINE

Diameter Inches	Threads per inch		Root Dia.	Tap Drill Size
	Whit.	B.S.F.		
$\frac{1}{16}$	60	—	·0412	56
$\frac{3}{32}$	48	—	·0671	49
$\frac{1}{8}$	40	—	·0930	40
$\frac{5}{32}$	32	—	·1162	31
$\frac{3}{16}$	24	—	·1341	28
$\frac{7}{32}$	24	—	·1654	18
$\frac{1}{4}$	20	—	·1860	11
$\frac{1}{4}$	—	26	·2001	5
$\frac{9}{32}$	20	—	·2172	2
$\frac{9}{32}$	—	26	·2321	B
$\frac{5}{16}$	18	—	·2414	D
$\frac{5}{16}$	—	22	·2543	G
$\frac{3}{8}$	16	—	·2950	N
$\frac{3}{8}$	—	20	·3110	O
$\frac{7}{16}$	14	—	·3460	S
$\frac{7}{16}$	—	18	·3665	$\frac{3}{8}$
$\frac{1}{2}$	12	—	·3933	X
$\frac{1}{2}$	—	16	·4200	$\frac{7}{16}$
$\frac{9}{16}$	12	—	·4558	$\frac{15}{32}$
$\frac{9}{16}$	—	16	·4825	$\frac{1}{2}$
$\frac{5}{8}$	11	—	·5086	$\frac{33}{64}$
$\frac{5}{8}$	—	14	·5336	$\frac{35}{64}$
$\frac{11}{16}$	11	—	·5711	$\frac{37}{64}$
$\frac{11}{16}$	—	14	·5961	$\frac{39}{64}$
$\frac{3}{4}$	10	—	·6219	$\frac{5}{8}$
$\frac{3}{4}$	—	12	·6434	$\frac{21}{32}$
$\frac{13}{16}$	10	—	·6844	$\frac{11}{16}$
$\frac{13}{16}$	—	12	·7059	$\frac{23}{32}$
$\frac{7}{8}$	9	—	·7327	$\frac{47}{64}$
$\frac{7}{8}$	—	11	·7586	$\frac{49}{64}$
$\frac{15}{16}$	9	—	·7952	$\frac{13}{16}$
$\frac{15}{16}$	—	11	·8215	$\frac{53}{64}$
1	8	—	·8399	$\frac{27}{32}$
1	—	10	·8720	$\frac{7}{8}$

TAPERS PER INCH AND FOOT

MORSE

Number	Taper per Inch	Taper per Foot
0	0·05208	0·625
1	·05000	·600
2	·05016	·602
3	·05016	·602
4	·05191	·623
5	·05250	·630
6	·05216	·626

JARNO

Number	Taper per Inch	Taper per Foot
2 to 20	0·0500	0·600

DECIMAL EQUIVALENTS OF MILLIMETRES

mm.	Inches	mm.	Inches
·1	·00394	22·0	0·86614
·2	·00787	23·0	·90551
·3	·01181	24·0	·94488
·4	·01575	25·0	·98425
·5	·01968	26·0	1·02362
·6	·02362	27·0	1·06299
·7	·02756	28·0	1·10236
·8	·03149	29·0	1·14173
·9	·03543	30·0	1·18110
1·0	·03937	31·0	1·22047
2·0	·07874	32·0	1·25984
3·0	·11811	33·0	1·29921
4·0	·15748	34·0	1·33858
5·0	·19685	35·0	1·37795
6·0	·23622	36·0	1·41732
7·0	·27559	37·0	1·45669
8·0	·31496	38·0	1·49606
9·0	·35433	39·0	1·53543
10·0	·39370	40·0	1·57480
11·0	·43307	41·0	1·61417
12·0	·47244	42·0	1·65354
13·0	·51181	43·0	1·69291
14·0	·55118	44·0	1·73228
15·0	·59055	45·0	1·77165
16·0	·62992	46·0	1·81102
17·0	·66929	47·0	1·85039
18·0	·70866	48·0	1·88976
19·0	·74803	49·0	1·92913
20·0	·78740	50·0	1·96850
21·0	·82677		

INCHES INTO MILLIMETRES

Inches	mm.		Inches	mm.
$\frac{1}{16}$	1·6		1	25·4
$\frac{1}{8}$	3·2		2	50·8
$\frac{3}{16}$	4·8		3	76·2
$\frac{1}{4}$	6·4		4	101·6
$\frac{5}{16}$	7·9		5	127·0
$\frac{3}{8}$	9·5		6	152·4
$\frac{7}{16}$	11·1		7	177·8
$\frac{1}{2}$	12·7		8	203·2
$\frac{9}{16}$	14·3		9	228·6
$\frac{5}{8}$	15·9		10	254·0
$\frac{11}{16}$	17·5		11	279·4
$\frac{3}{4}$	19·1		12	304·8
$\frac{13}{16}$	20·6			
$\frac{7}{8}$	22·2			
$\frac{15}{16}$	23·8			

INDEX